# HTML5 Programming with JavaScript

## FOR DUMMIES

A Wiley Brand

## by John Paul Mueller

FOR DUMMIES

A Wiley Brand

**HTML5 Programming with JavaScript® For Dummies®**

Published by
**John Wiley & Sons, Inc.**
111 River Street
Hoboken, NJ 07030-5774
www.wiley.com

Copyright © 2013 by John Wiley & Sons, Inc., Hoboken, New Jersey

Published simultaneously in Canada

For general information on our other products and services, please contact our Customer Care Department within the U.S. at 877-762-2974, outside the U.S. at 317-572-3993, or fax 317-572-4002.

For technical support, please visit www.wiley.com/techsupport.

Wiley publishes in a variety of print and electronic formats and by print-on-demand. Some material included with standard print versions of this book may not be included in e-books or in print-on-demand. If this book refers to media such as a CD or DVD that is not included in the version you purchased, you may download this material at http://booksupport.wiley.com. For more information about Wiley products, visit www.wiley.com.

Library of Congress Control Number: 2013936244

ISBN 978-1-118-43166-5 (pbk); ISBN 978-1-118-46209-6 (ebk);
ISBN 978-1-118-61188-3 (ebk); ISBN 978-1-118-49418-9 (ebk)

Manufactured in the United States of America

10 9 8 7 6 5 4 3 2 1

# About the Author

**John Mueller** is a freelance author and technical editor. He has writing in his blood, having produced 91 books and over 300 articles to date. The topics range from networking to artificial intelligence and from database management to heads-down programming. Some of his current books include Windows command-line references, books on VBA and Visio, several books on C#, and an IronPython programmer's guide. His technical editing skills have helped more than 63 authors refine the content of their manuscripts. John has provided technical editing services to both *Data Based Advisor* and *Coast Compute* magazines. He's also contributed articles to magazines like such as Software Quality Connection, DevSource, InformIT, SQL Server Professional, Visual C++ Developer, Hard Core Visual Basic, asp.netPRO, Software Test and Performance, and Visual Basic Developer. Be sure to read John's blog at http://blog.johnmuellerbooks.com.

When John isn't working at the computer, you can find him outside in the garden, cutting wood, or generally enjoying nature. John also likes making wine and knitting. When not occupied with anything else, he makes glycerin soap and candles, which comes in handy for gift baskets. You can reach John on the Internet at John@JohnMuellerBooks.com. John is also setting up a website at http://www.johnmuellerbooks.com. Feel free to take a look and make suggestions on how he can improve it.

# Dedication

Dedicated to people who have given me hope and who have helped me realize new potential as an author; on the occasion of their 50th anniversary, Bill and Karen Bridges.

# Author's Acknowledgments

Thanks to my wife, Rebecca, for working with me to get this book completed. I really don't know what I would have done without her help in researching and compiling some of the information that appears in this book. She also did a fine job of proofreading my rough draft. Rebecca keeps the house running while I'm buried in work.

Russ Mullen deserves thanks for his technical edit of this book. He greatly added to the accuracy and depth of the material you see here. Russ is always providing me with great URLs for new products and ideas. However, it's the testing Russ does that helps most. He's the sanity check for my work. Russ also has different computer equipment than mine, so he's able to point out flaws that I might not otherwise notice.

Matt Wagner, my agent, deserves credit for helping me get the contract in the first place and taking care of all the details that most authors don't really consider. I always appreciate his assistance. It's good to know that someone wants to help.

A number of people read all or part of this book to help me refine the approach, test the coding examples, and generally provide input that all readers wish they could have. These unpaid volunteers helped in ways too numerous to mention here. I especially appreciate the efforts of Eva Beattie, Glenn Russell, Osvaldo Téllez Almirall, and Gerald Wilson, Jr., who provided general input, read the entire book, and selflessly devoted themselves to this project.

Finally, I would like to thank Kim Darosett, Katie Feltman, Virginia Sanders, Katie Crocker, and the rest of the editorial and production staff at Wiley for their assistance in bringing this book to print. It's always nice to work with such a great group of professionals.

## Publisher's Acknowledgments

We're proud of this book; please send us your comments at `http://dummies.custhelp.com`. For other comments, please contact our Customer Care Department within the U.S. at 877-762-2974, outside the U.S. at 317-572-3993, or fax 317-572-4002.

Some of the people who helped bring this book to market include the following:

### *Acquisitions and Editorial*

**Senior Project Editor:** Kim Darosett

**Acquisitions Editor:** Constance Santisteban

**Copy Editor:** Virginia Sanders

**Technical Editor:** Russ Mullen

**Editorial Manager:** Leah Michael

**Editorial Assistant:** Annie Sullivan

**Senior Editorial Assistant:** Cherie Case

**Cover Photo:** © kertlis/iStockphoto

### *Composition Services*

**Project Coordinator:** Katherine Crocker

**Layout and Graphics:** Amy Hassos, Joyce Haughey

**Proofreaders:** Jessica Kramer, Lisa Stiers

**Indexer:** Ty Koontz

---

### Publishing and Editorial for Technology Dummies

**Richard Swadley,** Vice President and Executive Group Publisher

**Andy Cummings,** Vice President and Publisher

**Mary Bednarek,** Executive Acquisitions Director

**Mary C. Corder,** Editorial Director

### Publishing for Consumer Dummies

**Kathleen Nebenhaus,** Vice President and Executive Publisher

### Composition Services

**Debbie Stailey,** Director of Composition Services

# Table of Contents

# Introduction

**H**ave you people-watched lately? If not, you really should. People-watching is both fun and educational. At one time, you wouldn't see people using computers wherever they went because computers were large, cumbersome devices that no one wanted to take out of the office. Today, you have a hard time finding people who aren't using a computing device of some sort to perform some task. Developers have an incredible opportunity today to affect people in every walk of life and in any situation imaginable because people carry their computing devices with them far and wide to hold every bit of information they find valuable.

The tools that developers use to create applications must change to reflect this new reality, and HTML5 and JavaScript are the most appropriate tools to accomplish the goals developers have today. You can use the combination of HTML5 and JavaScript to create applications that run on any device using just about any new browser. *HTML5 Programming with JavaScript For Dummies* is your gateway to an incredible new future of development where you aren't limited to a specific platform or some vendor's concept of what tools you should use to create applications. This book helps you gain the skills required to create the new sorts of applications that developers have always wanted to write.

## About This Book

*HTML5 Programming with JavaScript For Dummies* is about possibilities. It focuses on getting started writing code quickly and efficiently. You see lots of coding examples, all of which demonstrate principles you need for writing applications that people want to use today. The latter part of the book actually shows some application programming techniques you can use directly in production applications. The method used to accomplish this goal is the same method that all smart developers use today — borrowing code from someone else. This book emphasizes the use of templates and libraries to make your coding experience fun and simple rather than cumbersome and boring, as it might have been in the past.

Don't worry about becoming immediately lost in detail. Like every *For Dummies* book, this one takes things slowly, and all the examples are explained thoroughly so that you know precisely how they work. You'll find that you advance quickly because this book takes advantage of the best possible techniques that knowledgeable developers use to make their lives simple. Working with libraries such as jQuery greatly decreases the work you have to do while simultaneously making the application you create look professional, and best of all, work everywhere on every device.

Of course, every developer needs to be aware of at least the basics, and the introductory chapters of the book do just that — they tell you how things work under the cover. Sometimes you need this information in order to make the best use possible of all those third-party offerings. However, as the text often states, there's no need to reinvent the wheel. Your JavaScript applications will look professional because you're using professionally written code to develop them. This book shows you how to create some truly impressive results in an incredibly short timeframe.

# What You Don't Have to Read

Most of the chapters contain some advanced material that will interest only some readers. When you see one of these specialized topics, feel free to skip it. Most of this advanced material appears in sidebars. The sidebar title always indicates the nature of the advanced material.

You can also skip any material marked with a Technical Stuff icon. This material is helpful, but you don't have to know it to work with HTML or JavaScript. I include this material because I find it helpful in my programming efforts and believe that you will, too.

# Foolish Assumptions

You might find it difficult to believe that I've assumed anything about you — after all, I haven't even met you yet! Although most assumptions are indeed foolish, I made these assumptions to provide a starting point for the book.

It's important that you're familiar with the platform and browser you want to use because the book doesn't provide any handholding in this regard. To focus on HTML5 and JavaScript as fully as possible, the book covers browsers marginally and platform requirements not at all. You really do need to know how to install applications, use the browser, and generally work with your chosen platform before you begin working with this book.

Knowing a little about HTML is helpful but not essential. Any experience you have with programming will be helpful as well. The book doesn't assume you have any knowledge of JavaScript.

# Conventions Used in This Book

This book uses special typeface to emphasize some information. For example, entries that you need to type appear in **bold**. All code, Website URLs, and onscreen messages appear in `monofont type`. When I define a new word, you see that word in *italics*.

Because you use multiple applications when you're working with JavaScript, I always point out when to move from one application to the next. However, the testers for this book tried out the code with the Internet Explorer, Firefox, and Chrome browsers on the Macintosh, Linux, and Windows platforms. One tester also checked at least some of the code using a Windows 8 phone. In most cases, you shouldn't experience any problem working with your application unless specifically noted in the application description. Please let me know at `John@JohnMuellerBooks.com` if you ever experience a problem with one of the examples.

# How This Book Is Organized

This book contains several parts. Each part demonstrates a particular JavaScript concept. In each chapter, I discuss a particular topic and include example programs that you can use to discover more about JavaScript on your own. It isn't necessary to read the book cover-to-cover — you can peruse the topics you find most interesting as you would with any reference book. However, you'll get more from the book if you do read it cover-to-cover. You can find the source code for this book on the Dummies.com Website at `http://www.dummies.com/go/html5programmingwith javascript`.

## Part 1: Understanding the Basics of JavaScript

This part of the book helps you gain a perspective of what the language can do for you as a developer and then shows you some simple examples of how the language works. Chapter 1 exposes you to JavaScript by presenting simple examples — you aren't expected to fully understand how they work, but you do gain an understanding of what JavaScript is like and how it could potentially help you create amazing browser-based applications. Chapter 2 spends time exploring some common tools you should consider using when writing your JavaScript applications. Chapter 3 begins exploring how HTML5 and JavaScript work together to create a useful programming environment.

# Part II: Speaking the JavaScript Language

Before you can do anything with JavaScript, you need to know how to speak the language. Chapters 4, 5, and 6 introduce you to the essential elements of the JavaScript language in the form of variables and objects. Everything in JavaScript is an object. Before you can do anything else, you need to understand these objects and discover how to use them.

# Part III: Meeting JavaScript's Control Structures

Complex applications rely on control structures to organize tasks, optionally perform them, and perform them repetitively. Chapter 7 focuses on functions, which are the JavaScript method of organizing tasks in easily understood and reusable pieces. Chapter 8 tells you how to make decisions using JavaScript code. Finally, Chapter 9 discusses techniques for performing tasks repetitively. Taken together, these three chapters help you create complete and useful JavaScript applications.

This part of the book also discusses errors. Errors can happen in every application, even when that application has no errors in it. A user can enter incorrect data or an environmental factor can cause various sorts of data degradation and loss. Many errors are completely out of your hands. However, recovering from these errors is completely within your grasp, which is the topic of Chapter 10.

# Part IV: Interacting with Users and HTML

This part of the book focuses on user interactions. The basis of interaction in JavaScript is the Document Object Model (DOM), which is the focus of Chapter 11. To react to user actions and external activity, your application must handle events. Chapter 12 describes all sorts of events and how you can handle them within your application.

Creating a good presentation also helps you motivate users to interact with your application. Chapters 13, 14, and 15 discuss various kinds of presentation techniques you use to create successful applications with JavaScript.

## *Part V: Extending JavaScript Further*

JavaScript is an astounding language that lets you interact with users in new ways that reflect the modern reality of computing device usage. This part of the book exposes you to just a subset of the truly amazing things you can do to extend JavaScript to help you create robust applications. Chapter 16 focuses on XML, which is a technique you can use to store data of all sorts without much effort at all.

One of the techniques you can use to make users more receptive to your applications is to make the application faster and more efficient. That's the purpose of Asynchronous JavaScript and XML (AJAX). It helps you create efficient applications as described in Chapter 17.

The most incredible feature of JavaScript is the support it enjoys from third party developers. This book can only introduce you to one such library (and even this one library can help you create new applications quickly). Chapters 18, 19, and 20 introduce you to a third-party library named jQuery, which can help you add interactions and special effects to your applications. This library also provides access to a number of interesting widgets that you can use to give your applications a professional appearance.

## *Part VI: The Part of Tens*

This part of the book contains two top ten lists of things related to JavaScript that you'll find handy as you work your way through your first applications. Chapter 21 contains some parting coding examples and ideas on how to make your coding environment more fun, efficient, and productive. Chapter 22 is all about the future. It discusses some ideas of where application development will go in the future.

## *The companion Website*

This book contains a lot of code, and you might not want to type it. In fact, it's probably better if you don't type this code manually. Fortunately, you can find the source code for this book on the Dummies.com Website at `http://www.dummies.com/go/html5programmingwithjavascript`. The source code is organized by chapter, and I always tell you about the example files in the text. The best way to work with a chapter is to download all the source code for it at one time.

# Icons Used in This Book

As you read this book, you'll see icons in the margins that indicate material of interest (or not, as the case may be). This section briefly describes each icon in this book.

Tips are nice because they help you save time or perform some task without a lot of extra work. The tips in this book are timesaving techniques or pointers to resources that you should try to get the maximum benefit from JavaScript or HTML5.

I don't want to sound like an angry parent or some kind of maniac, but you should avoid doing anything marked with a Warning icon. Otherwise, you could find that your program melts down and takes your data with it.

Whenever you see this icon, think *advanced* tip or technique. You might find these tidbits of useful information just too boring for words, or they could contain the solution you need to get a program running. Skip these bits of information whenever you like.

If you don't get anything else out of a particular chapter or section, remember the material marked by this icon. This text usually contains an essential process or a bit of information that you must know to write JavaScript programs successfully.

There are times when a topic is so immense that you really need additional information about it. Often, the topic covered is outside the scope of this book, and discussing it in the book would become distracting and would divert attention away from programming HTML5 with JavaScript. Paragraphs marked with this icon contain links to online sources you can use to discover more about a topic that will interest you, but you don't need to know about it in order to understand the code in the book.

# Where to Go from Here

It's time to start your HTML5 programming with JavaScript adventure! If you're a complete JavaScript novice, you should start with Chapter 1 and progress through the book at a pace that allows you to absorb as much of the material as possible. If you're in an absolute rush to get going with JavaScript as quickly as possible, you could possibly skip to Chapter 2 with the understanding that you may find some topics a bit confusing later.

Everyone should read Chapter 2 because it contains some setup information you need to use the examples effectively. The book assumes that you have some type of Web server set up to run examples that require it. Because Apache runs on all of the target platforms for this book (Linux, Windows, and Mac OS X), I recommend you install this particular Web server. In addition, Apache is the most popular server on the Internet, so you'll definitely encounter it at some point.

Advanced readers, those who already have a basic understanding of JavaScript, can save time by reading Chapter 2 and then moving directly to Chapter 11. If you're really in a rush to get to the best material in the book, you can always try to start with Chapter 17 and then go back to earlier chapters as necessary when you have questions. However, it's important that you understand how each example works before moving to the next one. Every example has important lessons for you, and you could miss vital content if you start skipping too much information.

Occasionally, Wiley's technology books are updated. If this book has technical updates, they'll be posted at `http://www.dummies.com/go/html5 programmingwithjavascriptupdates.`

# Part I
# Understanding the Basics of JavaScript

 Visit http://www.dummies.com for more great *For Dummies* content online.

# In this part . . .

- ✔ Discover why JavaScript is such an important addition to your programming toolbox.

- ✔ Create a simple example that demonstrates the basics of using JavaScript.

- ✔ Obtain a basic list of tools you can use to make writing JavaScript applications easier.

- ✔ Uncover the hidden developer features found in most browsers.

- ✔ Install Apache on your system to use as a test site.

- ✔ Understand basic JavaScript programming language terminology.

- ✔ Determine when visitors have JavaScript turned off in their browsers.

# Chapter 1

# HTML, Say Hello to JavaScript

. . . . . . . . . . . . . . . . . . . . . . . . . . . . . . . . . . . . . . . . . . . .

. . . . . . . . . . . . . . . . . . . . . . . . . . . . . . . . . . . . . . . . . . . .

*J*avaScript is a text-based scripting language that's interpreted by a client system to perform tasks in various settings. The most common setting is within browsers. A developer wants to do something special, such as accept input from a form, and JavaScript makes it possible.

JavaScript appears in many other places. For example, Windows has long allowed the use of JavaScript to create applications, and now it has an even bigger role with Windows 8. (See `http://msdn.microsoft.com/ library/windows/apps/br211385.aspx` for details.) Special versions of JavaScript also support application development on the Macintosh. (See `www.latenightsw.com/freeware/JavaScriptOSA` as an example.) In fact, you can even run Linux in a browser by using a JavaScript emulator. (See `www.webmonkey.com/2011/05/yes-virginia-that-is-linux-running-on-javascript` for details.) The point is that JavaScript is a language that appears in all sorts of places on many different operating systems. When you discover JavaScript, you open an exciting new world of programming that works on myriad platforms — a dream that developers have had for a very long time.

This book doesn't explore all of the possible environments in which you can use JavaScript. I doubt very much that you could examine the topic in any detail with an entire shelf of books. What you'll encounter is how JavaScript is used with HTML5, the newest version of the HyperText Markup Language (HTML). HTML5 and JavaScript are made for each other. By combining these two languages, you create a robust environment for Web applications. Modern Web applications can perform an amazing array of tasks —

everything from word processing to database entry. The use of HTML5 and JavaScript together makes it possible for anyone or any organization to move applications from the desktop to the *cloud* (a special location on the Internet used to store applications and data), where any device capable of running JavaScript can access and use them. In short, combining HTML5 with JavaScript can free users from using a specific device to interact with any application you can imagine.

Of course, any book on a programming language must begin with some basics and present some ground rules, which is precisely what you find in this chapter. You discover a little more about what JavaScript is and how it can help you create interesting applications. You'll also begin creating some basic JavaScript applications in this chapter. They won't do too much at first; you'll gain a sense of what JavaScript can do after you've worked with it some more.

JavaScript can work on any platform that supports it and in any browser that supports HTML5. To see what level of support your browser provides, go to `http://html5test.com` and enable JavaScript support (if asked). This site tells what your browser can and can't do with JavaScript so that you know whether your browser can use specific features in this book. (You may want to print the results so that you have a reference to them as you progress through the book.) For the purpose of making things easier for everyone, the scripts in this book were tested with the latest version of Firefox available at the time of writing on a Windows 7 system. (See Chapter 2 for more on the many benefits to using Firefox for developing browser-based applications.) You may see slight variations in screen output and functionality when you use a different browser or operating system.

# Introducing JavaScript

Originally, the Internet allowed only *static pages* — pages that presented fixed content that couldn't change. Yes, there were links and other features that let you move to other pages, but the content on them didn't change. JavaScript was originally conceived as a means for making Web pages *dynamic* — making it possible for users to interact with them and receive something in return. In fact, that's the basic idea behind JavaScript today, but the interactions have become complex enough that you can call them applications. The following sections introduce you to what JavaScript is all about and why you need to add this language to your programming toolbox.

## Discovering the history of JavaScript

You won't find a complete history of JavaScript in this book because so many people have already written about it. There are many histories of JavaScript on the Internet. One of the better histories is at `http://java script.about.com/od/reference/` `a/history.htm`. This short history will provide you with a good overview of the most important facts about the creation of JavaScript. You can find a more detailed history of JavaScript at `http://www.howto create.co.uk/jshistory.html`.

## Java and JavaScript aren't long-lost relatives

Some programmers have confused Java and JavaScript over the years, partly because of the naming similarities. It turns out that JavaScript was originally named LiveScript. Netscape saw how popular Java had become and decided to rename LiveScript to JavaScript to play off that popularity. In reality, Java and JavaScript are completely different languages, and you shouldn't confuse the two. There's nothing similar between Java and JavaScript. For example, whereas Java is a *compiled* language (one that's turned into a native executable using a special application) that requires a plug-in to run in your browser, JavaScript is an *interpreted* language (a text description of what to do that requires an interpreter, another sort of special application, to execute) that requires no special plug-in because the browser provides native support for it.

There's nothing unusual about the similarity in naming between Java and JavaScript. Vendors have used naming similarities for many products in order to obtain some sort of benefit from the popularity of similarly named products. The most important thing to remember is that you can't use any Java functionality, documentation, or tools to create your JavaScript applications. The two languages are quite different.

## Recognizing the benefits of JavaScript

JavaScript is an amazing language that can perform a wide variety of tasks when you know how to use it. In fact, in many respects, JavaScript is unique in the programming world because you don't have to perform any special tricks to get it to work in most environments. Not every environment is completely compatible with JavaScript, but you can usually get essential features of an application to work no matter which environment runs the application you create. With this in mind, you want to know what JavaScript can do for you as a developer because having this information makes it easier for you to convince management and other developers to work with you on JavaScript solutions.

The following sections discuss the most commonly cited benefits of JavaScript (although you'll almost certainly find other benefits in online articles such as the ones described at `http://ezinearticles.com/?What-Are-the-Benefits-of-JavaScript?&id=4743036`).

### Using JavaScript in any browser

JavaScript is quite flexible because it's an interpreted language. Interpreted languages are distributed as plain text. Every computer platform ever created can understand plain text. Even old mainframes can understand plain text, at some level, which means that plain text is the most common form of computer communication ever created. A special browser feature, the *interpreter,* reads the text description of what to do and then performs those tasks within the browser environment. Every browser has this special feature built-in so you never need to download a special plug-in when working with JavaScript — the support you need is already available. Because the JavaScript language is essentially the same in every browser, the same text description of what tasks to perform works everywhere. This text description is the JavaScript language that you use throughout the book to create the example applications.

It's important to realize that the browser's interpreter must recognize all of the JavaScript key words and programming constructs. As JavaScript has improved, it has added new features that older interpreters don't understand. Consequently, you can't expect a really old interpreter to completely understand a JavaScript application that uses all of the latest features. In many cases, the application may still run, but with reduced functionality. In other cases, the program may crash simply because the interpreter doesn't know what to do. This is why you need to know which platforms support the combination of HTML and JavaScript you want to use in your Web pages and why you need to test your browser at `http://html5test.com` to ensure the examples in this book will work for you.

### Using JavaScript with any operating system

Many programming languages rely on special operating system features. Native code programs — those that speak the operating system's special language — are especially attached to a particular operating system because the language relies on the special operating system features. JavaScript has no such reliance. All JavaScript cares about is the browser in which it runs. The browser interacts with the operating system and takes care of all of those low-level tasks so JavaScript can be generalized to work with any operating system.

### Using JavaScript with any device

Some developers are used to the idea that their applications will work only on certain devices. In fact, most developers are happy when they can get an application to work on just one *platform* (the combination of a specific device matched with a specific operating system) successfully. JavaScript has no such limits.

If you have a device that has an HTML5-compatible browser with JavaScript support, it's quite likely that the applications in this book will work. (That said, I've tested the applications only on the systems specified in the book's introduction, so your results will vary depending on device and browser compatibility.) Even mobile devices will use JavaScript without problems. For example, if you have a Blackberry, it's quite likely that the examples in this book will work on it without problem. (See `http://www.sencha.com/blog/html5-scorecard-rim-blackberry-playbook-2` for details on Blackberry support for HTML5.)

Most developers will find it quite amazing that the application created with JavaScript could potentially work on platforms that didn't even exist at the time the application was written! The idea that JavaScript is everywhere will surprise many people. Don't be surprised when the Android user sitting next to you in the doctor's office is using the application you wrote in JavaScript for the PC. JavaScript doesn't care where it runs.

### Accessing common platform features

As previously mentioned in this chapter, JavaScript requires an interpreter, and that interpreter translates JavaScript key words into something the underlying platform can understand. Unlike some other languages, JavaScript doesn't exist within a *sandbox* — a special programming environment that limits access to operating system features to reduce potential security problems. This means that JavaScript can tell the interpreter that it wants to save a file somewhere, and then the interpreter will do its best to satisfy that need using platform-specific functionality. JavaScript doesn't care how or where the file is saved — it simply cares that the file is saved. In short, JavaScript insulates your application from the platform in a way that makes it possible to create truly amazing applications.

There's never a free lunch when it comes to applications, however. JavaScript can perform simple tasks, such as saving a file. The catch is that you can't depend on it to use unique operating system features. For example, Windows supports file encryption, but you can't access that feature from JavaScript. As a consequence, the file you save to disk isn't encrypted unless the encryption is part of the standard platform method for doing things. Never assume that you can perform special platform tasks with JavaScript. Even so, you probably won't even miss these special features, because JavaScript works fine without them.

# Seeing How JavaScript Fits into an HTML Document

Now that you know a little more about JavaScript, it's time to see JavaScript in action. The following sections guide you through the process of creating a simple HTML5 document and adding some JavaScript code to it. You don't need to understand the underlying theory of why this application works yet. In addition, you don't need to fully understand the JavaScript language *constructs* (keywords used to build a Java application) yet — just follow along with the simple example to see what JavaScript can do.

This section is a lot more fun when you try the example in a number of browsers. Yes, you can get the gist of what's happening by using a single browser, but it will amaze you to see the application perform the same way no matter which browser you use. To get the most out of the following sections, try the example in two or more of your favorite HTML5-compatible browsers that include JavaScript support.

## Starting an HTML5 document

HTML has gone through a lot of changes over the years. In order to identify the various kinds of HTML, the World Wide Web Consortium (W3C) has created a number of specifications that define precisely what an HTML document of a particular type should look like. These standards are publicly available — although no one but a computer scientist can really understand them. You can see the HTML5 standard at `http://www.w3.org/TR/2011/WD-html5-20110525/`.

Make sure you get the full benefit of using this book by downloading the companion source code from `http://www.dummies.com/go/html5programmingwithjavascript`. The companion source code will greatly enhance your experience with the book and make working with JavaScript considerably easier. Make sure you also check the blog entries for this book at `http://blog.johnmuellerbooks.com/categories/263/html5-programming-with-javascript-for-dummies.aspx`. The blog entries answer commonly asked questions, provide additional examples, and help you better use the book content to perform tasks.

For the purposes of this book, you can start any HTML5 document like this (you can access this entire example in the `Test.HTML` file found in the `\Chapter 01\Simple JavaScript Example` folder of the downloadable source code for this book):

```
<!DOCTYPE html>
<html>
    <head>
        <title>JavaScript Example</title>
    </head>
    <body>
        <h1>My First JavaScript Example</h1>
        <p>This is a JavaScript test.</p>
    </body>
</html>
```

Each section of this example performs a specific task. For example, the `<!DOCTYPE html>` declaration tells you that this is an HTML5 document. Other sorts of HTML documents have other declarations. When a browser that understands HTML5 sees this declaration, it treats the rest of the document as an HTML5 document and allows use of HTML5 features.

The `<html>` tag begins and ends the document as a whole. Every HTML document also includes two other tags: a `<head>` tag where you place heading information (such as the page's title), and a `<body>` tag where you place the content you want displayed to the end user. This document includes a `<h1>` tag (first-level heading) and a `<p>` tag (paragraph). Figure 1-1 shows how this document looks in Firefox on a Windows 7 system. (Your screen may look a little different.)

**Figure 1-1:**
A typical
view of
a simple
HTML5
document.

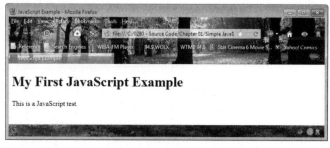

## Understanding the alert ( ) function

The first bit of JavaScript code you discover in this book is the `alert()` function. All that this function does is display a message box. You probably see the `alert()` function used on sites you visit several times a day because most developers use it relatively often to display updates and other information. Given the utility of the `alert()` function, it's a good addition to your JavaScript toolbox. The `alert()` function takes a message as input.

## Creating the JavaScript examples

This book contains a lot of JavaScript examples. You can type them if you want using any text editor or an editor designed specifically for working with JavaScript such as Komodo Edit (`http://www.activestate.com/komodo-edit`). The important thing is that the editor creates text without any formatting. If the editor adds formatting, then the JavaScript interpreter won't be able to read the file. Each example will include a suggested filename that you should use for your example. Simply save the file to a location you can easily find on your hard drive and then open it using your browser. Opening the file in your browser will cause the JavaScript to run automatically so that you can see how your code works. Chapter 2 provides more information on tools you can use to make your experience working with JavaScript a lot easier.

## Using the <script> tag

It's time to try the `alert()` function out. Type the following line of code after the `<p>This is a JavaScript test.</p>` line of code in your initial Web page:

```
<script language="JavaScript">
    alert("Hello World");
</script>
```

The `<script>` tag tells the browser to treat the text that follows as a script, rather than as text for display. The `language` attribute tells the browser that the code is in JavaScript and not some other language. When you display the page in a browser, the user sees a dialog box like the one shown in Figure 1-2.

**Figure 1-2:**
The alert()
function
displays a
simple mes-
sage box.

To dismiss the message box, the user simply clicks OK. There's nothing fancy about the `alert()` function, but it can convey simple messages, and it's so standard that any browser can display it, even if the browser wouldn't ordinarily work well with newer versions of JavaScript. Use the `alert()` function when you need to tell the user something and don't need to obtain any input in return.

# *Placing the code in the page heading*

Creating a script that runs immediately when you display the page probably works in some cases, but not in others. For example, you may not have anything to say to the user until the user performs some action. In this case, you place the script between the beginning and ending of the <head> tag. You also give the script a name so that you can access it at any time. Add this code under the <title> tag in the page you created earlier:

```
<script language="JavaScript">
   function SayHello()
   {
      alert("This is the SayHello() function!");
   }
</script>
```

As in the preceding section, you place the script within a <script> tag and tell the browser what language you're using to create the script. The function keyword tells the browser that this is a particular section of named code, which has a name of SayHello in this case. The curly braces ({}) tell the browser where the script code begins and ends. In this case, the script consists of a single line of code that contains the alert() function.

You could save the page at this point, and it would load just fine, but you can't access the SayHello() function. To access the SayHello() function, you must provide content that tells the browser to perform the tasks that are contained within the function. To make this happen, add the following lines of code after the <p> tag in <body> section of the page:

```
<input type="button"
       value="Click Me"
       onclick="SayHello()" />
```

This form of the <input> tag creates a button (specified by the type attribute). The button has Click Me as a caption as specified by the value attribute. When the user clicks the button, the browser performs the task defined by the SayHello() function as specified by the onclick attribute. Load the page in your browser and dismiss the initial message box. You see the button added to the page, as shown in Figure 1-3.

The <input> tag can create a number of controls on a page — buttons are only one such control. You change the kind of control that <input> creates through the type attribute. Later chapters show more of the <input> tag options at your disposal. For now, all you need to know is that <input> is a handy tag type to know about.

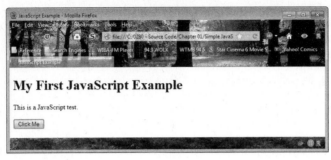

**Figure 1-3:**
The <input>
tag lets you
add a button
to the page.

The advantage of using named code and a button is that you can access the message box as often as needed. Whenever the user clicks Click Me, the browser displays the message box shown in Figure 1-4. Try it now. You must dismiss the dialog box before the browser returns control to the page, but you can display the dialog box as many times as desired.

**Figure 1-4:**
You can
display this
dialog box
as often
as desired
without
reloading
the page.

## Relying on external files

When you use a particular script regularly, you can do one of two things:

- ✔ Use cut and paste techniques to place the script everywhere you need it.
- ✔ Place the script in an external file.

The problem with cutting and pasting is that you end up with lots of copies of the same script. If you need to make a change to the script, you have to change every copy you create, which is error prone and time consuming. Using an external file means that you create the script only once and then use it everywhere. The script is easy to change because you change it in only one location.

Begin this part of the example by creating a new file using any means you like (such as a favorite text editor or an application specially designed for working with JavaScript). Name it `External.JS`. JavaScript files normally have a `.JS` file extension. Place this code inside the `External.JS` file:

```
function ExternalSayHello()
{
    alert("This is the ExternalSayHello() function!");
}
```

This code functions exactly like the code that appears in the <head> tag of the example page. It displays a message box using the `alert()` function. However, the functions you create in `External.JS` must have unique names. You can't have two functions with the same name in the same page. Notice that this function has a name of `ExternalSayHello` to differentiate it from the `SayHello()` function you created earlier in the chapter.

You have to tell the page where to access this code. To do this, you create a different sort of <script> tag entry in the <head> tag area of the page. This <script> tag looks like this:

```
<script src="External.JS">
</script>
```

The `src` attribute tells the browser to load all of the code found in `External.JS`. You access any function that appears in `External.JS` precisely the same way you would any code that appears in the <head> tag. To see how this works, add a new button directly after the first button you created in the preceding section using the following code:

```
<input type="button"
       value="Test External"
       onclick="ExternalSayHello()" />
```

This button works and acts precisely the same as the other button you created. The only difference is that it calls `ExternalSayHello()` instead of `SayHello()` when the user clicks the button. Figure 1-5 shows how the page looks with the additional button on it.

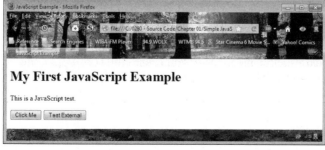

**Figure 1-5:**
The page has two buttons on it now.

Unless you provide additional formatting, the browser simply places the but-tons side by side on the page as shown. When the user clicks Test External, the browser displays the message box shown in Figure 1-6. As with the Click Me button, you can display this message box as often as needed.

**Figure 1-6:**
Click Test
External
to see this
message
box.

This is the ExternalSayHello() function!

OK

# Chapter 2

# Assessing Tools of the Trade

. . . . . . . . . . . . . . . . . . . . . . . . . . . . . . . . . . . . . . . . . . . . . .

. . . . . . . . . . . . . . . . . . . . . . . . . . . . . . . . . . . . . . . . . . . . . .

*M*ost development efforts require the use of tools. JavaScript is no different. You need tools to create, test, and *debug* (remove errors from) the applications you create. Fortunately, the tools you need to work with JavaScript are few, and you can obtain all of them without paying a cent. JavaScript is unique; there are few other languages that provide anything close to this level of support. With most languages, you have to invest at least a little money to obtain a truly usable set of tools. This chapter shows how to build a useful suite of tools that will work with the three target platforms for this book: Windows, Mac OS X, and Linux. However, many of these tools work just fine on other platforms, and you should feel free to expand the list as needed to meet your particular needs.

It pays to categorize the way you use tools. Doing so ensures that you can focus on the requirements of that specific tool and helps you avoid needless tool duplication (which can lead to all sorts of problems later, such as figuring out which tool you used to perform a task such as writing the code). This chapter is broken down into three main tool categories:

✔ **Browsers:** You can't test every browser in existence — doing so would require years, and your users aren't willing to wait that long to see your next application design achievement. (Testing applications in multiple browsers is needed because not every browser supports every HTML5 tag, amongst other issues.) However, you do need to test the browsers you expect users to work with most often, and you need to have a browser that includes tools necessary to ensure your JavaScript application works as expected. Choosing a good set of browsers is an essential first step in JavaScript development.

✔ **Editors:** JavaScript is a pure text language, so you can use any text editor to create your JavaScript application. The fact that you don't need a *compiler* (a special program used to turn human readable source code into bits that your computer understands) for JavaScript means that the requirements for an editor are significantly smaller than for other languages. However, using an editor specifically designed to write JavaScript applications can help you in significant ways. For example, a dedicated JavaScript editor can provide help in using the built-in JavaScript functions.

✔ **Testing environments:** It's possible to check your JavaScript application by opening the page from the hard drive in your browser. The browser really doesn't care about the source of the page. Unfortunately, local testing ensures only that the code will work; it doesn't test the code in the same environment the user will rely upon. To ensure that your JavaScript application works as anticipated, you need a hosting environment. Because the Apache server works on every one of the target platforms for this book, is available at no cost, and currently enjoys a 64.5 percent market share (as stated at `http://w3techs.com/technologies/overview/web_server/all`), this book uses the Apache server for testing purposes.

As you visit each of these tool categories, think about how you work with Web applications today and how you expect to work with them as your skills improve. It also pays to consider the platforms you plan to support, as well as those that users will use even if you hadn't planned to support them. (For example, many businesses are now finding a need to support applications on mobile devices, such as smartphones, even though the original application was never designed to work in this environment.)

# Researching Browsers and Their Debugging Tools

There are probably thousands of browsers available on the market today, and each browser has a number of versions. For example, Firefox has at least 16 versions and a number of minor builds within each of those versions. In short, you need to know which browsers your users rely on most often and then also choose a browser for your own needs.

Getting the user selection is relatively easy in many cases — just take a poll. If you don't know which users will rely on your application or you lack the resources to take a poll, then you can always choose to support the browsers with the greatest market share. A number of sites provide this sort of information, but the most flexible of these sites is NetMarketshare (`http://www.netmarketshare.com/browser-market-share.aspx?qprid=2&qpcustomd=0`). You can choose to define the market share based on the browser group, operating system, platform, device, or any combination of the four. Unfortunately some information on this site requires a paid subscription. You can also obtain the information from other sites, such as the W3Schools site at `http://www.w3schools.com/browsers/browsers_stats.asp`. The point is that you should have some basis on which to make a decision about which browsers to check; otherwise, you spend considerable time testing as many browsers as possible and may not create a usable application for any of them because of the conflicts you encounter.

When choosing browsers, make sure you verify that they actually provide the required support before you spend time working with them. Not every browser supports JavaScript fully, and even more don't support HTML5. The introduction to Chapter 1 discusses a test site you can use to check HTML5 readiness, but you can also find charts online that provide the information, such as the ones at HTML5 & CSS3 Readiness (`http://html5readiness.com`) and HTML5 Accessibility (`http://html5accessibility.com`). (CSS stands for Cascading Style Sheets.)

This book shows all of the example output using the Firefox browser because it provides the best flexibility and the greatest number of plug-in development tools. In addition, Firefox looks about the same no matter which platform you use it on, and I wanted to be sure as many readers as possible would be able to see the example output the same way it appears on my screen. However, the examples are also tested using Google Chrome and a native browser on each of the target platforms (Internet Explorer on Windows and Safari on the Macintosh — Firefox happens to be the native browser on the version of Linux used for the book).

The browser you choose to use needs to have some sort of debugging tools with it. Otherwise, you can't easily find the errors in your application and will drive yourself crazy trying to fix them. With this in mind, the following sections explore some browsers you may want to work with when creating JavaScript applications. These browsers are extremely popular, and they provide built-in debugger support, plug-in debugger support, or a combination of the two.

## *Catching up with Firefox*

Firefox (`http://www.mozilla.org/firefox/new`) comes with some basic tools for performing development tasks. These tools will likely serve most of your needs in the book.

Firefox is available for most of the platforms you need to support (including Windows, Mac OS X, and Linux). It works equally well on both desktop and mobile devices (you can check the list of supported phones at `http://www.mozilla.org/firefox/mobile/platforms`), so the application you test for one will normally work with the other. However, even though Firefox seems to work everywhere, it isn't the most popular browser out there, so you need to weigh the advantages in tools and general availability against the number of people actually using Firefox. The following sections tell you more about the technologies you can use to turn Firefox into a great developer tool.

### Exploring the developer tools

You see the tools when you choose Tools➪Web Developer. The following list describes the entries on this menu:

- ✔ **Developer Toolbar:** This tool displays a toolbar at the bottom of the browser window that contains a textbox where you can type debugging commands. In addition, there are buttons you can use to access the Web Console, Inspector, and built-in Debugger tools.

- ✔ **Web Console:** This tool displays a pane at the bottom of the browser that contains log entries for the current page. You can obtain information that relates to the network connection, JavaScript, Cascading Style Sheets (CSS), and general logging. Most of the information you see is focused on error or warning data. The log entries can also provide information of various sorts.

- ✔ **Inspect:** You use this tool to select a specific area of the displayed page so that you can see the code associated with it. It's also possible to perform tasks such as copying the information or deleting it from the page.

- ✔ **Responsive Design View:** A Responsive Design View helps you see the pages you create from different perspectives without actually creating a test environment to produce them. For example, you can configure the display to different resolutions so you can see how the page will appear in those environments. The tool also comes with a rotate feature that mimics the rotation offered by devices such as smartphones.

- ✔ **Debugger:** You use this tool to create an environment where you can inspect JavaScript code as it executes. The debugger offers features such as setting breakpoints, stepping through the code, and inspecting variable values. You won't find any advanced features, and it's not possible to do things such as setting watches, but the debugger does provide enough information to perform simple debugging tasks.

- ✔ **Scratchpad:** This tool provides a simple text editor where you can type JavaScript and then execute it. You can save the resulting code, if desired. The Scratchpad provides direct access to other Firefox development tools, such as the debugger. This is an extremely basic editor, but it does work.

- ✔ **Style Editor:** When you first start this tool, you see all the styles on the current page. You can use the tool to create new styles, edit existing styles, import styles you've saved to disk, or delete styles you no longer need.

✔ **Page Source:** This tool displays a text editor view of the source code for the current page precisely as the browser sees it. In some cases, this means that the text is essentially unformatted and difficult to see. You can use the text editor to modify the page source and save it to disk.

✔ **Error Console:** You use this tool to obtain a list of the current errors, warnings, and messages for the displayed page. Click the links associated with each entry to see the associated code. In most cases, the code is formatted so that you can see it in an easily understood format.

✔ **Get More Tools:** This special entry takes you to a page that shows additional development tools. It's important to note that you can easily find additional Firefox development tools by searching for them. However, this page provides a good starting point for obtaining the additional tools you need. Here are some of the more interesting tools on this page:

- *Greasemonkey:* A plug-in that provides access to a wealth of JavaScript scriptlets you can use to modify the behavior of a page.

- *Stylish:* This tool makes it possible to add skin and theme support for many sites and to modify the appearance of Firefox itself. The reason a developer would want to use this tool is to make it easy for users to customize the appearance of a page without a lot of work on the developer's part.

- *iMacros for Firefox:* Many developers rely on macro recorders to perform repetitive work (such as filling out forms) automatically. Otherwise, the developer spends considerable time interacting with the page as a user rather than fixing problems as a developer.

- *ColorZilla:* Working with color can be problematic even for designers. This tool makes it possible for you to grab the perfect colors you see onscreen and use them as needed on your page. You can also generate gradients and work with color in other ways without driving yourself crazy. (As an alternative, you can always try Rainbow Color Tools, which is available from the same page.)

- *Pixlr Grabber:* Sometimes you need to grab screens and pull images from your site to perform tasks such as creating help files. This tool makes it easy to grab, edit, and share these images as needed.

- *fontinfo:* Deciding which font to use on your site can prove perplexing because there are thousands (possibly millions) of font variations just for the standard font families. This tool makes it possible for you to learn the details of a font used on a favorite site so that you can use the same font (or a variation of it) on your own site.

### Examining developer plug-ins

One of the features that people like about Firefox is that it supports a robust set of plug-ins, or *add-ons* in Firefox parlance. (This book uses *plug-ins* for consistency because each vendor seems to use a different term to refer to the same sort of software.) If you don't like how a particular plug-in works, there are usually other plug-ins you can try. In other words, Firefox offers a highly customizable environment that you can tweak to meet your specific requirements. As your JavaScript skills grow and the kinds of applications you create change, you can modify your Firefox environment to match.

The negative side of Firefox is that it can consume a considerable amount of resources on your system. It isn't quite the resource hog that Internet Explorer is, but you'll find that you need to provide enough memory for Firefox to work properly. As you add more plug-ins, Firefox consumes more resources. Of course, this makes sense because you're adding software to an existing setup. The use of third party plug-ins can also cause stability problems at times and potentially open security holes, so you need to choose plug-ins with care.

The following list provides you with some ideas of plug-ins you may want to investigate for your Firefox installation:

✔ **JSView (**`https://addons.mozilla.org/firefox/addon/jsview`**):** Most boilerplate (commonly used) JavaScript is stored in external files because using an external file offers significant advantages to the developer. Unfortunately, most development tools view only the code stored with the current page. This tool helps you view the code that appears in external files so that you can better understand how the page works.

✔ **Foundstone HTML5 Local Storage Explorer (**`https://addons.mozilla.org/firefox/addon/foundstone-html5-local-storage`**):** HTML5 includes a new feature that provides access to local storage. Unfortunately, your browser probably doesn't know anything about local storage. This tool makes it possible for you to view, modify, and delete items in local storage as you work through JavaScript applications that work with local storage.

✔ **HTML5toggle (**`https://addons.mozilla.org/firefox/addon/html5toggle-toggle-html5-su`**):** In some cases, you need to know whether a page will work when a browser lacks HTML5 support. This plug-in makes it possible to turn HTML5 support off so you can see how the page works without it.

✔ **HeadingsMap (**`https://addons.mozilla.org/firefox/addon/headingsmap`**):** Discovering how a page is structured is important when working with complex pages that you didn't create (or created with the help of someone else). This tool creates a document map that you can use to learn the page structure and interact with various page elements.

✔ **Local Load (**`https://addons.mozilla.org/firefox/addon/local-load`**):** Use this plug-in to load common JavaScript libraries from a local source rather than over an Internet connection. Using this utility can save considerable development time by making it possible for you to load and test your pages more quickly.

✔ **HTML5 WebSQL for Firefox** (`https://addons.mozilla.org/`
`firefox/addon/html5-websql-for-firefox`)**:** If your JavaScript
application relies on database support, this plug-in may provide the
required database connectivity for you without a lot of extra coding on
your part. This plug-in uses the SQLite (an open source database manager) support provided with Firefox to provide the required database
connectivity.

Firefox provides access to hundreds of plug-ins that a developer could find
useful in a given circumstance. There simply isn't room in the chapter to discuss them all. This list presents a few of the plug-ins that I've tried personally
for various development tasks. Your best chance at finding the support you
need is to browse through the list of available plug-ins online and try a few of
them. You can always uninstall plug-ins that don't work as expected.

## Meeting Google Chrome

You may decide that you really don't want to use Firefox. Google Chrome
(`http://www.google.com/chrome`) makes a good alternative browser.
Like Firefox, you can find versions of Chrome for Windows, Macintosh, and
Linux operating systems. In addition, Google provides Chrome support for a
number of mobile platforms.

From a pure support perspective, Chrome and Firefox are about equal. In addition, like Firefox, Chrome provides great HTML5 and JavaScript support. In
fact, you can develop your applications using either browser and be almost
certain that the application will behave precisely the same way in the other
browser. (There are some small differences between the two browsers when
you use some of the more esoteric features.)

To access the developer tools in Chrome, you click the Customize and
Control Google Chrome button, which appears in the upper-right corner
of the display and looks like three dashes stacked one on top of the other.
Choose the Tools submenu and you see these development options:

✔ **View Source:** This tool displays a browser view of the source code for
the current page with appropriate white space added so that you can
see it clearly. The output includes line numbers to make it easy to refer
to a specific line in the source code. Unfortunately, you can't edit the
source code using this view, so you still need a text editor to work with
the code.

✔ **Developer Tools:** The Developer Tools window contains a number of
views that you can use to interact with the current page. The next section of this chapter discusses these views in greater detail.

✓ **JavaScript Console:** You can use the JavaScript Console window to interact with the JavaScript code in the current window, or experiment with JavaScript code of your own. The actual Console view provides an interactive environment where you can experiment with JavaScript. The "Working with the JavaScript Console window" section, later in this chapter, provides additional information about this window.

If you read about Firefox development tools in the "Catching up with Firefox" section earlier in this chapter, you might get the idea that working with Firefox and Google Chrome at the same time means learning two completely different toolsets. Fortunately, you really don't have to pull your hair out while spending a lot of time working through two toolsets. You can find some tools that work the same with both browsers on whatever platform you use. For example, Web Developer (`http://chrispederick.com/work/web-developer`) provides a consistent interface and precisely the same toolset for both Chrome and Firefox on the Windows, Mac OS X, and Linux platforms. So, you can learn how to use this single tool and use it to test your applications in a number of environments.

### Working with the Developer Tools window

The Developer Tools window can provide you with all sorts of information about the page you're working with. For example, you can discover where each element comes into play when working with the visual page. Simply highlight an area in the code, and you see that element selected in the output. For example, if you highlight `<h1>Browser Information</h1>` in the Developer Tools window, you see the Browser Information heading highlighted in the output. Figure 2-1 shows a typical example of the kind of information you see when working with the Developer Tools window.

Notice the icons that appear across the top of the Developer Tools window. Each of these icons selects a different function that this tool can perform. The following list provides an overview of each function:

✓ **Elements:** Displays a hierarchical listing of the elements within the page. You can select each element, see where it appears in the output, and discover the properties of that element. The information includes details such as the effect of styles on that particular element.

✓ **Resources:** Provides a listing of the resources that the page requires. You can obtain information about code, Web SQL (a kind of database manager created by the World Wide Web Consortium, W3C), IndexedDB (another sort of database manager created by Mozilla), local storage, session storage, cookies, and the application cache. All of this information helps you understand how the page interacts with its environment and what it expects the system to provide.

**Figure 2-1:**
Use the
Developer
Tools
window to
determine
how the
page is put
together.

✔ **Network:** Creates a graphic display of how the page interacts with the network. For example, if the page requires access to an external JavaScript file, the graph shows the time required to perform a Domain Name System (DNS) lookup, connect to the external server, send the request, wait for the server to process the request, and then receive the file.

✔ **Sources:** Displays the sources used to create a particular page, including external sources, such as external JavaScript files. You can view each of these sources, set breakpoints in them, single-step through them, and perform other debugging tasks. When an application is paused, you can view variable information, check the call stack, and perform other debugging tasks.

✔ **Timeline:** Defines the way the application behaves by providing output in graphic form. For example, you can trace the handling of events within the application.

✔ **Profiles:** Tracks the execution speed of individual elements of your JavaScript application to aid in tuning application performance. For example, you can see the effect of clicking a button or calling a method. The profile helps you see where the application spends most of its time so that you have a better idea of where to tune the application.

✔ **Audits:** Performs an audit on application behavior.

✔ **Console:** Displays a list of errors, warnings, and log entries associated with the current page. Each entry provides links that you can click to obtain further information. For example, you can click a link to see where the fault appears in the source code. Another link takes you to the Network function so that you can see the effect of the fault on application performance.

### Working with the JavaScript Console window

The JavaScript Console window is part of the Developer Tools window. Normally, you see the warnings, errors, and log entries for the application in this window. However, you can also use the JavaScript Console window for other tasks. For example, you can type code into it to see what happens. For example, type **alert("Hello");** and press Enter, and you see a dialog box appear with the word *Hello* in it.

Using the JavaScript Console window can help you understand your code better, and it's especially useful when working through the examples in this book. The "Checking browser and version" section, later in this chapter, discusses a new JavaScript object that you haven't seen yet. You can try it now to see what it contains. Type **navigator.userAgent** and press Enter. You see the output shown in Figure 2-2.

**Figure 2-2:** A console can help you play with JavaScript and learn new things about it.

The `navigator.userAgent` object contains all kinds of useful information about the browser that requested the page. You can use this information to discover capabilities about the browser and determine whether it will work with your application. Later examples in the book will help you understand how to use the information that the `navigator.userAgent` object provides.

## Checking out native browsers: Internet Explorer or Safari

Depending on the requirements for your application, you may find yourself working with what most developers would term a *native browser* — the browser that ships with a particular operating system. For example, when working with Windows, you think of Internet Explorer as the native browser because that's what most users see when they first start the operating system. Likewise, the Macintosh comes with Safari as the native browser. Various versions of Linux have different native browsers, depending on what the vendor for that version of Linux chooses. The versions of Linux that many developers use rely on Firefox as the native browser, but that selection isn't set in stone, and you may have a different experience. The bottom line is that a native browser is the one that comes with the operating systems that you target with your application.

Generally speaking, the native browser may not be the one that's best for running your application, but you must test the application with it because many users won't want to add another browser to their system. For example, most sites that track browser usage say that Internet Explorer still enjoys a nearly 50 percent market share compared with 19 percent for Firefox and 17 percent for Chrome. (See http://arstechnica.com/business/2012/04/internet-explorer-market-share-surges-as-version-9-wins-hearts-and-minds for details.) However, HTML5 testing shows that Internet Explorer 9 scores an anemic 142 points out of a possible 500, whereas Firefox scores 382, and Chrome scores 434. When writing your code initially, you want a browser with strong development features and good support for both HTML5 and JavaScript, but the reality is that you'll need to write the application in such a way that it does support the native browsers, even when those browsers don't provide the level of support you'd like.

The sites that tell you about market penetration of various browsers (such as the arstechnica site mentioned in the previous paragraph) also tell you about browser version penetration in many cases. In looking at the statistics these sites provide, you discover that many users don't upgrade browsers as often as you might think. For example, some users (about 10 percent) are still running Internet Explorer 6, which has no support whatsoever for HTML5. Even though the tool you use provides full HTML5 support, the user may not have any support. Of course, you can't wait for every user to upgrade before you create an application, so the next best strategy is to detect the browser version and display a message saying the user doesn't have the support required to run the application and suggesting strongly that the user upgrade. The next section of this chapter, "Checking browser and version," discusses techniques you can use to verify that the user has a usable version of a browser for your application.

Don't get the idea that native browsers are completely useless or that you can't perform development work with them. For example, Internet Explorer includes a set of developer tools similar in some respects to the Developer Toolbar option for Firefox or the Developer Tools option for Chrome. To access these features, you click Tools (the gear icon) and then choose F12 Developer Tools from the menu. You see a window open at the bottom of the display with developer options in it. These options make it possible to examine the HTML, CSS, the browser console, scripts, an application profiler, and network activity (requests that your application makes outside the browser). The main problem with native browsers is that you can generally test them only on a single platform, so you can't be sure that your application will work everywhere you need it to work.

## Checking browser and version

Developers don't get to choose which browser a user relies upon in many cases. To determine whether a particular user can work with your application, you need to detect the user's browser and then determine whether that browser is acceptable. Creating the code required to perform this task isn't impossible, but it can be hard. Articles like the one at `http://www.java scripter.net/faq/browsern.htm` tell you how to perform this task, but one look at the code should tell you that it's a complex task. (You can see the output from this example code at `http://www.javascripter.net/faq/ browserv.htm.`)

Fortunately, developers perform some tasks so often that other developers have created libraries that provide the required functionality so you don't have to write the code. One such library is jQuery (`http://jquery. com`). You can simply add an external JavaScript statement to your code, as explained in Chapter 1, and use it. This library doesn't require that you download anything, and because it's easily accessible online, you don't have to worry about your user having it either.

The following example shows how to detect the name and version of the user's browser. If you want, for now you can simply load the example to see how the code works. Later examples will help you understand how this code works — all that's important for now is that you see that it's quite possible to discover the name and version of any browser without writing a lot of code to do it. (You can find complete code for this example in the `\Chapter 02\BrowserDetect` folder of the downloadable code as `BrowserDetect. HTML.`)

```
<!DOCTYPE html>
<html>
    <head>
        <title>Detect a Browser</title>
        <script
            src="http://code.jquery.com/jquery-latest.js">
        </script>
    </head>
    <body>
        <h1>Browser Information</h1>
        <p id="name"></p>
        <script language="JavaScript">
            var browser =
                $.uaMatch(navigator.userAgent).browser;
            $('p[id="name"]').html(
                "Browser Name: <span>" + browser + "</span>");
        </script>
        <p id="version"></p>
        <script language="JavaScript">
            $('p[id="version"]').html(
                "Version Number: <span>" + $.browser.version +
                "</span>");
        </script>
    </body>
</html>
```

Make sure you get the full benefit of using this book by downloading the companion source code from `http://www.dummies.com/go/html5 programmingwithjavascript`. The companion source code will greatly enhance your experience with the book and make working with JavaScript considerably easier. Make sure you also check the blog entries for this book at `http://blog.johnmuellerbooks.com/categories/263/html5-programming-with-javascript-for-dummies.aspx`. The blog entries answer commonly asked questions, provide additional examples, and help you better use the book contact to perform tasks.

This is an HTML5 page, so it starts with the HTML declaration, `<!DOCTYPE html>`. As with the examples in Chapter 1, this example begins with a basic structure that includes the `<html>`, `<head>`, `<title>`, and `<body>` tags.

The code begins with the first `<script>` tag that uses the `src` attribute to tell the browser where to find the jQuery library. You can copy this information as shown to any page where you want to use jQuery. Anyone who uses the application will automatically have access to jQuery as long as the browser can access the Internet. (You can also download a copy of jQuery for local access from the jQuery site.)

The <body> of the page starts out with a <h1> tag that contains the page's heading. The next step is to provide a place for jQuery to put the browser's name. In this case, the example uses a <p> (paragraph) tag that has an id of name. The first <script> creates a var (variable) named browser and places the browser's name in it. The browser name is always provided to your application as part of the JavaScript navigator.userAgent object, but working with this object is time consuming, so this code shows a one-line method for obtaining the information.

It's time to display the name onscreen. The $ (dollar sign) is a special symbol that refers to the jQuery library, which is also called an Application Programming Interface (API). The bit of code that says, $('p[id="name"]'). html, tells jQuery to use the <p> tag with an id value of name to hold some HTML. The code then tells jQuery to create some text, a <span>, and then place the name of the browser within that span. All this information appears in the <p> tag after the script executes.

Next comes a second <p> tag. This one has an id attribute of version. The accompanying script starts out the same as before. The entry $('p[id="version"]').html tells jQuery to place some HTML in the <p> tag with an id attribute of version. In this case, jQuery provides what you need as a property. All the code has to do is tell jQuery to place the value in browser.version within the <p> tag to display the browser's version number. When you run this example, you see output similar to what's shown in Figure 2-3.

**Figure 2-3:**
Detecting the browser name and version is made easier when using jQuery.

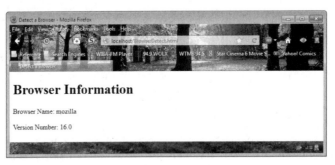

**Browser Information**

Browser Name: mozilla

Version Number: 16.0

# Discovering Programs to Write JavaScript

Both HTML5 and JavaScript are *pure text* (text that includes no formatting information whatsoever) interpreted languages, so you don't need anything special to work with them. Of course, it's always nice to have access to an application that will help you write code correctly. Much as a word processor includes a spelling and grammar checker to ensure your prose is correct, *dedicated editors* (those designed to create JavaScript code such as Komodo Edit) do have advantages over pure text editors. The following sections give you some idea of applications you can use to write your HTML5 and JavaScript code.

## Using a text editor

Some people actually do write their code using a text editor. It's not possible to write the code very quickly in such an environment, and the lack of any sort of checks means you'll make mistakes, but you can use any pure text editor to work through the examples in this book. For example, if you're working with Windows, you could use Notepad (a pure text editor) to create the examples. Mac users can use TextEdit for the task, while Linux users usually have access to either Vi or Vim. When working with TextEdit, you must set it up to create pure text output as described at `http://support.apple.com/kb/TA20406`.

Pure text editors have a number of advantages. Because they're already on the system, you don't have to download anything. In addition, a pure text editor doesn't cost anything, and most of them are simple to use because they contain no special features. You can be up and running with a pure text editor, especially one that comes with the operating system, in a matter of seconds.

Even though pure text editors work fine, it's important to compare them with dedicated editors. The following list describes the disadvantages of using pure text editors:

- **Lack of code checking:** A lack of code checking means that your code could contain errors that you'll discover only after you start running the application.

- **Lack of language helps:** Dedicated editors come with aids of all sorts. You usually find a help file as a minimum. Pop-up messages tell you how to complete a particular line of code in some cases and provide additional information about the function you're using in others. In sum, dedicated editors make it easier to type code correctly the first time.

- **Slower typing:** Some dedicated editors provide an autocomplete feature. You start typing the name of a function, and the editor automatically provides suggestions on how to complete the function name. Pressing Enter usually completes the name so you don't have to finish typing it. In fact, dedicated editors can provide suggestions on several levels — making it possible to complete an application in less time.

- **No code highlighting:** It may not seem very useful at first, but most dedicated editors provide *code highlighting* — the display of code in different colors. Keywords may appear in one color, function names in another, and variables in yet another color. The use of highlighting makes it possible to spot specific code features quickly and reduce the time required to make edits later.

✔ **Absence of community support:** Developer and user groups tend to support a dedicated editor, which means that you can obtain assistance with problems that you encounter. When working with a pure text editor, you're generally on your own in obtaining support.

## Using a dedicated editor

There are myriad dedicated editors on the market. In fact, you could possibly write a book just to discuss the advantages and disadvantages of various editors and still not cover the topic completely. Dedicated editors abound, and you have to choose which editor to use carefully. A good dedicated editor can greatly reduce your development time, make debugging significantly easier, and reduce the cost of creating the application. The reason that most developers rely on dedicated editors is that they make things easier, and everyone likes a reduction in workload whenever possible.

To make it easier to choose a dedicated editor, consider these criteria:

✔ **Cost:** You can obtain a great many dedicated editors today at no cost. Many of these editors include good support and receive updates relatively often. The editors that you pay for often include some type of incentive. For example, you might receive phone-based support, rather than the community support offered by a free editor.

✔ **Languages:** Many dedicated editors support more than one programming language. If at all possible, try to obtain a single editor that supports all the languages you want to use (or at least, as many as possible). Every editor has a learning curve, so reducing the number of editors you need to know has definite advantages.

✔ **Complexity:** Some dedicated editors are needlessly complex or have a flawed user interface that increases the amount of work you need to do. As complexity increases, so does the editor's learning curve. Every level of increased complexity means that you spend more time learning the editor rather than writing good code.

✔ **Functionality:** Some dedicated editors are incredibly easy to learn but lack the features needed to write good code. When you find yourself having to work around the lack of functionality in an editor, it's time to look for one that has the functionality you need. There's a balance between functionality and complexity. You need enough functionality to get the job done, but not such a big list of useless features that the interface becomes hard to use.

✔ **Flexibility:** The best dedicated editors provide some level of community support. A vendor may not have the resources required to provide every possible feature. By providing a method of extending the editor, the vendor can offload some development tasks to the community and end up with a better overall offering. In addition, the use of extensions makes it possible for you to pick and choose which features to include in the editor so that you can better manage the functionality versus complexity issue.

✔ **Availability:** Most developers today need to work with more than one platform, which means that your development tools also need to work on those platforms. Even though you use your dedicated editor mainly on your preferred platform, having it available for use on all of the platforms you must support is a plus. Having the editor available on these other platforms makes it possible to perform quick fixes without having to constantly go back to your desk and then run tests on the host machine.

A number of good JavaScript editors are available on the market. A personal favorite is Komodo Edit because it works on all three of the platforms I use and has support for a number of languages that I work with, but you should use the browser that meets your particular needs and tastes. The following list contains some free JavaScript editors that you might try while working through the examples in this book:

✔ **Free JavaScript Editor (**`http://www.yaldex.com/Free_ JavaScript_Editor.htm`**):** This is a moderately complex editor that provides support for JavaScript, HTML, AJAX, CSS, and DHTML. The free edition appears feature complete when you install it, but many of the features have a 21-day trial limit. Most of the editing features work beyond the trial date, so this editor works fine if you want to use the browser's debugger. If you want to be able to mix and match plug-ins to customize an editor for your specific needs, this is the product to get. The vendor's page is brimming over with plug-ins you can get to meet specific coding requirements. This is a Windows-only product.

✔ **HTML-Kit (**`http://www.htmlkit.com/download`**):** This editor focuses on mobile development. It includes an interesting preview feature that makes it possible to see how your pages will look on a tablet (such as the iPad) or smartphone. This editor works on both Windows and Macintosh systems. The free version will plague you with ads and nag you to buy the full version. However, the free version does appear to be feature complete, and you can use it to decide whether you want to buy the full version. This editor supports plug-ins so you can extend it as needed.

- ✔ **jEdit** (`http://www.jedit.org/index.php?page=download`): This editor provides good support for more languages and file types than Komodo Edit (you can get syntax highlighting for over 200 file types). However, it's also more complex, and the learning curve is relatively steep. You can find versions of this product for Windows, Mac OS X, Linux, OS/2, and VMS systems. There's no paid version of this product, so what you see on the site is what you get in the download.

- ✔ **Komodo Edit** (`http://www.activestate.com/komodo-edit/downloads`): This editor provides good support for JavaScript and a host of other languages, including Perl, PHP, Python, Ruby, and Tcl. The editor works on Windows, Macintosh, and Linux systems. The paid version of this product supports additional languages and a wealth of additional features, but the free version is perfectly usable for JavaScript coding. The biggest lack in the free version is a debugger, but you can easily use the debugger that comes with your browser to make up the difference.

- ✔ **Notepad++** (`http://notepad-plus-plus.org/download`): This is an extremely simple editor replacement for the Windows Notepad. It can perform tasks such as syntax highlighting, but it lacks any form of advanced feature, including a debugger. You can extend this product by using plug-ins. This is a Windows-only product, and there's no paid version. This is the option to use if you want to get right to coding and you're confident that the browser debugger will fulfill all your needs.

- ✔ **Scriptly** (`http://scriptly.webocton.de/9/34/start/english page.html`): This editor has a moderate number of features. It includes syntax highlighting and multi-document support. You also gain access to a number of advanced features, such as database support. The editor supports a number of file types including: HTML, PHP, CSS, JavaScript, Smarty, SQL, XML, and INI. You can also define your own custom file types and provide syntax highlighting for them. You can extend this product by using plug-ins. This is a Windows-only product, and there's no paid version.

Some JavaScript editor advertisements are misleading. A vendor will provide a free and paid version of the editor. The download page can make it appear that the free version is fully functional, when it really isn't. Make sure you read all the fine print when working with such an editor. Often you find that the free editor will work for a certain number of days, offer reduced functionality, or lack support from the vendor. Make sure you can live with the limitations of the free editor or you might find yourself buying the paid version to complete your project.

# Hosting Your Site

It's quite possible to test your application by simply loading the page into a browser. In fact, that's how you normally start testing. Unfortunately, loading a local page into a browser isn't how the Internet works, and if you stop your testing at this point, you never know whether your page will work as intended. To completely test your page, you must place it on a server and then load the page from the server. Of course, you don't want to perform this task by using a production server — one that everyone who uses your site will see. So, what you need is a test server. The following sections explore two ideas for working with servers in a way that makes it easier to test your applications.

## Quickly looking at Web hosting

Web hosting is an option to consider if your organization's resources are limited, if you don't want to support additional servers, or if you're working with a team composed of members from a number of geographical areas. A hosted site is also a good choice if you plan to make the site public after the application is finished and you don't want to host it on your own equipment. Providing more than a brief overview of this option is outside the scope of this book, but you do need to be aware that the option exists. If you want to know more of the details of hosting, *Web Design All-in-One For Dummies* by Sue Jenkins (Wiley) provides some extremely helpful information.

The main benefit of Web hosting is that you use the servers set up, configured, and maintained by someone else for a fee. When the development effort is done, you simply terminate the agreement with the host. The costs of this approach can be much lower than when you set up your own equipment if you intend to use the hosted site only for a short time. Long-term developers are usually served better by other options, including setting up a local server on the developer's system.

The least expensive hosted sites often rely on Linux servers, but you can also find sites that use Windows servers for an additional price. It pays to shop around because different host sites have different prices, packages, and terms. Read reviews of sites whenever possible to make the comparison process easier. For example, you can find a review of the top ten Web hosting sites at `http://webhostingchoice.com`.

When shopping for a hosting site, make sure you check on site features. For example, it pays to check on issues such as potential *bandwidth throttling* (the act of limiting the amount of data that the hosted site can accept, even though it should be possible to accept more) or charges for higher than usual bandwidth usage. The host also needs to provide any database or other service features that your application will require.

# Using JavaScript from your computer

You can host JavaScript applications from your computer when you have a server such as Apache or Internet Information Server (IIS) installed. There are many options available for creating a Web server setup on your system. This book relies on Apache because there's a version of Apache for most environments. In addition, Apache is free and highly extensible. Apache also has the majority of the market, as shown at http://w3techs.com/technologies/overview/web_server/all.

The main Apache download site is at http://httpd.apache.org/download.cgi. The following sections provide quick installation instructions for the three main programming platforms discussed in this book, but be assured that Apache will install on a considerably larger number of platforms than those covered here.

### Installing Apache on Windows

Sometimes finding the files you need on the Apache site can prove daunting. You can find the list of mirrors for downloading the Windows binaries at http://www.apache.org/dyn/closer.cgi/httpd/binaries/win32. The following steps will get you started:

1. **Download the latest binary from the mirror site closest to you.**

   The easiest option is to download the Microsoft Installer (.MSI) file.

2. **Double click the MSI file (such as httpd-2.2.22-win32-x86-no_ssl.msi) that you just downloaded.**

   You see the installation wizard Welcome screen.

3. **Click Next.**

   You see the license screen for the product.

4. **Choose the I Accept the Terms in the License Agreement option and then click Next.**

   You see a Read this First screen.

5. **Read about any special requirements for installing Apache on your system and then click Next.**

   You see a Server Information screen that contains the information used to configure the server, as shown in Figure 2-4.

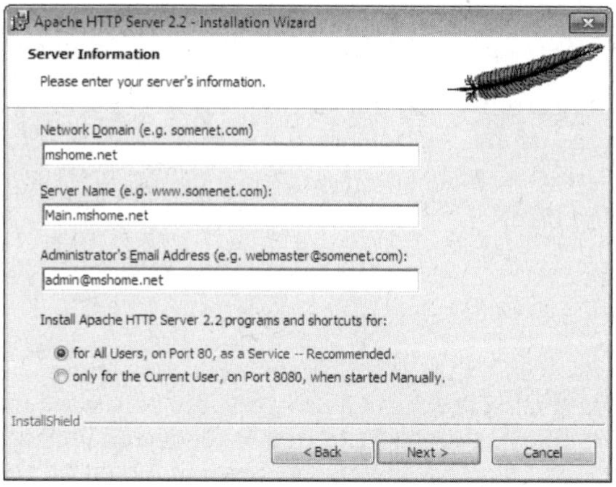

**Figure 2-4:**
Choose the server con-figuration that your system will use.

6. **Accept the default configuration by clicking Next.**

   You see a Setup Type screen where you can choose between a typical and a custom installation, as shown in Figure 2-5.

**Figure 2-5:**
Define how you would like to perform the installation.

7. **Perform a typical installation by clicking Next.**

   You see a Destination Folder screen where you can choose the installa-tion location of the Apache server.

8. **Accept the default installation location by clicking Next.**

   The installation wizard indicates that it's ready to perform the installation.

9. **Click Install.**

You see a dialog box showing the installation process. During the installation process, Windows may display a User Account Control (UAC) dialog box asking your permission to let the installation program make changes to your system. Click Yes if you see this dialog box. You may also see a command prompt open, display some text, and automatically close. This is perfectly normal. After the installation is complete, you see a Success dialog box.

10. **Click Finish.**

    Your Apache installation is ready to use.

### Installing Apache on Mac OS X

The amazing thing is that you don't have to install Apache on your Mac — the server is already installed. However, the server may not be enabled, so you can't use it immediately. When working with pre-10.8 versions of the Mac OS X, open up System Preferences. Look under Sharing and check Web Sharing. Your Apache installation should be enabled.

The 10.8 version also has Apache installed, but Apple has decided to make things a bit harder. Before you do anything, you need to configure Apache for your particular setup. The following steps will help you configure and start Apache on your system.

1. **Open a Terminal window (found at /Applications/Utilities/Terminal).**

2. **Type** nano /etc/apache2/users/USERNAME.CONF **and press Enter.**

    You see the nano editor open with the USERNAME.CONF file loaded.

3. **Type the following code into the editor, replacing *USERNAME* with your username:**

```
<Directory "/Users/kdarosett/Sites/">
Options Indexes Multiviews
AllowOverride AuthConfig Limit
Order allow,deny
Allow from all
</Directory>
```

4. **Press Ctrl+O.**

    Nano saves the changes you've made.

5. **Press Ctrl+X.**

    Nano closes.

6. **Type one of the following commands to interact with Apache:**

    - *To start Apache:* Type **sudo apachectl start**.

    - *To stop Apache:* Type **sudo apachectl stop**.

- *To restart Apache:* Type **sudo apachectl restart**.

- *To find the version of Apache installed on your system:* Type **httpd -v**.

Some Macintosh sites are going to say that you really do need the latest version of Apache. You do need it if you're creating a public site or you require the latest features that Apache provides. However, when testing JavaScript applications, you generally don't require the latest version of Apache — any version that can serve up Web pages will do. JavaScript works at the client and the version of the browser is more important than the version of the server.

## Installing Apache on Linux

Some Linux systems have Apache installed. If this is the case on your system, you should be able to open a browser, type **localhost** in the address bar, press Enter, and see a message. In most cases, when using newer Apache setups, you see a simple message, "It works!" Older versions of Apache display other messages, but the point is that you'll see a message. Installing Apache is one of the installation options that you receive when working with most versions of Linux and this is the easiest way to install Apache.

The actual installation process for Linux varies by system. Each vendor seems to have a slightly different procedure for installing applications. The following steps will help you through the installation for Fedora, CentOS, and Ubuntu Linux. They also act as an aid for other flavors of Linux. Make sure you're familiar with your particular Linux configuration before you begin the installation.

1. **Open a terminal window and type** su - **to enter super-user mode.**

   The server asks for your password.

2. **Type your password and press Enter.**

   You're now in super-user mode.

3. **Start the Apache installation for your system:**

   - *When working with Fedora or CentOS,* you type **yum install httpd** and press Enter. The server begins the package installation.

   - *When working with Ubuntu,* you type **sudo apt-get install tasksel** and press Enter, followed by **sudo tasksel install lamp-server** and press Enter. The server displays a list of packages. You select the package you want to install and the server begins the installation.

4. **Follow any additional prompts for your particular installation.**

   In general, the installation proceeds automatically because Apache expects you to edit the httpd.CONF file to make any required changes.

**5. Start the server:**

- *When working with Fedora or CentOS,* type **service httpd start** and press Enter. The server starts and is now ready for use.

- *When working with Ubuntu,* type **sudo /etc/init.d/apache2 start** and press Enter. The server starts and is now ready for use.

## Testing your installation

No matter where you install Apache, testing the server is easy. Open a browser window and type **localhost** as the address bar. When you press Enter, you see a simple message, "It works!"

You'll also want to test Apache with something other than the default page. To do this, you need to find the file storage on your system. Files are stored in the \htdocs subdirectory where applications are installed on your system. When working with Windows installation, you find the files in the \Program Files (x86)\Apache Software Foundation\Apache2.2 \htdocs or \Program Files\Apache Software Foundation\Apache2.2\ htdocs folder. Copy the example for this chapter, BrowserDetect.HTML, to that folder. Type **http://localhost/BrowserDetect.HTML** in the address bar and press Enter. You see the name and version number of your browser, but this time through the Web server instead of as a loaded file.

One of the better reasons to work with Apache is that it relies on text-based configuration files. The main configuration file is httpd.CONF, and it appears in the \conf subdirectory of the installation. For example, you find it in the \Program Files (x86)\Apache Software Foundation\Apache2.2\ conf or \Program Files\Apache Software Foundation\Apache2.2\ conf folder on a Windows system. This file always contains the location of the various folders that Apache uses, so if you find that you can't locate a particular folder for your setup, refer to the httpd.CONF file for additional information.

# Chapter 3

# Integrating HTML5 and JavaScript

- - - - - - - - - - - - - - - - - - - - - - - - - - - - - - - - - - - - -

## In This Chapter

▶ Performing simple output tasks

▶ Understanding the format of JavaScript statements

▶ Creating JavaScript comments to document your code

▶ Alerting users to the need to turn on JavaScript support

- - - - - - - - - - - - - - - - - - - - - - - - - - - - - - - - - - - - -

*T*he previous two chapters introduce you to JavaScript and the tools needed to work with it, but they don't really discuss JavaScript as a language. Now that you have a better idea of what JavaScript can do, how you can interact with it, and why you want to use it, it's time to start working with the language. This chapter provides you with some introductory information about JavaScript that you need in order to begin working with the language in earnest. These introductory topics make it possible for you to perform tasks such as creating output with your JavaScript applications so that you can see the result of the code you create.

Part of working with JavaScript is understanding how JavaScript statements work. A *statement* is simply a request for the JavaScript interpreter to do something. It's a command. You tell JavaScript what to do and how to do it, and JavaScript responds. When you give a command incorrectly, JavaScript doesn't produce the results you expect. As part of discovering techniques for creating and using JavaScript statements, you also need to know how to document them. That means creating *comments* for your code.

In Chapter 2, you discover one technique for learning which browser the user has so that you can ensure your application will run. However, the user can have the right browser and still not be able to run your application when the browser is configured not to allow JavaScript to run. To address that issue, this chapter discusses techniques you can use to alert the user to the need to turn on JavaScript support so that the application can run properly.

One of the unwritten rules to remember about JavaScript is that it depends on a trust relationship between the user and you. When the user enables JavaScript support for your site to run the application you create, it's a sign of trust on the user's part. To maintain that trust, you must know how to create good JavaScript code that works as anticipated and doesn't damage the user's system. Part of the emphasis of this chapter is gaining and maintaining the user's trust in your applications — an essential component in any Web-based application experience.

# Creating Simple Output

When writing applications, you must confront some issues before being really ready for them. It's a chicken-or-egg scenario — which technique should you address first? That's how it is with application output. To see how some programming techniques work, you need to know how to write output to the application screen. Of course, you really need to know more about JavaScript before you can master the technique of writing anything to the screen.

The following sections provide a sort of half step. You discover just enough about writing information to the screen to provide useful output for acquiring other techniques that will eventually help you create better output. The need to discover something simple in order to have a foundation on which to build more advanced techniques is a common issue when learning a new language, so don't be too worried if you feel a little lost at first.

## Writing to an HTML element

HTML documents are made up of individual elements. An *element* is any tag that you use to hold content, such as a `<div>`, `<p>`, or `<input>` tag. You can write information to any of these elements by using JavaScript. The following example shows how you can write to specific elements. (You can find this example in the `\Chapter 03\Output Text` folder of the downloadable code as `HTMLOutput.HTML`.)

```
<!DOCTYPE html>

<html>
<head>
   <title>Outputting Data to HTML</title>
   <script language="JavaScript">
      function WriteText()
      {
         document.getElementById("myText").innerHTML =
            "Clicked!";
      }
```

```
    </script>
</head>

<body>
    <h1>Creating HTML Element Output</h1>
    <div><p id="myText">Change Me</p></div>
    <div><input id="btnClickMe"
                type="button"
                value="Click Me"
                onclick="WriteText()" />
    </div>
</body>
</html>
```

In this case, the page contains a <p> tag with an id of myText. This paragraph contains the text Change Me. In addition, there's an <input> tag that creates a button the user can click. When the user clicks the Click Me button, the application calls the WriteText() function that appears in the <head> of the document within the <script> tag.

JavaScript has several global objects you can access with your code. One of the most important objects is document, which refers to the entire HTML document. Of course, you don't want to change the entire document; you want to change just one element within the document. The getElementById() function retrieves any element that has an id attribute by the name of that attribute, which is myText in this case.

At this point, you have access to the entire <p> element with the name myText. You want to change the text within that element. The innerHTML property provides access to the text within the <p> element. You can either read the content or modify it. Using innerHTML =, as shown in the code, modifies the content. It makes the content equal to whatever follows, which is Clicked! in this case.

When you try the example, you initially see a page with some text and a button. Click the button, and the value of the text changes. This technique works with any element that displays text. You could just as easily use it with a <span> or any other tag that can display text.

This technique works only when you interact with elements that contain text within an opening and closing tag, such as <p>. When working with an <input> or other element that uses attributes to hold content, you need to use a different method. In this case, you must access the attribute within the control and make the change there, as shown here:

```
document.getElementById("btnClickMe").setAttribute(
    "value", "Clicked!");
```

In this case, you ask JavaScript to obtain access to the btnClickMe <input> element in the document and then to set the value attribute to Clicked!. The result is the same as when working with the <p> tag, but the approach is slightly different. The innerHTML property is useful only for elements that have a value assigned to that property.

## *Creating direct document output*

In some cases, you don't want to interact with an existing element, so you create a new element that contains the content you want to see. For example, you can add a new <p> tag that contains the text you want to see. JavaScript provides a number of ways to accomplish this task. In fact, you see more examples of this sort of output as the book progresses. The simplest way to perform the task is to create an inline script like the one shown in the following example that adds the required output. (You can find this example in the \Chapter 03\Output Text folder of the downloadable code as DirectOutput.HTML.)

```
<!DOCTYPE html>

<html>
<head>
    <title>Direct Document Output</title>
</head>

<body>
    <h1>Creating Direct Output</h1>
    <script language="JavaScript">
        document.write("<p>This is direct output</p>");
    </script>
</body>
</html>
```

The focal point of this example is the call to the document.write() function. This function lets you write any text you want to the document object. In this case, the example creates a new <p> tag that contains a simple message.

You could easily create this text by adding the <p> tag directly. Later chapters show how this particular technique comes in handy. For example, you could use it to check for a condition and then add the appropriate text based on the condition. What you need to see in this example is that writing to the document using a script is indeed possible.

The `document.write()` function can produce unexpected results when used incorrectly. You normally use this function when the page is drawing itself onscreen. The next section of this chapter demonstrates a potential side effect of using this function incorrectly. It's essential to remember that the `document.write()` function writes directly to the `document` object and will overwrite everything in the `document` object when used after the document has been displayed onscreen.

## Avoiding potential problems with output

It's a good idea to start looking at potential coding errors from the outset while you discover JavaScript. *Bugs* (coding errors) can cause all sorts of problems for users who will, in turn, cause all sorts of problems for you. One of the more interesting errors that you can encounter is writing information to a `document` object incorrectly. The following example shows one situation where you see the incorrect result from using the `document.write()` function. (You can find this example in the `\Chapter 03\Output Text` folder of the downloadable code as `BadOutput.HTML`.)

```
<!DOCTYPE html>

<html>
<head>
   <title>Incorrect Output</title>
   <script language="JavaScript">
      function WriteText()
      {
          document.write("Oops!");
      }
   </script>
</head>

<body>
   <h1>Creating HTML Element Output</h1>
   <div><p id="myText">Change Me</p></div>
   <div><input id="btnClickMe"
               type="button"
               value="Click Me"
               onclick="WriteText()" />
   </div>
</body>
</html>
```

Notice that the `document.write()` function is called after the page is completed. When you use the `document.write()` function in this way, it overwrites everything that appears in the `document` object. When you click the

Click Me button on the page, you see the word Oops! onscreen and nothing else. In fact, the page won't even finish loading because the browser doesn't know what to do with it. To stop the loading process, you must manually click your browser's Stop Loading button.

At this point, if you use your browser's ability to view the page source (normally, this involves right-clicking the page and choosing an option such as View Source or View Page Source from the context menu), you'll see a single word, Oops!. The page no longer contains a <!DOCTYPE> declaration, <html>, <head>, or <body> tags, or any of the other information it used to contain. The document.write() function has overwritten everything. Now, this isn't always an incorrect result — you may actually need to overwrite the page with new material, but you need to create an entirely new page when doing so.

# Working with JavaScript Statements

It's essential to understand how JavaScript statements work. You've seen a number of examples of JavaScript statements in both this chapter and the previous two chapters without really exploring them in detail. The following sections provide you with information on how statements work so that you can better understand the examples you've already seen and those that will follow.

## Understanding the dot syntax

JavaScript uses what's known as a *dot syntax* — a period between elements of a complete statement. In general, a complete statement begins with an object or variable. Objects can have functions, properties, and events associated with them. Here's a short explanation of each of these elements:

- ✓ **Object:** An entity that contains everything associated with a particular aspect of an application. For example, the document object contains everything needed to display a page onscreen.

- ✓ **Property:** A description of a particular object feature. For example, the document object provides access to a cookie property that contains the cookie resources for a page. Cookies are part of a page and describe the data that the page relies on to function properly.

- ✓ **Function:** An action you can perform with an object. For example, the document object provides access to the write() function that makes it possible to add new information (or overwrite information when the page is complete).

✔ **Event:** An action that the object or an external source has performed with an object. The event is a notification that this action has occurred. For example, the document object provides a click event. When you assign a function to the onclick notification and a user clicks the document, JavaScript calls the function you provide (called an *event handler*). You've already seen events used with the various buttons in the example applications.

You use dot syntax to describe to JavaScript how to interact with the objects, properties, functions, and events in an application. For example, when you write document.write("This is some direct output"), you're telling JavaScript to

1. Access the document object.

2. Find the write() function within that object.

3. Send "This is some direct output" to the write() function.

4. Tell the write() function to execute.

The dot syntax can go down as many levels as needed to fully describe what you want JavaScript to do. For example, when you type document.body. bgColor, you tell JavaScript that you want to change the background color of the body element of the current document. You can combine elements as needed to provide a full description of what you want to accomplish to JavaScript using dot syntax. The rest of the book shows you all kinds of examples of dot syntax in action.

## Adding multiple statements to a single script

So far, many of the examples in this book rely on a single statement. A statement is a single command that you want JavaScript to perform. Each statement always ends with a semicolon (;). In real applications, you seldom complete an application using a single statement — you combine statements to obtain a specific result. JavaScript executes the statements in the order that you type them. JavaScript doesn't require that you place each statement on its own line, nor does it require you to place a single statement on one line. Formatting the code by placing each statement on a separate line and indenting some elements is for your benefit.

Here's an example of three statements within a single function. (You can find the full code for this example in the \Chapter 03\Statements folder of the downloadable code as MultipleStatements.HTML.)

```
<script language="JavaScript">
    function WriteText()
    {
        document.getElementById("First").innerHTML =
            "Changed First"; alert("Check First!");
        document.getElementById("Second").innerHTML =
            "Changed Second";
    }
</script>
```

The first statement changes a <p> element with an id of First. The second statement displays an alert() so that you can verify that the first statement executed without doing anything else. The third statement changes a <p> element with an id of Second.

The use of white space is for your benefit. This example is a little hard to read because the alert() function doesn't appear on its own line. You could easily miss the alert() tucked in after the <p> element change. The white space (indentation and new lines) makes your code easier to work with and understand.

When you run this example, you see a heading and two paragraphs. The first paragraph says First Statement, and the second paragraph says Second Statement. Click the Click Me button and you see that the first paragraph changes and that the browser displays an alert(), as shown in Figure 3-1. Notice that the second paragraph hasn't changed because the script hasn't gotten to that point yet.

**Figure 3-1:**
JavaScript executes one statement at a time and in the order you provide.

## Defining basic code blocks

You've probably noticed that the coding examples use curly brackets to show where a function begins and ends. A left (opening) curly bracket ({) always shows the beginning of the function, and a right (closing) curly bracket (}) always shows the ending of the function. The combination of an opening and closing curly bracket defines a *code block*. JavaScript relies on code blocks to help organize code and to define the beginning and ending of a particular task. You see more uses for code blocks as the book progresses.

There's an important rule when working with JavaScript: A code block always consists of a pair of curly brackets. It's an error to have one without the other. Developers most often make a mistake of creating an opening curly bracket without the corresponding closing curly bracket. This is another good reason to use an editor specially designed for use with JavaScript. Most JavaScript editors automatically create a closing curly bracket when you type the opening curly bracket. Editors also provide other aids, such as showing the location of the other member of a pair when you select either the opening or closing curly bracket. (Check out Chapter 2 for more on choosing a dedicated JavaScript editor.)

## Understanding case sensitivity

JavaScript is a case sensitive language. This means that you must exercise care in how you type. For example, there's an `alert()` function, but not an `Alert()` function, supplied as part of JavaScript. The `color` property is completely different from the `Color` property, which is different still from the `cOlor` property. Although you see the same word each time, the word is capitalized differently, so JavaScript sees it as a different word.

Even though it's perfectly legal to do so, giving two variables the same name and differentiating them only by case is an incredibly bad idea. Doing so will almost certainly result in serious application errors that will be tough (if not impossible) to find. Always give variables distinct names and don't rely on case to differentiate between them.

## Using white space effectively

White space is essential for humans, but JavaScript doesn't require it. For example, you can write an `alert()` in any of the following ways, and all of them will execute without problem:

```
alert("Hello");
alert( "Hello" );
alert(                              "Hello"                    );
```

The first and second lines are relatively easy to read. The third could present a problem because the human viewer may have trouble seeing where the message is in all that white space.

The use of white space is important. For example, you could place the function on a single line like this (even though the code appears on multiple lines in the book, the actual code would be on a single line):

```
function WriteText() {document.getElementById("First").
        innerHTML ="Changed First";alert("Check
        First!");document.getElementById("Second").
        innerHTML ="Changed Second";}
```

This code is incredibly hard to read. It works, but human developers would have a hard time maintaining it. It's far better to add white space so you can see where lines of code begin and end like this:

```
function WriteText()
{
    document.getElementById("First").innerHTML =
        "Changed First";
    alert("Check First!");
    document.getElementById("Second").innerHTML =
        "Changed Second";
}
```

Every statement appears on its own line. Continuations appear indented so you can tell that they're a continuation. The entire code block appears indented, and you can clearly see the opening and closing curly brackets. This second version is a lot easier to maintain.

## Using the line continuation character

JavaScript provides a line continuation character, the backslash (\), that you can use in your code to break up long lines. In practice, you seldom see the line continuation character used because JavaScript also allows for natural breaks.

For example, you can naturally break lines between statement components. When you want to set a property to a new value, the description of which property to change can appear on one line and the new value on the second line. However, there are times when you need to use the line continuation character, such as when working with long segments of text like this. (You can find the full code for this example in the \Chapter 03\Statements folder of the downloadable code as LineContinuation.HTML.)

```
function WriteText()
{
   document.getElementById("LongParagraph").innerHTML =
      "This is a really long line of text that won't \
      easily fit on a single line.";
}
```

This example actually contains two line breaks. The first is a more traditional natural line break — the second relies on the line continuation character. You must use the line continuation character in the second case because the break appears in the middle of a line of text. If you don't use the line continuation character in this case, JavaScript displays an error message. JavaScript displays the entire line of text as you expect, as shown in Figure 3-2.

**Figure 3-2:**
Use the line continuation character as needed to break up lines of text.

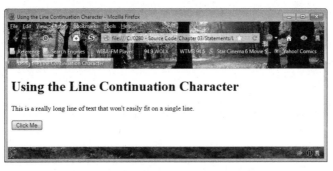

# *Writing Comments in JavaScript*

Comments are an important part of your JavaScript application. While you may easily remember what an application does for a day or two after you write it, trying to figure out what complex applications are doing one or two years later can prove difficult. In fact, there are documented cases where companies have had to rewrite applications from scratch because no one could figure out how the application worked due to a lack of comments. No one has an infallible memory, so comments are an important way for you to keep track of what your application does.

JavaScript doesn't care about your comments. It ignores them, so you can write the comments any way that you want. The content is there to help you. Good comments explain details such as

✔ Why you wrote a particular function or other code block

✔ What task the code block is supposed to perform

✔ Who requested the code block

✔ Why you used a particular technique for writing the code block

✔ Which resources you used to create the code

✔ How the code was created and tested

✔ Who worked on the code (including contact information)

✔ When the code was created

A growing number of people insist that some forms of code are self-documenting. However, JavaScript is *never* self-documenting, and if you leave out the comments, you may find yourself working late nights and weekends trying to figure out your code later.

JavaScript provides two methods for creating comments, as described in the following sections.

## Creating single-line comments

Most developers use what are called *single-line comments*. A single-line comment can appear anywhere on a line. To create a single-line comment, you type two forward slashes (//) and then the comment text. Here are examples of single-line comments. (You can find the full code for this example in the \Chapter 03\Comments folder of the downloadable code as MultipleStatements.HTML.)

```
function WriteText()
{
    // Change the first statement, then wait so the
    // user can see the change.
    document.getElementById("First").innerHTML =
        "Changed First";
    alert("Check First!"); // Wait here.

    // After the user clicks Click Me, show the
    // change to the second statement.
    document.getElementById("Second").innerHTML =
        "Changed Second";
}
```

Each line begins with a double slash (//) to indicate that it's a comment line. Notice that you can begin a comment after the code in a line, as shown in the line with the `alert()` call in it. Everything after the double slash is treated as a comment.

Use white space to help delineate sections of code that are covered by a single comment. The addition of white space makes the comments easier to find, and it also makes it easier to see how much code the comment affects.

## Creating multi-line comments

Sometimes you have more than one or two lines worth of comment to write. In this case, you can create *multi-line comments*. A multi-line comment begins with a slash and an asterisk (/\*) and ends with an asterisk and slash (\*/). Here's an example of a multi-line comment. (You can find the full code for this example in the \Chapter 03\Comments folder of the downloadable code as MultipleStatements.HTML.)

```
<script language="JavaScript">
   /* This function makes changes to the text on the
    * page after the user clicks Click Me as a
    * demonstration of modifying page elements using
    * multiple lines of code.
    *
    * Written by: John Mueller */

   function WriteText()
   {
      // Change the first statement, then wait so the
      // user can see the change.
      document.getElementById("First").innerHTML =
         "Changed First";
      alert("Check First!"); // Wait here.

      // After the user clicks Click Me, show the
      // change to the second statement.
      document.getElementById("Second").innerHTML =
         "Changed Second";
   }
</script>
```

In this case, the comment is used to create a description of the function. These blocks often appear in team projects to help members interact with each other. For example, this comment would tell someone on the team who wrote the block of code shown in the example.

## Preventing code execution by using comments

Developers often use single-line comments to prevent a line of code from executing. *Commenting out* code is a common technique where a developer adds two forward slashes (//) in front of a line of code that the developer suspects is causing problems in the application. Professional code editors often include features that make it easy to comment out lines of code and then add them back into the application as needed.

# Alerting Visitors That JavaScript Has Something to Say

Many users are wary of enabling JavaScript support for sites because they don't want to download a virus or have other bad things happen to their systems. In addition, people have become less receptive to using scripts because they sometimes do things the user doesn't want, such as grab the user's identity. When a user enables JavaScript for your application, it represents a trust relationship between the user and you.

Of course, the user needs to know that your site requires JavaScript in order to enable it. The following sections present just two of the many ways to tell a user that your site requires JavaScript to work.

## Using the <noscript> tag

The <noscript> tag is a special tag that the browser reacts to when scripting support isn't available on the local system. This is a standard tag that every browser currently on the market should support, so it represents the safest and most reliable way to tell a user that your site requires JavaScript support.

However, some people have complained that the <noscript> tag can also cause some unwanted effects with some devices, such as flickering on smartphones. If you receive user complaints about this issue, you may have to resort to the technique described in the next section of the chapter, even though it's less reliable. (You can find this example in the \Chapter 03\JavaScript Notification folder of the downloadable code as UsingNoScript.HTML.)

```
<!DOCTYPE html>

<html>
<head>
    <title>Using the NoScript Tag</title>
</head>

<body>

    <h1>Using the NoScript Tag</h1>
    <noscript>
        <p>Please enable JavaScript to use this page!</p>
    </noscript>
    <script language="JavaScript">
        document.write(
            "<p>You have JavaScript enabled!</p>");
    </script>

</body>
</html>
```

This approach is quite simple. When you try the example, you see one of two messages. If you have JavaScript enabled, you see "You have JavaScript enabled!" Otherwise, you see "Please enable JavaScript to use this page!" Try disabling JavaScript support in your browser and refreshing this page to see the alternative message.

## Using styles

The styles approach relies on the use of Cascading Style Sheets (CSS) to create a condition where a message is displayed when scripting is disabled. The problem with this approach is that not every browser supports it. Yes, newer browsers do support this technique just fine, but if you encounter users with older browsers, your application could experience problems. The following example shows how to use this technique. (You can find this example in the \Chapter 03\JavaScript Notification folder of the downloadable code as UsingStyles.HTML.)

```
<!DOCTYPE html>

<html>
<head>
    <title>Using Styles</title>
    <script language="JavaScript">
        document.write(
            '<style>#NoJS { display: none; }</style>');
```

```
        </script>
    </head>

    <body>

        <h1>Using Styles</h1>
        <p id="NoJS">
            Please enable JavaScript to use this page!
        </p>
        <script language="JavaScript">
            document.write(
                "<p>You have JavaScript enabled!</p>");
        </script>

    </body>
</html>
```

This technique relies on a simple trick. When scripting is enabled, the first script creates a style for the first <p> tag that hides the information in that paragraph by adding the display: none style. The presence of scripting support also lets the second script run, which displays the "You have JavaScript enabled!" message.

When scripting is disabled, the first script can't run, so there's no special style for the <p> tag with an id of NoJS. This means that the "Please enable JavaScript to use this page!" message is displayed. However, because there's no scripting support, the second script also fails, which means you won't see the JavaScript-enabled message. Try this example by enabling, then disabling, JavaScript support on your browser.

# Part II
# Speaking the JavaScript Language

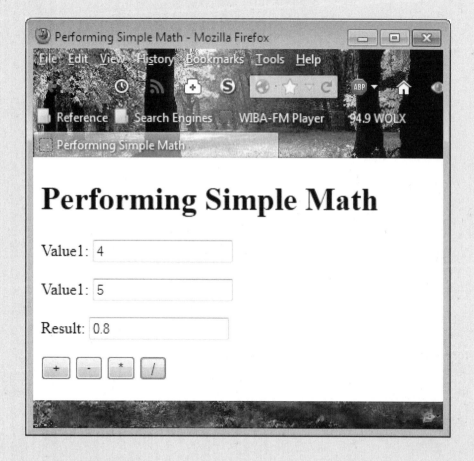

# *In this part* . . .

- ✔ Understand JavaScript objects and discover how to use them.

- ✔ Create and use Boolean, number, text, and array objects.

- ✔ Develop custom objects to use in your applications.

- ✔ Pass data using object literals.

- ✔ Discover the details of using the `Object`, `Number`, `String`, `Date`, and `RegExp` objects.

# Chapter 4

# Embracing JavaScript Variables

*T*he purpose of most applications is to work with data in some way. *Data* are defined as any kind of information you want to interact with in some fashion — anything from simply displaying it to creating new information or manipulating existing information to see it in new ways. *Variables* provide storage containers for data. You store the data until you need to use it in the application, take the data out, do something with it, and then put it back into the variable when you're done. The term variable is appropriate because you can store different data items in a variable — the content is, well, variable. The variable content changes to meet application needs. This chapter helps you understand how variables work in JavaScript and how you can use them to perform tasks within your application.

The chapter divides variables into a number of types. Just as you wouldn't normally store food in shoe boxes or cleaning equipment in jewelry boxes, you use different kinds of variables to store certain types of data. Knowing which kind of container to use for your data is an important part of keeping it safe.

In addition, this chapter discusses one sort of data *collection*. Think of a collection in the same way as you think of storage shelves. Each shelf contains boxes, each of which contains an item. The kind of collection discussed in this chapter is the *array,* a type of collection supported by most programming languages. Arrays provide simple, yet effective, means of collecting like data together so that you can access it with greater ease — just as using shelves makes it easier to locate and access items in boxes.

# Understanding Simple Variables

The title for this section should tell you something. Yes, there are multiple variable types. Simple variables act as storage containers and nothing more. In some cases, that's all you really need — nothing fancy, just a place to put your data for a while. JavaScript also supports a number of complex variable types, such as objects and arrays, but for now, think about the beauty of simple storage. The following sections describe how you can use simple variables to meet a wide range of application needs.

## Seeing variables as storage bins

Some developers become confused when working with variables because they make the variables too complicated. A variable is nothing more than a storage bin. If you look in your computer's memory, a variable is simply a series of electrical impulses, 1s and 0s, placed in a certain physical location for later retrieval. In short, a variable really is a storage bin — a place to put data.

In the "Discovering variable types" section, later in this chapter, you discover how JavaScript differentiates between kinds of variables. The differentiation is for your benefit. As far as the computer is concerned, data consists of 1s and 0s stored as electrical impulses in a specific physical location in memory — nothing more. Humans need to categorize the data to see it in a useful way, but the computer doesn't.

It may surprise you to learn that the computer has no concept of characters, Booleans (true/false values), or any other human data construction. Everything is 1s and 0s — even characters. When you see the letter *A* onscreen, the computer sees it as the number 65. Actually, the computer sees the binary version of 01000001. A lowercase *a* is actually a value of 01100001 (97 decimal) — the computer doesn't even have any concept of uppercase or lowercase letters.

The point is that when you think about variables, you see all sorts of shades of meaning. However, you also need to remember that variables are simply physical memory locations to the computer that just happen to have a particular sequence of electrical impulses in them.

# Declaring variables

To use a variable, you must tell JavaScript to create it. After all, when you want to store something in a box in real life, you must first acquire the box. There's no JavaScript store where you go to buy a box — you simply tell JavaScript you need one by using the var keyword, followed by the variable name. To place something in the box immediately, you use the assignment operator (=), which assigns the value to the box, and you must also provide what you want to store in the variable.

Here's an example that creates a variable named AVariable and stores the value 5 in it. (You can find this example in the \Chapter 04\Simple Variables folder of the downloadable code as DeclareVariables.HTML.)

```html
<!DOCTYPE html>

<html>
<head>
    <title>Declaring Variables</title>
    <script language="JavaScript">
        function UseVariable()
        {
            // Create a variable.
            var AVariable = 5;

            // Display it onscreen.
            alert(AVariable);
        }
    </script>
</head>

<body>
    <h1>Declaring Variables</h1>
    <input type="button"
           value="Click Me"
           onclick="UseVariable()" />
</body>
</html>
```

When a user clicks the Click Me button, the application calls UseVariable(). The UseVariable() function creates AVariable and places the value 5 in it. The function then calls on alert() to display the content of AVariable onscreen where the user sees a message box with the value 5 in it.

Unlike many programming languages, JavaScript doesn't require you to do anything fancy to create a variable. All you need to do is use the var keyword, followed by a variable name. To assign a value, you add an equals sign (=) followed by a value.

## Understanding the computer view of variables

Here's an example of how the computer looks at data: You may have a variable that contains the number 23 and another variable that contains two characters, 2 and 3. The two characters form a *string* — a string of characters. The computer sees the number 23 as 00010111. However, it sees the string 23 as 00110010 00110011. That's two separate memory locations — one for each character. The number and the character form of 23 have no distinction to the computer, even though the values are quite different. If you confuse them, you would create errors in your application.

## Discovering variable types

As previously mentioned, the notion of a variable type is for your convenience — the computer doesn't actually understand variable types. To make things easier for developers though, JavaScript assigns a type to variables. A variable can hold characters, for example, or numbers. Each variable has its own variable type. You need to know about variable types to aid in debugging. In addition, using variable types makes it less likely you'll use the data incorrectly by confusing a number with a letter. The computer sees the data differently, but you may not (see the "Understanding the computer view of variables" sidebar for details).

JavaScript uses a simple variable type system. For example, you need to know only that a variable contains a number — not what type of number is stored there. Some programming languages make a distinction between *integer values* (those that are whole numbers) and *floating point values* (those with a decimal part), but JavaScript doesn't.

You also need to know that JavaScript is a *dynamic* language, which means that you can assign values of different types to the same variable. JavaScript actually changes the type of the variable to match the data it contains. It's best though if you place a single type within a given variable to avoid becoming confused.

The following list describes the types that JavaScript supports:

✔ **String:** A *string* holds characters. Each character is a letter, like the letters you see in this book. You must enclose string values in either double or single quotes. For example, `var Name = "John Doe"` and `var Name = 'John Doe'` both assign the string, `John Doe`, to the variable `Name`. You can also combine quotes to achieve special effects. For example, `var Statement = 'My name is "John Doe"'` assigns the string `My name is "John Doe"` to the variable `Statement`. Notice that John Doe is enclosed in double quotes.

✔ **Number:** Humans see all numbers as being alike. Even though 4 is slightly less than 4.1, humans see both as numbers. A computer sees 4 as an integer and 4.1 as a floating point (real) number. The two values are actually handled by different parts of the computer processor. Because of this difference, most computer languages provide separate types for integers and floating point numbers. However, like humans, JavaScript sees all numbers as being the same. Whether you create an integer or a floating point value, JavaScript sees the variable as a number. To create a number, you provide the usual variable declaration with a number that isn't enclosed in any form of quote like this: `var MyNumber = 15`.

✔ **Boolean:** Computers need to make decisions based on user input, data, or application state. Decisions rely on Boolean variables, which are either true or false. You can use various statements to test the truth of a Boolean variable or a Boolean expression (an equation that results in a value of `true` or `false`).

Boolean variables are named after George Boole, a 19th century mathematician you can read about at `http://www.buzzle.com/articles/boolean-origination-history-and-origin-of-boolean-logic.html`.

✔ **Array:** An *array* is a kind of collection. You can create a collection of any sort of variable that JavaScript supports. For example, an array of strings can contain the client name list. Arrays are extremely useful collections that you use often in JavaScript to conveniently manipulate data in ways that would otherwise require a lot of code (and head scratching).

✔ **Object:** Most real-world data is complex. For example, when you see a customer, the customer has a name and other features (properties), you can perform certain tasks for the customer (methods), and the customer can make requests of you (events). To model real-world data, computers require objects. Using objects makes it possible to describe the real-world data in terms that a computer can manipulate.

✔ **Null:** The word `null` is a special kind of keyword that means nothing. You can set a variable to the `null` type when you don't want it to contain anything. JavaScript also sets variables to `null` when there isn't any information it can supply for that variable. A `null` variable may not seem very useful, but it's incredibly useful because you can test for `null` data and then perform tasks based on that test.

✔ **Undefined:** When a variable is *undefined,* it means that JavaScript knows that the variable exists, but the variable doesn't contain any information. An undefined variable is one that hasn't been initialized to contain any data yet. You can test for undefined variables by using the `undefined` keyword.

You can declare any variable directly by inserting a value into it, as described in the preceding section. However, you may want to create a variable, declare it as a certain type, but not fill it with anything immediately. In this case, you use the `new` keyword to create the variable. Here are examples of creating variables by using the `new` keyword:

```
var MyString = new String();
var MyNumber = new Number();
var MyBoolean = new Boolean();
var MyCollection = new Array();
var ComplexData = new Object();
```

At their lowest level — a level that most developers really don't care about — all JavaScript variables are objects. Yes, the variable has a type, and that type determines how JavaScript interacts with it, but JavaScript uses objects to hold all variable data. JavaScript lacks the concept of a *value type* (one stored on the stack) and uses *reference types* (those stored on the heap as objects) exclusively.

## Understanding undefined and null variables

Many developers have problems understanding undefined and null variables. An undefined variable is one that hasn't been initialized yet — a null variable is one that's set to a value of `null`. In both cases, the storage that the variable represents is empty — it contains no data.

JavaScript provides two keywords that you need to know about when working with undefined and null variables. Interestingly enough, the keywords are `null` and `undefined` — imagine that! You can use these keywords to test variables to determine whether they match the criteria for being null or undefined. The following example shows how to perform such a test. (You can find the full source code for this example in the `\Chapter 04\Simple Variables` folder of the downloadable code as `TestNullAndUndefined. HTML`.)

```
function UseVariable()
{
    // Create an undefined variable and test it.
    var MyVariable;
    alert(MyVariable + " has a type of: " +
        typeof(MyVariable));

    // Define the variable and test again.
    MyVariable = "I Am Defined!";

    alert(MyVariable + " has a type of: " +
        typeof(MyVariable));
```

```
    // Empty the variable of data and test again.
    MyVariable = null;
    alert(MyVariable + " has a type of: " +
        typeof(MyVariable));
}
```

In this example, the code begins by creating `MyVariable` but doesn't initialize it. As far as JavaScript is concerned, `MyVariable` exists, but it doesn't contain anything. When the code uses the `alert()` function to display the content of `MyVariable`, you see the word, undefined, in the resulting dialog box. The alert function also uses the `typeof()` function to determine the type (kind) of `MyVariable`, which is also undefined, so the output reads `"undefined has a type of: undefined"`.

The next step is to define `MyVariable` by assigning a value to it. When the code calls `alert()` again, the output changes. This time, you see `"I Am Defined! has a type of: string"` when the browser displays the dialog box. Notice that JavaScript automatically detects the change in type. If you were to assign a numeric value to the same variable and display it again, you'd see that the type changes to number.

Now that `MyVariable` is initialized and contains a value, the code empties it by assigning it a value of `null`. The `null` keyword is special because it lets you create an empty variable. This time `alert()` displays something interesting, it tells you that `"null has a type of: object"`. That's right, `MyVariable` remains initialized, but it's empty, so it has a value of `null` but a type of `object`.

# *Working with Booleans*

Boolean variables have only two possible values: `true` or `false`. Computers need a way to determine whether something is true or false in order to make decisions. The decision-making process makes it possible for a computer to perform a task, to choose between two tasks, or to stop performing a task. Chapters 8 and 9 help you understand the decision making process better. For now, all you need to really understand is that Boolean variables are traditionally used to make a decision or to tell the user the truth value of the Boolean variable (possibly as the result of performing a calculation or checking the status of data).

In most cases, you create a Boolean variable by assigning the variable a value of `true` or `false` like this: `var MyBoolean = true`. You can also assign a variable a Boolean value by using an expression that equates to true or false, such as `var MyBoolean = 3 < 4`. In this case, 3 is less than 4, so `MyBoolean` is true. The `<` symbol is an operator. (The "Understanding the operators" section, later in this chapter, describes the various operators that JavaScript supports.)

You can create Boolean values by using the `new` operator. The statement `MyBoolean = new Boolean();` creates a new Boolean variable that's initialized to `false`. You can also add a value or an expression between the parentheses. Some odd things happen in this situation. For example, if you provide `MyBoolean = new Boolean("Hello");`, JavaScript creates a Boolean variable with a value of `true`. The variable is true because the string you supplied isn't empty — it contains a value. This is one of several techniques you can use to test other variables for content in JavaScript.

The Boolean `new` operator accepts all sorts of inputs. The following list of inputs creates variables that contain a value of `false`:

- 0
- -0
- null
- ""
- false
- undefined
- NaN

The `NaN` keyword stands for Not a Number. It occurs when you perform certain esoteric math functions. In addition, some JavaScript functions return this value when you use them incorrectly. For example, if you call `parseInt("Hello")`, the `parseInt()` function returns `NaN` because `"Hello"` isn't a number and `parseInt()` can't turn it into a number.

# Working with Numbers

JavaScript supports both integer and floating point numbers by using a single type, number. This is probably the most important difference between JavaScript and many other languages. However, JavaScript does support the full range of standard *operators* (special characters used to perform tasks such as addition), and you can perform the full range of standard math tasks using it.

Numbers are values and not text. You can use numbers in comparisons and to aid in making decisions. In addition, you can use equations to create new numeric values. The most common method of placing a number in a variable is to use one of the assignment operators; however, you can also use the `new` operator to create a number, such as `MyNumber = new Number(10);`, which places the value `10` in `MyNumber`.

Most JavaScript applications perform some sort of math tasks (amongst other things). You need to perform math for all sorts of reasons — everything from calculating output for the user to positioning an item onscreen. Consequently, JavaScript, like most computer languages, provides strong support for numeric operations. The following sections provide an overview of the numeric functionality that JavaScript provides.

## Understanding the operators

JavaScript supports a number of operators. The easiest way to remember the various operators is to group them into categories. The following sections break the operators that JavaScript supports into categories to make them easier for you to work with and understand.

### Using the arithmetic operators

Arithmetic operators let you perform calculations by using JavaScript applications. The JavaScript operators perform basic math — you use functions to perform more complicated tasks. Table 4-1 shows the arithmetic operators.

| Table 4-1 | JavaScript Arithmetic Operators | |
|-----------|------------|-------------|
| *Operator* | *Example* | *Description* |
| + | MyNumber = 11 + 5; | The addition operator adds the values to the right of the assignment operator and places the result in MyNumber. For example, MyNumber would contain 16 in this case. |
| − | MyNumber = 11 − 5; | The subtraction operator subtracts the rightmost value from the leftmost value in the expression to the right of the assignment operator and places the result in MyNumber. For example, MyNumber would contain 6 in this case. |
| * | MyNumber = 11 * 5; | The multiplication operator multiplies the values to the right of the assignment operator and places the result in MyNumber. For example, MyNumber would contain 55 in this case. |

*(continued)*

**Table 4-1** *(continued)*

| Operator | Example | Description |
|---|---|---|
| / | `MyNumber = 11 / 5;` | The division operator divides the leftmost value by the rightmost value in the expression to the right of the assignment operator and places the result in `MyNumber`. For example, `MyNumber` would contain `2.2` in this case. |
| % | `MyNumber = 11 % 5;` | The modulus operator divides the leftmost value by the rightmost value in the expression to the right of the assignment operator and places the remainder in `MyNumber`. For example, `MyNumber` would contain `1` in this case. |
| ++ | `MyNumber++;` | The increment operator adds 1 to the value of `MyNumber`. For example, if `MyNumber` originally contained `5` in this example, it would end with a value of `6`. |
| -- | `MyNumber--;` | The decrement operator subtracts 1 from the value of `MyNumber`. For example, if `MyNumber` originally contained `5` in this example, it would end with a value of `4`. |

It's essential to remember precedence when working with arithmetic in JavaScript. When viewing the information in Table 4-1, the increment and decrement operators have the highest precedence. Multiplication, division, and modulus come second. Addition and subtraction are third. As a consequence, consider the case where you have a variable named `MyVariable` and assign it a value of 4. The following equation produces a result of 35:

```
MyVariable = ++MyVariable + 5 * 6;
```

In this case, `MyVariable` is incremented first because the increment operator has the highest precedence, changing the `MyVariable` content to 5. The sub-expression 5 * 6 comes next, which produces a value of 30. Finally, `MyVariable` is added to the value of 30 to produce a result of 35. The brief discussion of precedence at `https://developer.mozilla.org/docs/JavaScript/Reference/Operators/Operator_Precedence` provides additional details.

## *Using the assignment operators*

Assignment operators make it possible to place a numeric value into a variable. Table 4-2 shows the assignment operators that JavaScript supports.

| Table 4-2 | JavaScript Assignment Operators | |
|---|---|---|
| *Operator* | *Example* | *Description* |
| = | `MyNumber = 5;` | The standard assignment operator simply places the value into the variable. |
| += | `MyNumber += 5;` | The add-then-assign operator adds the value found in `MyNumber` to the value on the right side of the assignment and then places the result in `MyNumber`. For example, if `MyNumber` contains `11` at the outset, the result of this assignment is `16`. |
| -= | `MyNumber -= 5;` | The subtract-then-assign operator subtracts the value on the right side of the assignment from the value found in `MyNumber` and then places the result in `MyNumber`. For example, if `MyNumber` contains `11` at the outset, the result of this assignment is `6`. |
| *= | `MyNumber *= 5;` | The multiply-then-assign operator multiplies the value found in `MyNumber` by the value on the right side of the assignment and then places the result in `MyNumber`. For example, if `MyNumber` contains `11` at the outset, the result of this assignment is `55`. |
| /= | `MyNumber /= 5;` | The divide-then-assign operator divides the value found in `MyNumber` by the value on the right side of the assignment and then places the result in `MyNumber`. For example, if `MyNumber` contains `11` at the outset, the result of this assignment is `2.2`. |
| %= | `MyNumber %= 5;` | The modulus-then-assign operator divides the value found in `MyNumber` by the value on the right side of the assignment and then places the remainder (the modulus) in `MyNumber`. For example, if `MyNumber` contains `11` at the outset, the result of this assignment is `1`. |

## Using the comparison operators

Comparison operators make it possible to establish a relationship between the values of two expressions. The expressions can be an equation, a variable, or a value. The result is a Boolean value that you can then use to make decisions based on the relationship between the two expressions. For example, you might decide to perform a calculation only when one variable is less than another. Chapters 8 and 9 provide examples of how to use the comparison operators. Table 4-3 shows the comparison operators that JavaScript supports.

| Table 4-3 | | JavaScript Comparison Operators |
|-----------|---------|----------------------------------|
| *Operator* | *Example* | *Description* |
| < | 5 < 10 | The less-than operator determines whether the value on the left is less than the value on the right. In this case, the comparison would return true. |
| <= | 5 <= 10 | The less-than-or-equal-to operator determines whether the value on the left is less than or equal to the value on the right. In this case, the comparison would return true. |
| == | 5 == 10 | The equal-to operator determines whether the value on the left is equal to the value on the right. In this case, the comparison would return false. |
| >= | 5 >= 10 | The greater-than-or-equal-to operator determines whether the value on the left is greater than or equal to the value on the right. In this case, the comparison would return false. |
| > | 5 > 10 | The greater-than operator determines whether the value on the left is greater than the value on the right. In this case, the comparison would return false. |
| === | 5 === 10 | The exactly-equal-to operator determines whether the value on the left is equal to the value on the right. In addition, this comparison verifies that the type of the value on the left is the same as the type of the value on the right. In this case, the comparison would return false. Even though the type of the values is the same, the value of the two numbers is not. |
| != | 5 != 10 | The not-equal-to operator determines whether the value on the left is not equal to the value on the right. In this case, the comparison would return true. |
| !== | 5 !== 10 | The exactly-not-equal-to operator determines whether the value on the left is not equal to the value on the right. In addition, this comparison verifies that the type of the value on the left is different from the type of the value on the right. In this case, the comparison would return false. Even though 5 is not equal to 10, the type of the two values is the same, which means that this comparison fails. |

## Using the logical operators

Logical operators help you perform Boolean logic. You use them to perform tasks based on the truth value of one or more expressions. For example, if you wanted to determine whether Value1 is less than 2 and Value2 is greater than 4, you would express it as ((Value1 < 2) && (Value2 > 4)). Table 4-4 shows the logical operators and explains their use.

| Table 4-4 | | JavaScript Logical Operators |
|---|---|---|
| *Operator* | *Example* | *Description* |
| && | ((5 < 10) && (10 > 5)) | The AND operator combines two expressions such that both sub-expressions must evaluate to true for the entire expression to be true. In this case, the expression evaluates to true because both sub-expressions are true. |
| \|\| | ((5 < 10) \|\| (10 < 5)) | The OR operator combines two expressions such that one sub-expression or the other can be true and make the entire expression true. In this case, the expression evaluates to true because the first sub-expression is true. It doesn't matter that the second sub-expression evaluates to false. |
| ! | !true | The NOT operator changes the state of an expression to its opposite value. In this case, the expression evaluates to false because the expression is initially true. |

Developers often have problems figuring out the logical operators. In fact, many colleges teach entire courses on Boolean logic just to make it easier for mathematicians and developers to work through complex logic situations. The AND, OR, and NOT operators can make it possible to create complex comparisons using JavaScript, which means that your application can evaluate and respond to complex real-world events.

Table 4-5 shows the truth logic for the AND operator, and Table 4-6 shows the truth logic for the OR operator. Use these tables to figure out when an expression will evaluate to true or false based on the value of the individual sub-expressions.

| Table 4-5 | AND Operator Logic | |
|-----------|---------------------|---|
| *Expression 1* | *Expression 2* | *Result* |
| true | true | true |
| false | true | false |
| true | false | false |
| false | false | false |

| Table 4-6 | OR Operator Logic | |
|-----------|---------------------|---|
| *Expression 1* | *Expression 2* | *Result* |
| true | true | true |
| false | true | true |
| true | false | true |
| false | false | false |

### Using the grouping operators

JavaScript supports the use of parentheses as grouping operators. The left parenthesis, (, begins a group, and the right parenthesis, ), ends it. The use of parentheses is incredibly important in some situations because the parenthesis has *higher precedence* (is evaluated before) any other operator discussed in this chapter. Consequently, the expression 4 + 5 * 6 evaluates to 34, but the expression (4 + 5) * 6 evaluates to 54.

## Doing simple math

You now have the tools to create your first real application. In this case, the example performs simple four-function math. The resulting page can add, subtract, multiply, or divide two numbers. The interface part of the code includes three text inputs (one set for read-only use) and four buttons (one for each math function), as shown here. (You can find the complete source code for this example in the \Chapter 04\Numbers folder of the downloadable code as VariableMath.HTML.)

```
<body>
    <h1>Performing Simple Math</h1>
    <p>
        Value1:
        <input type="text" id="Value1" value="4">
    </p>
    <p>
```

```
        Value1:
        <input type="text" id="Value2" value="5">
</p>
<p>
        Result:
        <input type="text" id="Result" value=""
                readonly="true">
</p>
<input type="button"
        value="+"
        onclick="DoAdd()" />
<input type="button"
        value="-"
        onclick="DoSub()" />
<input type="button"
        value="*"
        onclick="DoMul()" />
<input type="button"
        value="/"
        onclick="DoDiv()" />
</body>
```

When you display the page, you see the entry fields and associated buttons. Figure 4-1 shows how they appear in Firefox. This figure also shows the result of performing a division using the two input numbers.

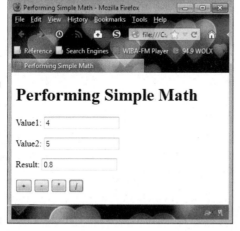

**Figure 4-1:**
The example provides inputs and buttons for performing simple math tasks.

Each button has a different JavaScript function associated with it. The essential tasks are the same in each case:

1. Obtain the input from `Value1` and convert it to a number.

2. Obtain the input from `Value2` and convert it to a number.

3. Change the value attribute of `Result` to reflect the math operation on `Value1` and `Value2`.

The attribute value you receive from the document is always in text form, so numeric conversion is essential. Otherwise, what you'd really do is create a combined string. For example, if `Value1` is 4 and `Value2` is 5, the result would read 45 — the combination of `Value1` and `Value2` as strings. Here's the code used to perform addition:

```
function DoAdd()
{
    // Obtain the current values of Value1 and Value2.
    var Value1 = new Number(
        document.getElementById("Value1").value);
    var Value2 = new Number(
        document.getElementById("Value2").value);

    // Set the result to reflect the addition
    // of the two numbers.
    document.getElementById("Result").setAttribute(
        "value", Value1 + Value2);
}
```

The code begins by creating a number using the `new` keyword. It obtains the current text value of `Value1` and converts it to a number type. Notice that you must use the `value` property. If you were to use the `getAttribute()` function instead, the code would return the initial value of `Value1`, not the current value. The code performs the same task with `Value2`.

At this point, the code has access to two numbers. It calls the `setAttribute()` function for `Result` and sets this attribute to the combination of `Value1 + Value2`.

The `DoSub()`, `DoMul()`, and `DoDiv()` functions look the same. The only difference is that each of these functions performs a different math task.

## Changing number formats

Formatting numbers is important. The presentation of a number affects how the viewer sees it. For example, dollar amounts have two decimal places, even if there's no decimal (cents) portion. Fortunately, JavaScript provides some simple functions you can use to control the presentation of numeric information. The following list provides a short description of each of these functions:

✔ `toExponential()`: Displays the number in scientific (exponential) format, even if JavaScript would normally display the number in standard format.

✔ toFixed(): Displays the number with a fixed number of digits after the decimal point.

✔ toLocaleString(): Displays the number by using the browser's locale information. For example, some countries use a comma for the decimal point, but others use a period.

✔ toPrecision(): Displays the number by using the specified number of digits for the entire number.

✔ toString(): Displays the number as a string in the specified radix (base). For example, you can use this function to convert a number into hexadecimal format.

The easiest way to understand numeric formats is to write a short program to display them. This example begins with something new — a global variable. You place the global variable, ThisNumber, in the <head> section of the page like this:

```
<script language="JavaScript">
   var ThisNumber = 22.5
</script>
```

A *global variable* is one that you can access anywhere on the current page. The following code creates a page that displays ThisNumber in all of the formats that JavaScript makes available. (You can find the complete source code for this example in the \Chapter 04\Numbers folder of the downloadable code as DisplayNumber.HTML.)

```
<body>
   <h1>Formatting Numbers</h1>
   <p>toExponential():
      <script language="JavaScript">
         document.write(ThisNumber.toExponential(5));
      </script>
   </p>
   <p>toFixed():
      <script language="JavaScript">
         document.write(ThisNumber.toFixed(5));
      </script>
   </p>
   <p>toLocaleString():
      <script language="JavaScript">
         document.write(ThisNumber.toLocaleString());
      </script>
   </p>
   <p>toPrecision():
      <script language="JavaScript">
         document.write(ThisNumber.toPrecision(5));
      </script>
   </p>
   <p>toString():
```

```
    <ul>
        <li>Binary:
            <script language="JavaScript">
                document.write(ThisNumber.toString(2));
            </script>
        </li>
        <li>Octal:
            <script language="JavaScript">
                document.write(ThisNumber.toString(8));
            </script>
        </li>
        <li>Decimal:
            <script language="JavaScript">
                document.write(ThisNumber.toString(10));
            </script>
        </li>
        <li>Hexadecimal:
            <script language="JavaScript">
                document.write(ThisNumber.toString(16));
            </script>
        </li>
    </ul>
</p>
```

Each output uses five places of precision as defined by that function, when the function allows you to specify the amount of precision. The `toString()` function is different in that it requires a *radix* (base) as input. For example, `toString(10)` displays the number in decimal format. Figure 4-2 makes the various numeric formats a lot easier to understand.

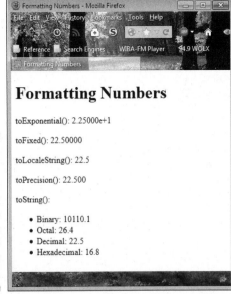

**Figure 4-2:** Presenting numbers correctly helps viewers understand their meaning.

# Working with Text

The string data type (text) is the presentation format that most humans think about when viewing information on the screen. Even though the underlying data is some other type, what a human sees is text. As far as JavaScript is concerned, strings are just one of many data types. Developers need to be aware of the difference between what the human sees and what JavaScript manipulates using application code. Even so, you find yourself working with strings regularly because strings lend themselves to certain tasks, such as searching for specific information and creating pretty displays.

Throughout this book you work with strings to create text output in various ways. The following sections get you started with text, but they're only the tip of a large iceberg.

## Concatenating text

Strings are made up of many different pieces of information in many cases. You've seen some examples of *concatenation* — the act of combining string pieces to create a larger whole — several times in the book already. In fact, it's hard to create any application without using concatenation. Essentially, concatenation involves adding strings together by using the plus sign (+).

Consider two strings: `ThisString` and `ThatString`. `ThisString` contains `"Hello "`, and `ThatString` contains `"World"`. When you see

```
var FinalString = ThisString + ThatString;
```

in an application, `FinalString` equals `"Hello World"`. Using the plus sign concatenates the two strings into a new string.

## Changing word and letter formats

JavaScript provides a wealth of string functions. This section covers only four formatting functions that you use to control the appearance of strings. The rest of the book contains other functions that affect your use of strings. It's amazing to think about all the ways in which you can use strings with JavaScript. Keeping this flexible nature in mind, here are four formatting functions to start off your library of JavaScript string functions:

- `toLocaleLowerCase()`: Changes all the characters in a string to lowercase versions while respecting lowercase rules for the current locale.

✔ `toLocaleUpperCase()`: Changes all the characters in a string to uppercase versions while respecting the uppercase rules for the current locale.

✔ `toLowerCase()`: Changes all the characters in a string to lowercase equivalents without regard to locale.

✔ `toUpperCase()`: Changes all the characters in a string to uppercase equivalents without regard to locale.

As with formatting numbers, the best way to see string formatting is to create an application to do it. As with the `DisplayNumber.HTML` page, this page begins with a global variable, `ThisString`, that contains `"This is a Sample String"`. The following code shows how to use the various functions. (You can find the complete source code for this example in the `\Chapter 04\Strings` folder of the downloadable code as `DisplayText.HTML`.)

```
<body>
    <h1>Formatting Strings</h1>
    <p>Original String:
        <script language="JavaScript">
            document.write(ThisString);
        </script>
    </p>
    <p>toLocaleLowerCase():
        <script language="JavaScript">
            document.write(ThisString.
            toLocaleLowerCase());
        </script>
    </p>
    <p>toLocaleUpperCase():
        <script language="JavaScript">
            document.write(ThisString.
            toLocaleUpperCase());
        </script>
    </p>
    <p>toLowerCase():
        <script language="JavaScript">
            document.write(ThisString.toLowerCase());
        </script>
    </p>
    <p>toUpperCase():
        <script language="JavaScript">
            document.write(ThisString.toUpperCase());
        </script>
    </p>
</body>
```

Unlike the number-formatting functions, you won't find any way to customize the string output. What you see depends on your browser and your locale. Figure 4-3 shows typical output from this application.

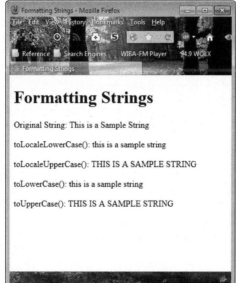

**Figure 4-3:** JavaScript provides a number of interesting string formatting functions.

# Working with Arrays

*Arrays* are a kind of collection. Each array contains zero or more like items that you can manipulate as a group. The following sections provide an extremely brief overview of arrays that will lead into other discussions found in the book.

## Creating an array

JavaScript provides three methods for creating arrays: regular, condensed, and literal. In general, one way is as good as another. Of the three, the regular method shown in the following listing is the easiest to understand, but the literal method is the most compact. (You can find the complete source code for this example in the `\Chapter 04\Arrays` folder of the downloadable code as `CreateArray.HTML`.)

```
<body>
    <h1>Creating Arrays</h1>
    <h2>Regular:</h2>
    <script language="JavaScript">
        // Create the array.
        var Colors = new Array();
        // Fill the array with data.
        Colors[0] = "Blue";
        Colors[1] = "Green";
        Colors[2] = "Purple";

        // Display the content onscreen.
        document.write(Colors);
    </script>

    <h2>Condensed:</h2>
    <script language="JavaScript">
        // Create the array and fill it with data.
        var Colors = new Array("Blue", "Green", "Purple");

        // Display the content onscreen.
        document.write(Colors);
    </script>

    <h2>Literal:</h2>
    <script language="JavaScript">
        // Create the array and fill it with data.
        var Colors = ["Blue", "Green", "Purple"];

        // Display the content onscreen.
        document.write(Colors);
    </script>
</body>
```

All three methods produce precisely the same array. The regular method creates the array first and then assigns strings to each array element by number.
The square brackets behind Colors indicate the element number, which
begins at 0 and increments by 1 for each element you add. Notice that when
using the condensed method you enclose the array elements in parentheses as part of the constructor. However, when using the literal method, you
enclose the array elements in square brackets. You can see the results of this
example in Figure 4-4.

## Accessing array members

Each array member has a unique number — an address of sorts. You access
array members by providing the array name and then the element number
within square brackets. Normally, you use a loop to access array members.
Chapter 9 discusses loops in detail. For now, just consider a loop as a means
of automating array access.

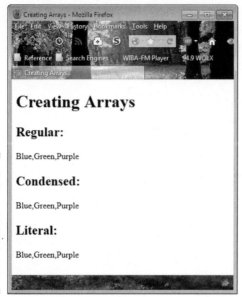

**Figure 4-4:**
Use any of
the meth-
ods that
JavaScript
provides
for creating
arrays.

The following code shows an example of how you might access an array, one element at a time, and display its content. (You can find the complete source code for this example in the \Chapter 04\Arrays folder of the download-able code as AccessArray.HTML.)

```
<body>
    <h1>Access Array Elements</h1>
    <script language="JavaScript">
        // Create the array and fill it with data.
        var Colors = ["Blue", "Green", "Purple"];

        // Define a loop to access each array element
        // and display it onscreen.
        for (i = 0; i < Colors.length; i++)
        {
            document.write(
                "Colors " + i + " = " +
                Colors[i] + "<br />");
        }
    </script>
</body>
```

This example uses a for loop. The for loop creates a counter variable (a number) named i that begins at 0 (the first element of the array) and con-tinues to increment (i++) until it has accessed all the array elements (i < Colors.length). The document.write() function outputs the Colors element number, the content (as Colors[i] where i is the element number), and an end-of-line tag. Figure 4-5 shows the output from this example.

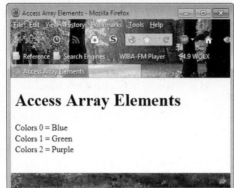

**Figure 4-5:**
Access
each array
element by
number.

# Chapter 5

# Working with Objects

## In This Chapter

▶ Specifying the features that define an object in JavaScript

▶ Working with objects

▶ Using object literals

▶ Making objects easier to use by naming them correctly

*A*t one time, programming was entirely about writing procedures. You wrote a procedure to perform a task in a way that the computer could understand. Even if you used a higher level programming language, the process was the same — writing a procedure telling the computer to do something in terms it could understand.

As computer science progressed, it was found that people could relate better to coding scenarios that model the real world rather than the abstract world of the computer. Object Oriented Programming (OOP) is a technique whereby the developer creates a model of a real-world entity and then manipulates that entity with code. The underlying infrastructure translates the model into terms that the computer can understand. Objects are simply models of items you interact with in the real world in some way.

Given that objects are models of real-world entities, you need some method of telling the computer what those real world entities look like. As a result, all OOP languages support some method of defining, creating, and using objects. The language wouldn't be much use otherwise because a language creator can't anticipate what objects will exist in your world.

One of the features that differentiate objects from procedures is the ability to *encapsulate* (create a package containing) the elements that define the object. JavaScript provides a means to encapsulate just data, when that's all you really need to work with. The special technique used to encapsulate just the data is called an *object literal*. This chapter shows how to create and use object literals to make it easier to work with your data in a JavaScript application.

The final section of this chapter discusses a topic that's controversial with many developers — naming variables and objects. JavaScript doesn't care what you call the objects and variables you create as long as the name doesn't violate any of the naming requirements that JavaScript must use to recognize the word as an object or variable. For example, your object or variable name must begin with a letter and not a number. In addition, you can't name an object or variable by using any of the keywords that JavaScript recognizes as code. The main reason to name objects and variables a certain way is to make your code easier to understand. A name such as `FirstName` is certainly much easier to understand than `Var21`. The first tells you that the variable contains someone's first name, but the second tells you nothing at all.

# Defining Objects

Think of programming objects in the same way you think of real-world objects. For example, you could create an object in JavaScript named apple and then describe what makes an apple unique to JavaScript. From that point on, you could create apple objects, define each apple's special characteristics, and interact with that apple by using code in the same way you'd interact with an apple in the real world. Of course, the apple isn't real — it's a model of a real-world apple, but the idea is that you can envision what this apple would look like based on the description you provide for it. The following sections describe objects in more detail so that you can create and use objects later in the chapter.

## Starting with the Object object

Everything in JavaScript is an object. However, JavaScript needs a definition of what an object is before it can do anything with objects. The `Object` object is the basis for all objects in JavaScript. Whenever you create an object, it uses `Object` as the starting point.

Before proceeding too far, you need to understand a little of the terminology used for objects. A description of an object is called a *class*. Think of a class as a blueprint for building the object. It isn't an object; rather, it's simply the instructions used to create an object later.

When you want to use a class to create an actual object, you *instantiate* the object, which means that you tell JavaScript to build an object based on the class you provide — much as an architect would ask a contractor to construct a building based on a blueprint. When you see code such as `var MyNumber = new Number();`, that code is telling JavaScript to use the `Number` class to instantiate a new object named `MyNumber`. The `new` keyword is the key here because it tells JavaScript to create a new object.

Any special instructions required to create an object based on the class definition appear within the class *constructor*. The constructor is a special method (see the "Understanding methods" section, later in this chapter, for a description of how methods work) that contains instructions for creating a new object based on the class description. For example, you might decide that the object should have certain default characteristics when JavaScript creates it, so these requirements appear in the constructor.

A constructor can also receive special instructions from the caller. For example, when you create an array by passing a list of items to it, such as var Colors = ["Blue", "Green", "Purple"];, what you're really doing is telling the constructor that you want to create the array with three predefined strings in it: Blue, Green, and Purple.

Every object has a special property called *this*. The this value of an object always refers to the particular instance of the object that you're working with now, rather than any other instance of the object. The this value of an object is important when you need to differentiate between elements that are internal to this specific object. In some cases, JavaScript may try to use elements that are provided by the parent or *base* class. For now, simply remember that this refers to the current object. Future examples will demonstrate how this works so you gain a better understanding of it.

The Object object also comes with some predefined properties and methods. As a consequence, every object you create in JavaScript has these predefined properties and methods, even though you didn't tell JavaScript to create them. The act of using Object as the basis for your classes and the resulting objects having the same properties and methods as Object is called *inheritance*. Just as you inherit certain characteristics from your parents, an object in JavaScript inherits features from its parent, which is Object. Classes can inherit from other JavaScript classes, but every JavaScript class inherits from Object.

The following list describes the most commonly used Object methods (there aren't any commonly used properties):

- ✔ toString(): Outputs the value of the object, such as the numeric value of a Number object, as a string.

- ✔ toLocaleString(): Outputs the value of the object, such as the numeric value of a Number object, as a string that includes localized formatting. For example, numeric values in some countries use a comma for the decimal point, but other countries use a period.

- ✔ valueOf(): Outputs the internal value of the object as a string. In this case, the value is the this value of this particular object, rather than the value of any other instance of the class.

## Understanding properties

A *property* defines a characteristic of an object. For example, when looking at the `Apple` object, the `Color` property would define the color of the apple. You use properties to define the features of an object — its value or anything concrete about the object that others need to know to interact with the object. For example, when you write `var Colors = ["Blue", "Green", "Purple"];`, the `length` property tells you how many items appear within the array.

## Understanding methods

A *method* is a task you can perform using the object. The term *task* is loosely defined in this case because the range of tasks you can perform with objects is quite broad. Think of the `Apple` object. The `bite()` method reduces the size of the apple by a value of one bite. When you write `Apple.bite()`, JavaScript removes one bite from the `Apple`. Using a more concrete example, when you write `var Colors = ["Blue", "Green", "Purple"];`, calling `var Item = Colors.pop();` places the last value, `Purple`, in `Item` and removes it from `Colors` by using the `pop()` method.

When working with methods, you sometimes need to provide information to the method in order for it to perform the required task. Each piece of information you provide is called an *argument*. Arguments are either *required* (which means you must provide them) or *optional* (which means you can provide them when desired). For example, calling `Colors.push("Yellow");` places a new string, `Yellow`, into the `Colors` array. The first argument you provide is required. However, this method also accepts optional arguments. Calling `Colors.push("Yellow", "Orange");` places two strings in the `Colors` array. The second string, `Orange`, is optional.

## Understanding events

An *event* is something that occurs outside of your application. Your application can monitor the event and react to it. For example, you can react to a user clicking a button on a form. The event needn't apply to a user though — often an event is generated by another application or even a different computer. In fact, your application can signal itself that something has happened (such as the expiration of a timer or the occurrence of an error).

Most JavaScript applications react to form-based events, such as a user click. The form *publishes* an event every time the user clicks a control. Some languages call this *firing* the event. Thinking about a user click, a button publishes a `click` event every time the user clicks the button. However, many JavaScript developers create special events using their custom classes, so you shouldn't limit yourself to the form-based events unless they actually do meet all your needs.

Your application won't react to the event unless it *subscribes* to the event. When working with a button, your application can subscribe by providing the name of an *event handler* to the `onclick` attribute of the button. For example, when you type `<input type="button" value="+" onclick="DoAdd()" />`, the `DoAdd()` method creates a subscription through the `onclick` attribute. When the user clicks the button, the button publishes a `click` event that's handled by `DoAdd()`. The button would still publish a `click` event even if there wasn't any subscription, but there wouldn't be an event handler to do anything with it.

# Using and Creating Objects

You've already used many built-in JavaScript objects in the previous chapters, but haven't really examined how those objects worked. In the sections that follow, you take another look at the built-in JavaScript object classes and begin viewing them as classes that you instantiate to create an object.

In addition, it's time to start looking at techniques you can use to build your own JavaScript classes. As your code becomes more complex, it helps to create classes to make the code manageable and to make it better able to model real-world data. Using your own custom objects will make it easier to understand what tasks the code is performing and reduce complexity. Objects also have benefits such as reducing the potential for errors.

## Using JavaScript objects

JavaScript comes with a host of built-in objects that help you perform general programming tasks. For example, each of the variable types discussed in Chapter 4 is a built-in object. You can create a new variable of any type you want using the techniques shown in that chapter. JavaScript also supports a number of other built-in objects that help you interact with the pages you create. The following sections describe these objects by basic type: browser, Document Object Model (DOM), and built-in.

### Exploring JavaScript browser objects

Here's a quick overview of some of the more interesting JavaScript browser objects — those that relate to how the browser performs tasks:

✔ `history`: Provides the means for examining and moving between URLs stored in the browser's history. You can see a complete list of the methods and properties associated with this object at `http://www.w3schools.com/jsref/obj_history.asp`.

✔ `location`: Contains information about the current URL. This object also provides the means to perform tasks such as loading a new page or reloading the current page. You can see a complete list of the methods and properties associated with this object at `http://www.w3schools.com/jsref/obj_location.asp`.

✔ `navigator`: Contains information about the current browser. For example, you can determine the browser type and version, and determine whether the browser has cookies enabled. You can see a complete list of the methods and properties associated with this object at `http://www.w3schools.com/jsref/obj_navigator.asp`.

✔ `screen`: Specifies the physical characteristics of the device used to display the page, including page height, width, and color depth. You can see a complete list of the methods and properties associated with this object at `http://www.w3schools.com/jsref/obj_screen.asp`.

✔ `window`: Provides access to the browser's window so that you can perform tasks such as displaying message boxes. When working with pages that contain frames, the browser creates a window for the entire HTML document and another window for each frame. You can see a complete list of the methods and properties associated with this object at `http://www.w3schools.com/jsref/obj_window.asp`.

### Examining built-in DOM objects

JavaScript also supports special objects for the DOM. The DOM is a platform and browser independent method of describing the content, structure, and style of documents. You can read more about DOM at `http://www.w3.org/DOM`. Every page you load into the browser is part of the DOM.

The following list provides a brief overview of the built-in DOM objects:

✔ `Attr`: Provides access to individual attributes within the document. You can see a complete list of the methods and properties associated with this object at `http://www.w3schools.com/jsref/dom_obj_attr.asp`.

✔ `document`: Provides access to the entire document. You can use this object to access any part of the document. In addition, this object lets you display information directly on the page and perform other tasks related to the user interface. You can see a complete list of the methods and properties associated with this object at `http://www.w3schools.com/jsref/dom_obj_core_document.asp`.

✔ `Element`: Contains an individual document element of any type supported as XML. This object provides access to attributes through the `Attr` object and properties through the `Node` object (described later in this list). You can see a complete list of the methods and properties associated with this object at `http://www.w3schools.com/jsref/dom_obj_element.asp`.

✔ Events: Supports access to existing events and creation of new ones. You can see a complete list of the methods and properties associated with this object at `http://www.w3schools.com/jsref/dom_obj_event.asp`.

✔ HTMLElement: Contains an individual HTML document element, such as a paragraph or a control. Use the `Element` and `Node` objects to gain access to element attributes and properties. You can see a complete list of the methods and properties associated with this object at `http://www.w3schools.com/jsref/dom_obj_all.asp`.

✔ Node: Defines the particulars of any given *node*, which can include the document as a whole, an element within the document, an attribute provided as part of an element, text, and comments. You can see a complete list of the methods and properties associated with this object at `http://www.w3schools.com/jsref/dom_obj_node.asp`.

✔ NodeFilter: Specifies which nodes appear as part of a `NodeIterator` used to traverse the list of nodes within a document. You can see a complete list of the methods and properties associated with this object at `https://developer.mozilla.org/en-US/docs/DOM/NodeFilter`.

✔ NodeIterator: Provides a method of obtaining a list of nodes within a document. Traversing the list of nodes can help you locate specific nodes and interact with them. For example, you might find all of the `<input>` tag nodes and add a particular attribute to them. You can see a complete list of the methods and properties associated with this object at `https://developer.mozilla.org/en-US/docs/DOM/NodeIterator`.

✔ NodeList: Contains an ordered list of all the nodes within the document or in a particular area of the document. You can see a complete list of the methods and properties associated with this object at `http://www.w3schools.com/jsref/dom_obj_nodelist.asp`.

✔ NamedNodeMap: Contains an unordered list of all the nodes within the document or in a particular area of the document. You can see a complete list of the methods and properties associated with this object at `http://www.w3schools.com/jsref/dom_obj_namednodemap.asp`.

JavaScript supports a number of additional built-in objects. The lists in this chapter simply describe the objects you use most often. If you want to see a complete list of the built-in JavaScript objects, check the latest specification at `http://www.ecma-international.org/publications/standards/Ecma-262.htm`.

### Using built-in objects

The example for this section shows how to use some of the built-in objects to create some interesting content for a page. The page contains a simple header and the following button:

```
<input type="button"
       value="Display Screen Stats"
       onclick="DisplayScreenStats()">
```

When the code calls DisplayScreenStats(), it queries the user about displaying the statistics onscreen. When the user clicks OK, the function obtains and displays the required information by creating the required nodes on the page. In other words, the example actually adds new tags to the page to contain the custom content.

Here's the code for the DisplayScreenStats() function. (You can find complete code for this example in the \Chapter 05\Objects folder of the downloadable code as UseObjects.HTML.)

```
function DisplayScreenStats()
{
    // Ask the user about displaying the screen
    // information.
    var DoIt = window.confirm(
        "Display the screen dimensions?");

    // If the user agrees, display the information.
    if (DoIt)
    {
        // Create a new <p> tag to store the data.
        var Para = document.createElement("p");

        // Create a new <br> tag to provide space.
        var Spacer1 = document.createElement("br");
        var Spacer2 = document.createElement("br");

        // Create the content for the <p> tag.
        var Content1 = document.createTextNode(
            "Width: " + window.screen.width);
        var Content2 = document.createTextNode(
            "Height: " + window.screen.height);
        var Content3 = document.createTextNode(
            "Colors: " + window.screen.colorDepth);

        // Add the content to the <p> tag.
        Para.appendChild(Content1);
        Para.appendChild(Spacer1);
        Para.appendChild(Content2);
        Para.appendChild(Spacer2);
        Para.appendChild(Content3);
```

```
        // Display the <p> tag on the page.
        document.body.appendChild(Para);
    }
}
```

You've seen the alert() function in action in the past. Unfortunately, this function limits you to displaying messages. The confirm() function creates a dialog box that contains two buttons: OK and Cancel. When the user clicks OK, DoIt contains true. Otherwise, DoIt contains false. Chapter 8 discusses the if statement in detail. All you need to know for now is that it tests DoIt and when DoIt is true, the function obtains and displays the screen statistics onscreen.

The document.createElement() method can create new elements for you. In this example, the code uses them to create a <p> tag and a <br> tag. The <p> tag holds the content you want to see onscreen, and the <br> tag creates space between the individual statistics. You can use this method to create any legal tag that HTML5 supports.

The technique shown here allows use of a particular piece of content only one time within a container element. Reusing content simply moves it from its original location to the last location where it's used. The inability to reuse content is the reason the example creates two spacers, rather than using a single spacer, even though both spacers are <br> tags.

The content is text, so you need to use the document.createTextNode() method to create a text node. Within this node, you place the content you want to display as part of the <p> tag. The window.screen object provides access to properties that contain information about the browser's window. In this case, the application displays the content of the width, height, and colorDepth properties.

At this point, all the function has to do is put the content together. The <p> tag is the container, so the code calls the Para.appendChild() method to add each bit of content to the <p> tag. Notice that the content can include both text nodes and other elements. You can use any mix of items that would normally appear on a Web page as HTML.

All you have at this point is a new <p> tag that no one can see. To display the <p> tag, the code calls document.body.appendChild() to add the <p> tag to the rest of the information on the page. Figure 5-1 shows the resulting screen information from my browser. The information from your browser will be different, but the page will essentially look the same.

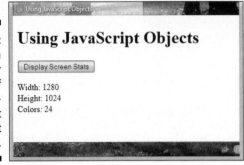

## Building custom objects

Most objects you create in JavaScript provide properties, methods, or both. Few custom objects require events unless you plan to create a new type of display element or something that works in the background, such as a timer. With this in mind, this section looks at the technique for creating a basic custom object that includes both properties and methods.

The example begins by creating the required elements of the class. You may be surprised to find out that you create classes using functions. After defining the class elements, the example creates an instance of the class, provides data for each of its properties, and then uses a method to output the class data as a formatted string. (You can find the full source code for this example in the `\Chapter 05\Objects` folder of the downloadable code as `CreateObjects.HTML`.)

```html
<!DOCTYPE html>

<html>
<head>
    <title>Creating New Objects</title>
    <script language="JavaScript">

        // Create a method to add to the customer
        // class.
        function formattedOutput()
        {
            // Return the formatted output consisting
            // of a string that contains the customer
            // data.
            return "The customer's name is: " +
                this.Name + " and age is: " +
                this.Age;
        }
```

```
            // Create the customer class.
            function customer()
            {
                // Define two properties for this class.
                this.Name = "";
                this.Age = 0;

                // Add a method for displaying the class data.
                this.formattedOutput = formattedOutput;
            }
    </script>
</head>

<body>
    <h1>Creating a New Customer</h1>

    <script language="JavaScript">
        // Instantiate the customer class.
        var ThisCustomer = new customer();

        // Add data to this instance of the customer
        // object.
        ThisCustomer.Name = "Sam Smith";
        ThisCustomer.Age = 22;

        // Output the data found in the ThisCustomer
        // object.
        document.write("<p>" +
            ThisCustomer.formattedOutput() + "</p>");
    </script>
</body>
</html>
```

The `formattedOutput()` function defines a method you can use with the class. All it does is obtain the current instance values and place them in a string. Notice the use of the `this` keyword. You want to work with this instance — not some other instance or the base class. It's essential to use the `this` keyword as needed or the method won't work as you expect. (For more on the `this` value of an object, see the earlier section "Starting with the Object object.")

The `customer()` function is actually the class definition. This class includes two properties, `Name` and `Age`, and one method, `formattedOutput`. Notice again how the `this` keyword is used. When working with properties, you want to assign values to the properties in this instance of the object. Likewise, the method works with this instance of the object. However, you assign the `formattedOutput()` function to the `formattedOutput` method associated with this instance.

To demonstrate how the class works, the code creates a `customer` instance named `ThisCustomer`. Notice that you use the `new` keyword just as you would with any other object. The code adds values to the Name and Age properties just as you would with any other object. Likewise, it calls the formattedOutput() method to display the data as a formatted string. Figure 5-2 shows the output from this example.

**Figure 5-2:** Objects you create work just like those that are built into JavaScript.

Creating New Objects

# Creating a New Customer

The customer's name is: Sam Smith and age is: 22

# Working with Object Literals

An *object literal* is a special kind of data collection. It contains named values that you use to make accessing a particular value easier. The idea is to create a package that you can send to somewhere with all the values required to perform a task. Because the values are named, you don't have to provide them in any specific order. In addition, the recipient doesn't have to work with the content in any specific way. This is a kind of object that lacks any sort of constructor and has no need for methods. The entire purpose of this technique is to make transferring data simpler and less error prone. You can see a real world example of how object literals are used at http://blog. smartbear.com/software-quality/bid/242126/using-the-google-maps-api-to-add-cool-stuff-to-your-applications. The following sections describe how to work with JavaScript object literals.

## Creating the name/value pairs

Object literals rely on name and value pairs to store information. You provide a name (also called a label) and a data value to go with it. The recipient can then retrieve the data by name. The following example shows a simple use of an object literal. (You can find the full source code for this example in the \Chapter 05\Object Literals folder of the downloadable code as CreateLiterals.HTML.)

```
<!DOCTYPE html>

<html>
<head>
    <title>Working with Object Literals</title>
</head>
```

```
<body>
    <h1>Create and Use Object Literals</h1>

    <script language="JavaScript">
        // Create the object literal.
        var customerData =
        {
            Name: 'Sally Jones',
            Age: 32,
            Birthday: new Date("01/15/1981")
        }

        // Display the object literal data onscreen.
        document.write(
            "<p>The customer's name is: " +
            customerData.Name +
            " age is: " + customerData.Age +
            " and date of birth is: " +
            customerData.Birthday.toDateString() + "</p>");
    </script>
</body>
</html>
```

In this case, `customerData` contains three values: `Name`, `Age`, and `Birthday`. Each of these labels has an associated value. Notice that you needn't worry about mixing data type — the object literal doesn't care. The important elements are to enclose the data within curly brackets, to provide a name for each value, to separate the value from the name by a colon, and to separate values with commas.

At this point, `customerData` is a package that you could send anywhere. The example uses the information directly after the object literal is created. Notice that you use standard dot syntax to access each of the values. The order of access doesn't matter because you access the values by name. Figure 5-3 shows typical output from this example.

**Figure 5-3:** Use object literals to create packages of data you can send anywhere.

Working with Object Literals

# Create and Use Object Literals

The customer's name is: Sally Jones age is: 32 and date of birth is: Thu Jan 15 1981

## *Adding new name/value pairs*

JavaScript supports a number of methods for adding new name and value pairs to an object literal. The easiest method of accomplishing this task is to simply type the name of a new property and assign a value to it. For example, if you wanted to add a property named `HairColor` to the `customerData` example and give the customer a hair color of brown, you'd simply type `customer Data.HairColor = "Brown";`. The new property would appear as part of `customerData` as if you had provided it as part of the original object literal.

# *Naming Variables and Objects Properly*

JavaScript doesn't care what you name variables and objects in your application. You could name a variable `Var22`, and JavaScript wouldn't care. However, you'd care months later when you forget what `Var22` means.

Variable and object names must follow these simple rules in JavaScript:

- ✔ The variable or object name must begin with a letter.

- ✔ You can alternatively begin the variable or object name with the dollar sign ($) or underscore (_), but most professionals recommend against using special characters because they can prove confusing.

- ✔ Variable names are case sensitive, so `Var` is different from `var`, which is also different from `VAR`.

The variable and object names you choose are for your benefit. You need to select variable or object names that mean something to you and will jog your memory months later when you've forgotten some of what the code does. A variable name such as `FirstName` is descriptive and will most definitely jog your memory when you need it.

It's also essential that you decide how to work with variable and object names when part of a team. JavaScript automatically uses camel case for its variables, properties, methods, events, and objects in most cases. *Camel case* is a technique where each word begins with a capital letter. Some developers insist that the first word appear in lowercase letters such as `firstName`, rather than `FirstName`, but there's no strict rule about this. (Starting a variable name with a capital letter is also called *Pascal case*.) However, using camel case for your variable names does make them much easier to read and understand.

Avoiding keywords is also a good idea. Yes, you can create a variable named `New` in your application, but now you've used a keyword as a variable, which will prove confusing to anyone viewing your code (including you when you review the code later). You should also avoid using standard JavaScript object names and other potentially confusing names for the objects and variables you create.

# Chapter 6

# Getting to Know the Standard JavaScript Objects

*In This Chapter*

▶ Using the basic JavaScript objects

▶ Creating, using, and searching strings

▶ Creating and using dates

C hapters 4 and 5 work together to introduce you to the concepts behind variables and objects. Those chapters help you understand why variables and objects are important. In this chapter, you move on to working with specific objects and using these objects to do something interesting. You've already been exposed to most of these objects at a very basic level, but it's time to look at them in more detail because you use these objects to perform a wide variety of tasks in most JavaScript applications. The better you know these objects, the faster and more accurately you can write code to perform special tasks using HTML5 and JavaScript.

As mentioned in Chapter 5, the basis for all JavaScript objects is the `Object` class. If you drill down into any object, you find the `Object` class mentioned in some way as the endpoint, the progenitor, of that object. In addition, JavaScript treats all variables as objects. In general, JavaScript objects provide properties and methods, but not events. You can create objects that have events, but doing so is unusual because JavaScript normally provides event support through the HTML tags used to create the user interface.

Strings are the most important JavaScript object to know how to use well because strings are the data type that humans understand best. Strings are used for everything from user interfaces to data searches. Although you must rely on other data types for calculations, most data types provide some method of creating string output because that's the format humans need to understand the data. This chapter helps you understand strings better, especially with regard to presentation and searches — the two ways strings are used most often.

Given that humans place a strong value on date and time, it's also important to know how to work with both in your applications. Computing the passage of time is an essential tool in the developer's toolbox. This chapter provides the essentials you need to know to work with both date and time, and to calculate time ranges so that you can mark the passage of time in your applications.

# Defining the Basic JavaScript Objects

It's time to look at some of the tasks you can perform with individual objects — including the creation of more complex custom objects based on the `Object` class. All objects inherit from `Object`, so the first section shows a more complete custom object example based on `Object`. The sections that follow examine individual features of the standard objects that JavaScript supplies.

## Understanding Object

The basis of all JavaScript objects is `Object`, even though you seldom see the word `Object` actually used anywhere in JavaScript code. Chapter 5 presents an extremely basic custom class and shows how to use it. This chapter explores how you can employ `Object` at a slightly deeper level. (The custom objects you see in later chapters build on this one.)

One of the problems with the example in Chapter 5 is that it shows how to create a method as a property. This is a perfectly acceptable technique, but the method shows up as a property when you work with most JavaScript editors. It really isn't a true method. Fortunately, there are ways to create true methods in your code. JavaScript supports two kinds of methods, in fact:

✔ **Static:** A static method is one that you can execute at any time without instantiating the class. Many objects provide static methods that you can use to learn about the class or to perform tasks such as data conversion. A static method doesn't have access to any instance data — it must be self-contained.

✔ **Instance:** An instance method is one that works with the data found in a particular instance of the object. To use this method, you must instantiate the object and perform any tasks required to configure it. Most developers are used to working with instance methods in other languages, and instance methods are the ones that are most intuitive.

The following code shows how to create a more advanced custom class based on `Object` that includes both a true static method and a true instance method. The example contains some customer information, and you use the methods to find out about the object and to display it as a formatted string onscreen. (You can find complete code for this example in the `\Chapter 06\Objects` folder of the downloadable code as `CreateObject.HTML`.)

```
function customer()
{
    // Add properties.
    this.Name = "";
    this.Age = "";
}

// Create a true static method.
customer.help = function()
{
    return "Defines a customer.";
}

// Create a true method for the instance.
customer.prototype.toString = function()
{
    return "Name: " + this.Name +
        " Age: " + this.Age;
};

function CreateCustomer()
{
    // Display the help.
    document.getElementById("Help").innerHTML =
        customer.help();

    // Instantiate the object.
    var ThisCustomer = new customer();

    // Add data to the object.
    ThisCustomer.Name = "Adrian Watts";
    ThisCustomer.Age = 22;

    // Display the data onscreen.
    document.getElementById("Output").innerHTML =
        ThisCustomer.toString();
}
```

The `customer()` function creates the properties for the class. There are two public properties for this object: `Name` and `Age`.

Creating true methods involves writing external declarations like the ones shown. You type the name of the class, a period, and the name of the method to create a static method. The `customer.help()` method displays a simple string describing the object.

When you want to create an instance method, you must include the `prototype` keyword between the class and the method names. The `customer.prototype.toString` declaration creates the `customer.toString()` instance method. Even though `prototype` is part of the declaration, you don't include it when accessing the instance method. An instance method does have access to instance data using the `this` keyword.

The `CreateCustomer()` function shows how to use this new class. Notice that you can call `customer.help()` without creating an instance of the class. However, to call `toString()` you must create an instance of the customer class as `ThisCustomer`. The code supplies data to the instance and then uses `ThisCustomer.toString()` to display the data onscreen, as shown in Figure 6-1.

**Figure 6-1:**
This latest version of the customer class includes both static and instance methods.

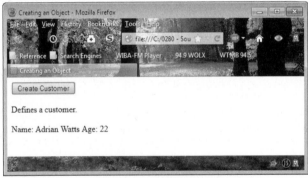

## Understanding Number

The `Number` object handles numeric data of all sorts for you. The section on changing number formats in Chapter 4 shows the methods that you have available for use with this object. Here's a list of the properties that this object provides:

- `constructor`: Displays a string showing the prototype used to define the object. In this case, you see "function Number() { [native code] }".

- `MAX_VALUE`: Displays the maximum value that the `Number` type can hold, which is 1.7976931348623157e+308.

- `MIN_VALUE`: Displays the minimum value that the `Number` type can hold, which is 5e-324.

- ✔ NEGATIVE_INFINITY: Represents negative infinity, the value that occurs after an underflow. The text output of this property is -Infinity.

- ✔ NaN: Represents a value that isn't a number. The text version of this property is NaN.

- ✔ POSITIVE_INFINITY: Represents positive infinity, the value that occurs after an overflow. The text version of this property is Infinity.

- ✔ prototype: Provides the means for adding both properties and methods to an object.

# Understanding String

You use the String object to work with all text in JavaScript. Because the String object is called upon to perform so many different tasks, it has quite an array of properties, methods, and HTML *wrapper methods* (code that is used to perform complex tasks through a single call). You've already seen some of the methods used in other areas of the book. The following sections describe the properties, methods, and wrapper methods supported by the String object.

### Properties that interact with JavaScript data

String properties tell you about the characteristics of the strings. They're akin to saying that the color of an apple is red, yellow, or green. Here's the list of String properties:

- ✔ constructor: Displays a string showing the prototype used to define the object. In this case, you see "function String() { [native code] }".

- ✔ length: Returns the length of the string in characters.

- ✔ prototype: Provides the means for adding both properties and methods to an object.

### Methods that interact with JavaScript data

The area where the String object really shines is in the methods it provides to manipulate data. Here's a list of standard methods you use within applications to interact with JavaScript data:

- ✔ charAt(): Obtains the character located at the specified index.

- ✔ charCodeAt(): Obtains the Unicode value of the character located at the specified index. The character value is the numeric equivalent of the character. For example, the letter A is 65, but the letter a is 97.

- ✔ concat(): Creates a single string from two or more separate strings.

- ✔ fromCharCode(): Converts a Unicode value to a character. For example, this method converts the number 65 to the letter A.

- ✔ `indexOf()`: Returns the first occurrence of a search string within a source string as a number value. For example, if you search for the letter *e* in *Rested*, this function returns a value of 1. You can also provide an optional starting position within the source string to begin the search.

- ✔ `lastIndexOf()`: Returns the last occurrence of a search string within a source string as a numeric value. For example, if you search for the letter *e* in *Rested*, this function returns a value of 4. You can also provide an optional starting position within the source string to begin the search.

- ✔ `match()`: Searches for matches between a regular expression (see the "Working with regular expressions" section, later in this chapter, for details) within a source string and returns the matches as numeric values.

- ✔ `replace()`: Replaces a match between a regular expression or search string with the specified replacement value in a source string. When working with a search string, only the first occurrence of the search is replaced. For example, if you replaced the letter *e* in *Rested* with the letter *u*, you'd see an output of *Rusted*.

- ✔ `search()`: Searches for matches between a regular expression within a search string and returns the first match as a numeric value.

- ✔ `slice()`: Removes the specified portion of a source string and returns that part as a new string. For example, if you start with the word *Rested* and provide a start position of 0 and an end position of 4, you receive Rest as output.

- ✔ `split()`: Divides a string into substrings based on a separator. For example, if you begin with "This is a string." and provide a separator of " " (a space), the output is an array of four substrings: This, is, a, and string.

- ✔ `substr()` and `substring()`: Returns the specified substring within a source string. You provide a starting point and optionally an ending point. For example, if you start with the word *Rested* and supply a starting point of 0 and an ending point of 4, either method returns Rest.

- ✔ `toLocaleLowerCase()`: Changes all of the characters in a string to lowercase versions while respecting lowercase rules for the current locale. The *locale* is the person's location or language. For example, some countries and languages use a comma for the decimal point, but other countries and languages use a period.

- ✔ `toLocaleUpperCase()`: Changes all of the characters in a string to uppercase versions while respecting the uppercase rules for the current locale.

- ✔ `toLowerCase()`: Changes all of the characters in a string to lowercase equivalents without regard to locale.

- ✔ `toUpperCase()`: Changes all of the characters in a string to uppercase equivalents without regard to locale.

✔ `valueOf()`: Returns the primitive value of a string's object. The primitive value is the series of characters, rather than the object itself.

From a low level perspective, primitive values are stored on the stack, and reference values (objects) are stored on the heap. Using primitive values can have certain performance benefits, but using reference values have specific flexibility benefits. You don't need to use primitives in most JavaScript applications, and a discussion of them is outside the scope of this book. You can discover more about primitives at `http://javascriptweblog.wordpress.com/2010/09/27/the-secret-life-of-javascript-primitives/` and `http://www.yaldex.com/javascript_tutorial_2/LiB0022.html`.

One of the issues that tend to cause problems for JavaScript developers who've moved from another language is that JavaScript relies on zero-based indexes. If you want to access the first letter in a string, for instance, you need to use an index value of `0`, not `1`, as you might initially think. Many of the `String` methods require that you provide indexes to tell the method what data to access in the string, so the use of the correct index value is essential.

### HTML wrapper methods

The `String` object is also called upon to create HTML output for display onscreen. With this in mind, you also have access to a number of HTML wrapper methods. These methods make it easier to create tags that you require to display information onscreen. Here's the list of HTML wrapper methods:

✔ `anchor()`: Creates an anchor tag. You must supply the name of the anchor tag as input. For example, if you have a string that contains Rested and provide an anchor name of `MyAnchor`, you receive `<a name="MyAnchor">Rested</a>` as output.

✔ `big()`: Displays the string using a larger font.

✔ `blink()`: Displays the string as blinking text. The `blink()` function doesn't work with Internet Explorer, Chrome, or Safari.

✔ `bold()`: Displays the string using a bold font.

✔ `fixed()`: Displays the string using a fixed pitch font (of the type used for source code on many sites).

✔ `fontcolor()`: Uses a specific color to display the text. You must supply the font color as a specific hexadecimal number, such as FF0000; or a color name, such as red; or with the `rgb()` function, such as `rgb(255, 0, 0)`, where the arguments are for red, blue, and green.

✔ `fontsize()`: Displays the string using the specified font size. You must supply a size between 1 and 7 as input. The precise font size will vary between browsers.

✔ `italics()`: Displays the string using an italics font.

✔ `link()`: Displays the string as a link. You must provide the URL for the link as input. For example, if you start with a string that contains `John's Blog` and provide `http://blog.johnmuellerbooks.com` as input, you receive `<a href="http://blog.johnmuellerbooks.com">John's Blog</a>` as output.

✔ `small()`: Displays the string using a smaller font.

✔ `strike()`: Displays the string using a strikethrough font.

✔ `sub()`: Displays the string as a subscript.

✔ `sup()`: Displays the string as a superscript.

## Understanding Date

Dates are an essential part of JavaScript programming because they make it possible to mark the passage of time. The `Date` data type includes both date and time values, so unlike many other programming languages, there's no `Time` data type in JavaScript. Because dates and times come in so many forms, the `Date` data type includes a wealth of methods. The properties are pretty much standard, as shown in the following list:

✔ `constructor`: Displays a string showing the prototype used to define the object. In this case, you see "function Date() { [native code] }".

✔ `prototype`: Provides the means for adding both properties and methods to an object.

The `Date` data type methods focus on presentation for the most part. The way in which your application presents the date or time is important because different groups expect to see these values a certain way. The following list provides an overview of the `Date` methods:

✔ `getDate()`: Obtains the day of the month as a numeric value from 1 through 31. See the "Getting today's date right" section, later in this chapter, for an example of how this output appears.

✔ `getDay()`: Obtains the day of the week as a numeric value from 0 through 6.

JavaScript returns many date and time elements as zero-based values. Exercise care when creating an application to account for the difference between the way JavaScript views the value and the way humans view it. For example, humans view day of the week values as being from 1 through 7, not 0 through 6 as JavaScript views them.

✔ `getFullYear()`: Obtains the year as a four-digit value. See the "Getting today's date right" section, later in this chapter, for an example of how this output appears.

JavaScript used to include a getYear() method. This method is deprecated, which means that current versions of JavaScript still likely support getYear(), but that support for this method won't appear in future versions of JavaScript. Always use the getFullYear() method when creating new applications to ensure your application will continue to work with newer browsers.

✔ getHours(): Obtains the hours as a numeric value from 0 through 23. See the "Getting today's date right" section, later in this chapter, for an example of how this output appears.

✔ getMilliseconds(): Obtains a three-digit millisecond value from 0 through 999. See the "Getting today's date right" section, later in this chapter, for an example of how this output appears.

✔ getMinutes(): Obtains the minutes as a numeric value from 0 through 59. See the "Getting today's date right" section, later in this chapter, for an example of how this output appears.

✔ getMonth(): Obtains the month as a numeric value from 0 through 11. See the "Getting today's date right" section, later in this chapter, for an example of how this output appears.

✔ getSeconds(): Obtains the seconds as a numeric value from 0 through 59. See the "Getting today's date right" section, later in this chapter, for an example of how this output appears.

✔ getTime(): Specifies the number of milliseconds that have passed since January 1, 1970 Universal Time Coordinated (UTC). There are 86,400,000 milliseconds in a day (24 hours/day × 60 minutes/hour × 60 seconds/hour × 1000 milliseconds/second).

Some Date methods specify UTC output, but others, such as get-Time(), rely on UTC without specifying it as part of their name. You may also know UTC as Greenwich Mean Time (GMT). Both terms specify a single starting point for time values used throughout the world. Having a single, coordinated time source is incredibly important to synchronize business and other activities. You can always obtain the current UTC/GMT time value at http://www.worldtimeserver.com/current_time_in_UTC.aspx. If you want to know all the technical specifics about UTC (including some minor differences with GMT), read the article entitled "Coordinated Universal Time (UTC) Explained" at http://www.timeanddate.com/time/aboututc.html.

✔ getTimezoneOffset(): Obtains the time difference between UTC time and local time in minutes.

✔ getUTCDate(): Obtains the UTC day of the month as a numeric value from 1 through 31.

✔ getUTCDay(): Obtains the UTC day of the week as a numeric value from 0 through 6.

✔ getUTCFullYear(): Obtains the UTC year as a four-digit value.

- ✔ getUTCHours(): Obtains the UTC hours as a numeric value from 0 through 23.

- ✔ getUTCMilliseconds(): Obtains a three-digit UTC millisecond value from 0 through 999.

- ✔ getUTCMinutes(): Obtains the UTC minutes as a numeric value from 0 through 59.

- ✔ getUTCMonth(): Obtains the UTC month as a numeric value from 0 through 11.

- ✔ getUTCSeconds(): Obtains the UTC seconds as a numeric value from 0 through 59.

- ✔ parse(): Changes the date string that you pass to the method into a numeric value that represents the number of milliseconds that have passed since midnight, January 1, 1970. The act of parsing a string always converts it to another data type — normally a type that the parsing class can easily understand. The parse() method is normally used directly with the Date class as a static method. See the "Understanding Object" section of the chapter for details on static and instance methods. This is a static method, which means you call it directly from the Date class, rather than creating an instance of the Date class to use it.

- ✔ setDate(): Sets the day of the month as a numeric value from 1 through 31.

- ✔ setFullYear(): Sets the year as a four-digit value.

JavaScript used to include a setYear() method. This method is deprecated, which means that current versions of JavaScript still likely support setYear(), but support for this method won't appear in future versions of JavaScript. Always use the setFullYear() method when creating new applications to ensure your application will continue to work with newer browsers.

- ✔ setHours(): Sets the hours as a numeric value from 0 through 23.

- ✔ setMilliseconds(): Sets a three-digit millisecond value from 0 through 999.

- ✔ setMinutes(): Sets the minutes as a numeric value from 0 through 59.

- ✔ setMonth(): Sets the month as a numeric value from 0 through 11.

- ✔ setSeconds(): Sets the seconds as a numeric value from 0 through 59.

- ✔ setTime(): Modifies the date and time by adding or subtracting a specific number of milliseconds from a value that starts at January 1, 1970.

- ✔ setUTCDate(): Sets the UTC day of the month as a numeric value from 1 through 31.

- ✔ setUTCFullYear(): Sets the UTC year as a four-digit value.

- ✔ setUTCHours(): Sets the UTC hours as a numeric value from 0 through 23.

- ✔ `setUTCMilliseconds()`: Sets a three-digit UTC millisecond value from 0 through 999.

- ✔ `setUTCMinutes()`: Sets the UTC minutes as a numeric value from 0 through 59.

- ✔ `setUTCMonth()`: Sets the UTC month as a numeric value from 0 through 11.

- ✔ `setUTCSeconds()`: Sets the UTC seconds as a numeric value from 0 through 59.

- ✔ `toDateString()`: Outputs the date portion of a `Date` object as a formatted string. See the "Getting today's date right" section, later in this chapter, for an example of how this output appears.

- ✔ `toISOString()`: Outputs the date and time of a `Date` object in ISO format. Typical output is 2012-11-26T18:26:32.976Z where the year, month, and day appear first, followed by the UTC hours, minutes, second, and milliseconds.

- ✔ `toJSON()`: Outputs the date and time of a `Date` object in JavaScript `Object` Notation (JSON) format. Typical output is 2012-11-26T18:26:32.976Z, where the year, month, and day appear first, followed by the UTC hours, minutes, second, and milliseconds.

- ✔ `toLocaleDateString()`: Outputs the date portion of a `Date` object as a formatted string that takes the user's locale into account. See the "Getting today's date right" section, later in this chapter, for an example of how this output appears.

- ✔ `toLocaleTimeString()`: Outputs the time portion of a `Date` object as a formatted string that takes the user's locale into account. See the "Getting today's date right" section, later in this chapter, for an example of how this output appears.

- ✔ `toLocaleString()`: Outputs both the date and time portions of a `Date` object as a formatted string that takes the user's locale into account. See the "Getting today's date right" section, later in this chapter, for an example of how this output appears.

- ✔ `toString()`: Outputs both the date and time portions of a `Date` object as a formatted string.

- ✔ `toTimeString()`: Outputs the time portion of a `Date` object as a formatted string. See the "Getting today's date right" section, later in this chapter, for an example of how this output appears.

- ✔ `toUTCString()`: Outputs both the date and time portions of a `Date` object as a formatted string that reflects UTC time, rather than local time.

JavaScript used to include a `toGMTString()` method. This method is deprecated, which means that current versions of JavaScript still likely support `toGMTString()`, but that support for this method won't appear in future versions of JavaScript. Always use the `toUTCString()`

method when creating new applications to ensure your application will
continue to work with newer browsers.

✔ UTC(): Outputs the number of milliseconds that have passed since
January 1, 1970 Universal Time Coordinated (UTC). This is a static
method, which means you call it directly from the Date class, rather
than creating an instance of the Date class to use it.

✔ valueOf(): Outputs the number of milliseconds that have passed since
January 1, 1970. The result is a native type rather than an object.

It isn't always possible to create date or time output that precisely matches
your needs, so Date provides methods such as getDay() and getHours()
that provide values you can string together to create custom output. Because
these values are Number types, you also have access to all of the Number
properties and methods when creating output. In addition, you can use
these values to perform calculations of various sorts in your application.
Consequently, these methods make it possible to create applications that
can view the passage of time in all sorts of ways.

# Understanding RegExp

Regular expressions rely on the RegExp object. The focus of this object is
a combination of *patterns,* which define the data you want to find, and *modifiers,* which determine how you want to find the data. You use regular expressions in a number of ways, and this book includes a number of examples of
them. (See the simple example in the "Working with regular expressions"
section, later in this chapter, as a starting point.) A regular expression makes
it possible to perform precise wildcard searches on data, which makes them
a little complex but also provides the user with incredible flexibility. The following sections break the regular expression into two parts: the search term
features and the object elements.

## Using the RegExp search term features

A search expression can consist of a number of elements. The most common
element is a simple string. If you want to search for Hello in the text, you
simply type **Hello**, and the application performs the search. You can include
any string, or part of a string, as part of a search.

Sometimes you need to find a range of values. You don't know the precise
value, but you do know that the value appears within a specific list of characters or terms. When you encounter this situation, you can use brackets to
define the range of values you're interested in seeing. You can combine these
bracketed values with any other regular expression values. When working
with brackets, you specify the value of a single character by using the bracketed range. The following list describes the kinds of values that you can place
within brackets:

✔ [abc]: Locates any character that appears within the brackets.

✔ [^abc]: Locates any character that doesn't appear within the brackets.

✔ [0-9]: Locates any digit between 0 and 9.

✔ [A-Z]: Locates any uppercase character in the range *A* through *Z*.

✔ [a-z]: Locates any lowercase character in the range *a* through *z*.

✔ [A-z]: Locates any character in the range from uppercase *A* through lowercase *z*.

✔ (red|blue|green): Finds any of the specific words or terms specified in the list. Notice that this particular search expression appears in parenthesis and the terms are separated by the pipe character (|).

When working with search expressions, there are no absolutes. For example, you can define a search expression that uses only part of a range, such as [A-C] to find the letters *A* through *C*. A character set need not be continuous. For example, you can specify the set [aeiou] to locate vowels. It pays to experiment with regular expressions to determine what's possible and what won't work with the RegExp object. Developers have come up with interesting solutions to problems in the past through simple experimentation.

In some cases, you need to specify special characters as part of the search, but your keyboard lacks the capability to type those characters. For example, you may want to find a specific term but only when it appears at the end of a line, so you need to include an end-of-line character as part of the search expression. Meta characters provide a means of telling RegExp that you want to search for these special characters. The following list contains the standard meta characters that RegExp understands. (Notice that you use a backslash with the vast majority of these characters, rather than the usual forward slash.)

✔ .: Represents any single character except an end-of-line character.

✔ \w: Represents an alphabetic character normally associated with words.

✔ \W: Represents a character that isn't associated with words.

✔ \d: Represents a digit — the numbers 0 through 9.

✔ \D: Represents a non-digit character.

✔ \s: Represents a whitespace character, including the tab, space, form feed, newline, and carriage return characters.

✔ \S: Represents a non-whitespace character.

✔ \b: Search at the beginning or end of a word.

✔ \B: Search for a character that doesn't appear at the beginning or end of a word.

✔ \0: Represents the null (NUL) character often used to terminate strings.

✔ \n: Represents the newline character.

✔ \f: Represents the form feed character.

✔ \r: Represents the carriage return character.

✔ \t: Represents the tab character.

✔ \v: Represents the vertical tab character.

✔ \xxx: Find the character specified by the octal number xxx. For example, the letter A is \101.

✔ \xdd: Find the character specified by the hexadecimal number xx. For example, the letter A is \x41.

✔ \uxxxx: Find the Unicode character specified by the hexadecimal number xxxx. For example, the letter A is \u0041.

Defining how many of something you want to find is also important. You can create search expressions that tell RegExp to find any number of a specific character in the source string. These expressions are called *quantifiers* because they specify how many of something to find. A quantifier expresses how it works with the value *n*, where *n* is any character. You replace *n* with the search expression you want to find. The following list describes the RegExp quantifiers:

✔ *n*+: Looks for any string that contains at least one *n*.

✔ *n**: Looks for any string that contains zero or more occurrences of *n*.

✔ *n*?: Looks for any string that contains zero or one occurrence of *n*.

✔ *n*{*X*}: Looks for a string that contains a sequence of X *n*'s. For example, if you want to search for five *A*'s in a string, you type A{5}.

✔ *n*{*X, Y*}: Looks for a string that contains a sequence of *n*'s in the range of *X* to *Y*. For example, if you want to search for a range of four through six *A*'s in a string, you type A{4,6}.

✔ *n*{*X,* }: Looks for a string that contains at least *X* number of *n*'s. For example, if you want to find a sequence of at least five *A*'s in a string, you type A{5,}.

✔ *n*$: Searches for *n* at the end of the string.

✔ ^*n*: Searches for *n* at the beginning of the string.

✔ ?=*n*: Finds a string that's followed by a specific string *n*.

✔ ?!*n*: Finds a string that isn't followed by a specific string *n*.

## Using the RegExp search modifiers

Search modifiers define how RegExp performs a search. For example, you can tell RegExp that you want to search for all instances of a search expression, rather than just one instance. The following list describes the search modifiers:

- ✔ i: Specifies that you want to perform a case-insensitive search where Abc is treated the same as aBc.

- ✔ g: Performs a global search where the search returns all possible matches, rather than returning just the first match.

- ✔ m: Searches on all of the lines in a search string that contains end-of-line characters rather than searching just the first line.

## Using the RegExp properties and methods

As with any other JavaScript object, the RegExp object provides access to certain properties. The following list describes the properties you get with RegExp:

- ✔ global: Returns true when the object has the g modifier set.

- ✔ ignoreCase: Returns true when the object has the i modifier set.

- ✔ lastIndex: Specifies the index at which to start the next search. Remember that the index is zero-based, so if you want to start searching at the second character, you provide a value of 1.

- ✔ multiline: Returns true when the object has the m modifier set.

- ✔ source: Contains the search expression used by RegExp.

RegExp also defines a number of useful methods. These methods help you interact with the regular expression itself, not the data that the regular expression is used to search. The following list describes the RegExp methods:

- ✔ exec(): Performs a test of the search expression against the search string and returns the result.

- ✔ test(): Performs a test of the search expression against the search string and returns true when the search expression appears within the search string.

JavaScript used to include a compile() method. This method is deprecated, which means that current versions of JavaScript still likely support compile(), but support for this method won't appear in future versions of JavaScript. There's no need for the compile() method because compilation occurs automatically when you create the RegExp object.

# *Introducing the String Object*

Strings are what most humans equate to computer data because people see output onscreen as strings. Fortunately, JavaScript provides a wealth of ways in which to interact with strings. The following sections provide two useful techniques for looking for information in strings.

## *Manipulating and searching strings*

Many string searches are simple. A user looks for a particular word or other data in a string, and your application finds it. The following example shows one technique for performing a simple search. (You can find complete code for this example in the `\Chapter 06\Strings` folder of the downloadable code as `SearchString.HTML`.)

```
<script language="JavaScript">
   // Define a global search string.
   var SearchString = "This is the search string!"

   function FindString()
   {
      // Obtain the value the user wants to find.
      var FindValue =
         document.getElementById("SearchString").value;

      // Perform the search.
      var Result = SearchString.indexOf(FindValue);

      // Display an appropriate result.
      // Check for a blank input first.
      if (Result == 0)
      {
         document.getElementById("Result").innerHTML =
            "You must provide an input value!";
      }

      // Check for a result that doesn't exist next.
      else if (Result == -1)
      {
         document.getElementById("Result").innerHTML =
            "The search string doesn't exist.";
      }

      // Display the location information.
      else
      {
```

```
                document.getElementById("Result").innerHTML =
                    'The search string "' + FindValue +
                    '" appears at character ' + Result;
        }
    }
</script>
```

In this example, the code begins by creating a global variable that contains a search string the user can interact with. You could change this string to anything you want for experimentation purposes.

The `FindString()` function is connected to the Find It button shown in Figure 6-2. The first task is to obtain the value that the user wants to find and place it in `FindValue`. The example then uses the `indexOf()` function on `SearchString` to locate `FindValue` and place the position in `Result`.

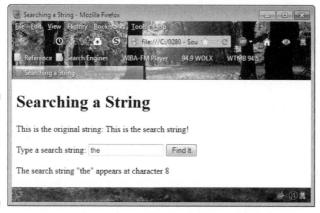

**Figure 6-2:**
Searching
strings
helps users
find infor-
mation.

The second task is to interpret the results. The example looks for one of three values in `Result`. When `Result` is 0, the user hasn't provided any input, and the example asks the user to provide some. When `Result` is -1, the user has supplied a search string that doesn't appear in the original string, and the example lets the user know that the search string wasn't found. When `Result` is a positive value, the application displays the position of the search string in the original string onscreen as shown in Figure 6-2.

## *Working with regular expressions*

Not all searches are simple. Sometimes a user needs to perform a complex search based in a regular expression — one in which there are wildcard search terms. The following example shows a simple way to implement such a search. (You can find complete code for this example in the `\Chapter 06\ Strings` folder of the downloadable code as `RegularExpressions.HTML`.)

```
<script language="JavaScript">
   // Define a global search string.
   var SearchString =
     "Use a regular expression to search a string!"

   function FindString()
   {
      // Obtain the value the user wants to find.
      var FindValue =
         document.getElementById("SearchString").value;

      // Obtain the modifiers the user wants to use.
      var Modifiers =
         document.getElementById("Modifiers").value;

      // Create a search pattern.
      var Pattern = new RegExp(FindValue, Modifiers);

      // Perform the search.
      document.getElementById("Result").innerHTML =
         SearchString.match(Pattern);
   }
</script>
```

The example begins by defining a global search string. It then defines the
FindString() function that's used to perform the actual search. Compare
this version of FindString() with the FindString() function in the
preceding section and you see they have some similarities, but that this version's much shorter (even though it's far more flexible).

The FindString() function obtains the search string and places it in
FindValue. It then obtains any search modifiers and places them in
Modifiers. The example creates a new RegExp object, Pattern, that's a
combination of the search string and search modifiers.

At this point, the code uses the match() function on SearchString to produce a result. The output is actually an array of values that you could use to
locate each incidence of the search term in the search string. The array elements appear onscreen separated by commas, as shown in Figure 6-3. Notice
that this search uses a bracketed regular expression for input. In addition,
the search modifiers appear in the second field after the search expression.
This example is fully capable of using any combination of regular expression
elements, so try various combinations to see how they work for you.

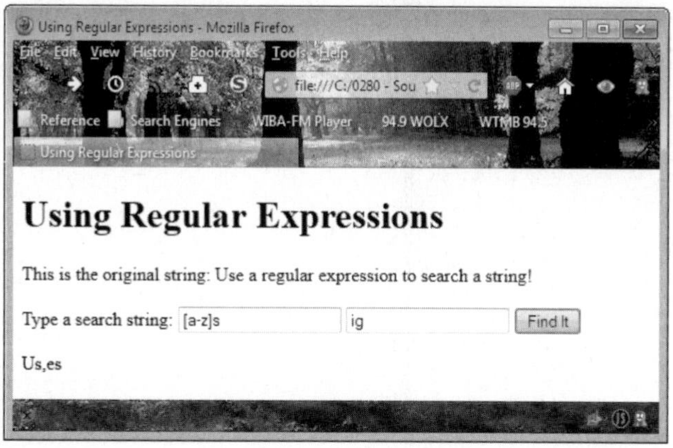

**Figure 6-3:**
Use regular
expressions
to perform
power
searches.

# Working with the Date Object

Dates are used in all sorts of ways, but the most common techniques you must master in JavaScript applications are formatting and time span calculation. People want dates and times formatted in a way they understand. In addition, dates and times are most useful when used to mark the passage of time, also known as a *time span*. The following sections show one example of each technique.

## Getting today's date right

JavaScript provides standardized methods of displaying dates. You can either use a standard approach for everyone or display time based on a person's locale. When none of the standard display techniques work, you can build your own custom display. The following example shows some of the most common techniques used to display a date, time, or both. (You can find complete code for this example in the \Chapter 06\Dates folder of the downloadable code as GetDate.HTML.)

```
<script language="JavaScript">
    var Today = new Date();
    document.write("<p>Full Date/Time: " +
        Today.toLocaleString() + "<br />");
    document.write("Full Date: " +
        Today.toLocaleDateString() + "<br />");
    document.write("Date Only: " +
        Today.toDateString() + "<br />");
    document.write("Full Time: " +
```

```
            Today.toLocaleTimeString() + "<br />");
    document.write("Time Only: " +
        Today.toTimeString() + "</p>");
    document.write("<p>Custom Date (m/d/y): " +
        (Today.getMonth() + 1) + "/" +
        Today.getDate() + "/" +
        Today.getFullYear() + "<br />");
    document.write("Custom Time (h:m:s:ms): " +
        Today.getHours() + ":" +
        Today.getMinutes() + ":" +
        Today.getSeconds() + "." +
        Today.getMilliseconds() + "</p>");
</script>
```

The example begins by creating a Date object, Today. Whenever you call the Date() constructor without any input value, you get the current date and time. Some languages have a special method or property you call to obtain the current date and time. JavaScript makes things simple by using the technique shown.

In many cases, all you need to do is call a particular method, such as toLocaleString(), to obtain the desired result. However, sometimes you need to build a custom presentation. The two custom examples — Custom Date (m/d/y) and Custom Time (h:m:s:ms) — show how to create a custom date or custom time output using functions such as getMonth(). Notice that when working with getMonth(), you must add 1 to the value because getMonth() outputs its information in the range 0 through 11. This is an example of a situation where you must adjust the JavaScript output to meet a user's needs. Figure 6-4 shows typical output for this example.

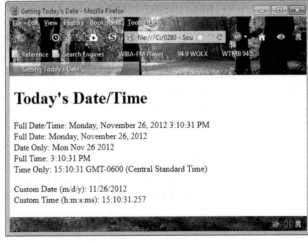

**Figure 6-4:** Date and time output format is important for user understanding.

**Today's Date/Time**

Full Date/Time: Monday, November 26, 2012 3:10:31 PM
Full Date: Monday, November 26, 2012
Date Only: Mon Nov 26 2012
Full Time: 3:10:31 PM
Time Only: 15:10:31 GMT-0600 (Central Standard Time)

Custom Date (m/d/y): 11/26/2012
Custom Time (h:m:s:ms): 15:10:31.257

# Calculating differences in dates

Determining the time span between events is an important part of many applications today. Imagine trying to quantify productivity without knowing a time span in which work is completed. Fortunately, JavaScript makes determining a time span relatively easy. All you need to do is subtract one date or time from another date or time to determine the interval as shown in the following example. (You can find complete code for this example in the \Chapter 06\Dates folder of the downloadable code as DateDifference. HTML.)

```
<body>
    <h1>Difference Between Dates</h1>
    <script language="JavaScript">
        var ThisDate = new Date("2/1/2013");
        var ThatDate = new Date("3/1/2013");
        document.write(
            "Difference between ThisDate and ThatDate: " +
            ((ThatDate - ThisDate) / 86400000) + " Days");
    </script>

    <h1>Difference Between Times</h1>
    <script language="JavaScript">
        var ThisTime = new Date(2013, 2, 1, 2, 30);
        var ThatTime = new Date(2013, 2, 1, 2, 51);
        document.write(
            "Difference between ThisTime and ThatTime: " +
            ((ThatTime - ThisTime) / 60000) + " Minutes");
    </script>
</body>
```

The example creates two date values and two time values. Each of the values actually contains both date and time. The application uses the Date object one way or the other, but that's the application's view of the object, rather than a determination the object has made. In fact, you can't create a time value without also defining a date as part of it.

The example shows two techniques for creating a Date object. You can supply a string or individual values as shown. You can also create a Date object by providing the number of milliseconds since midnight, January 1, 1970.

To determine the time span, you simply subtract one value from the other. The only problem is that the output is in milliseconds and most people don't understand milliseconds. The example shows how to convert a time span to days or minutes so that you see the easily understood output in Figure 6-5.

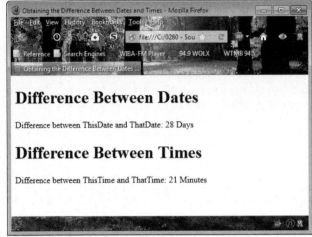

**Figure 6-5:**
Performing
date and
time calcu-
lations is an
important
part of many
applications.

# Part III

# Meeting JavaScript's Control Structures

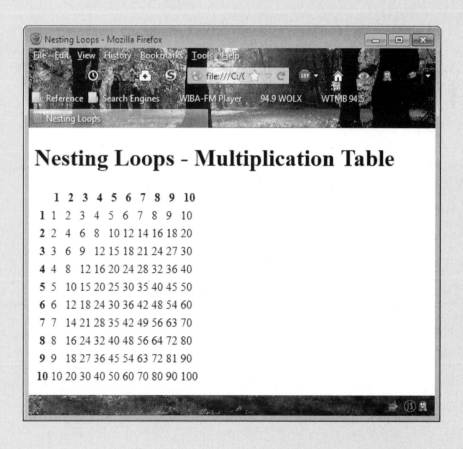

Create custom changes to an existing class such as String by using
the techniques described at http://www.dummies.com/extras/
html5programmingwithjavascript.

# In this part . . .

- ✔ Discover how to use functions to create neater applications that have fewer errors and are easier to maintain.

- ✔ Create applications that can make decisions of various sorts, which improves overall application flexibility.

- ✔ See how to repeat a set of steps as needed to complete a task a specific number of times.

- ✔ Understand how errors creep into applications, how to discover them, and what to do to fix them.

# Chapter 7

# Using Functions

*I*n previous chapters, you see a multitude of both built-in and custom functions, but you don't really work through all of the intricacies of functions. In addition, JavaScript offers far more in the way of functions than the few you see in earlier chapters. This chapter focuses on the JavaScript function. It begins by introducing you to more built-in functions, especially those provided by the `Math` object. After that, you begin creating your own custom functions.

This chapter introduces you to some new concepts when it comes to functions. For example, you discover the best time to separate code into a new function rather than keeping it part of an existing function. You also find some techniques for passing both required and optional parameters (arguments) to functions and returning data to the caller.

Perhaps the most controversial topic in the chapter is using private data with JavaScript. Some developers are of the opinion that JavaScript doesn't support private data, but it's possible to create private data so that you can create objects that have true encapsulation. However, the process isn't as straightforward as simply declaring variables private, which is why you really do need to read at least the last part of this chapter — even if you're already comfortable using JavaScript functions.

## Using the Built-In Functions

In previous chapters, you access a number of built-in functions for JavaScript, including the `alert()` and `confirm()` functions. Along with these two functions is a third function, `prompt()`, which lets you ask the user for written input. As with the `confirm()` function, you provide a text prompt to ask the user to provide a value. On return, you set the output of the function equal to the `prompt()` function and use the data in your application. The section on using the `default` option in Chapter 8 describes how to use the `prompt()` function.

Chapter 5 introduces you to working with objects of various sorts, including the nodes that are used to create a JavaScript document. The section on using JavaScript objects in Chapter 5 demonstrates techniques you use to add new elements to a document. In Chapter 11, you discover how the functions associated with the JavaScript document work in more detail.

Chapter 6 introduces you to a wealth of built-in functions in the form of object methods. All of these methods help you perform specific tasks with certain types of data. Using these methods makes it easier for you to create robust applications. Of all the methods provided by objects, these methods are the most common and likely the most important for many situations:

- ✔ `length()`: Returns the number of something. For example, when working with a string, `length()` returns the number of characters in the string. Likewise, when working with an array, `length()` returns the number of elements in the array. This method also appears as a property in some cases.

- ✔ `toLocaleString()`: Outputs the value of an object as a locale-specific string. For example, when the locale uses a comma for the decimal point, the viewer will see a comma, rather than a period, even if you use a period in your code. It's essential that you provide this support for people from other countries that visit your site.

Simply displaying data with locale in mind doesn't perform any data conversion. For example, the strings you create won't suddenly appear in French if you natively speak English. There's nothing magic about locale-specific methods. All that these methods do is change the presentation of the data as you provide it.

- ✔ `toString()`: Outputs the value of the object as a string. This method is often used for display purposes.

- ✔ `valueOf()`: Returns a native version of the object value. You need this method in situations where an object could cause problems. For example, when saving data to disk, you want the value, not the object, stored.

JavaScript also includes the concept of global functions. These functions are available without regard to any object from any place you use JavaScript on a page. The following list provides an overview of the most common global functions:

✔ decodeURI(): Decodes a Uniform Resource Identifier (URI).

Encoding replaces whitespace characters, such as a space, with whitespace equivalent values, such as %20. In addition, Unicode characters that would normally cause parsing problems, such as those with diacritical marks, are replaced with their Unicode equivalents. You can see a list of common URL encoded characters at http://www.degraeve.com/reference/urlencoding.php.

✔ decodeURIComponent(): Decodes a URI component, rather than the entire URI.

URIs normally have between three or five standard components:

- *Protocol:* The set of transport rules used to access the resource, such as HTTP, HTTPS, FTP, SMTP, or NNTP.

- *Host:* The name of the server used to provide access to the resource, such as blog.johnmuellerbooks.com.

- *Port number:* The port used to access the resource. In general, you don't provide this component because most sites use standard ports, which are assumed by the browser. For example, HTTP relies on port 80 for communication. When the server uses port 80, you don't need to include the port number as part of the URI.

- *Path:* The fully defined location of the resource on the server. In some cases, you don't provide a path, which means that the server provides the resource found on the default path.

- *Query string:* Name and value pairs that define additional information required to obtain the resource you want on the server.

✔ encodeURI(): Encodes a URI.

✔ encodeURIComponent(): Encodes a URI component rather than the entire URI.

✔ escape(): Encodes a string using the same techniques used for a URI. For example, escape("This string is encoded!") outputs This%20string%20is%20encoded%21.

✔ eval(): Accepts a string that contains a script and then executes the string content as a script. Many developers use this function to create self-modifying applications that provide good flexibility.

Using the eval() function in your JavaScript application is an incredibly bad idea for the following reasons:

- Using evaluated code opens your application to potential security problems through injection attacks.

- Debugging evaluated code is incredibly hard because none of the normal debugging tools will work.

- Evaluated code runs more slowly because the browser can't compile and then cache it.

✔ isFinite(): Returns `true` when a value is a finite, legal number.

✔ isNaN(): Returns `true` when a value is an illegal number.

✔ Number(): Changes an object's value to a native number.

✔ parseFloat(): Parses a string and returns a floating point number.

✔ parseInt(): Parses a string and returns an integer.

✔ String(): Converts an object's value to a string. This function provides the same output as the `toString()` method provided by most objects.

✔ unescape(): Decodes an encoded string by using the same techniques used for a URI.

# Working with the Math Object

The `Math` object is a special sort of object in JavaScript — you use it to access math-related functionality, rather than create new objects. This difference with objects such as `Number` or `String` is the reason that `Math` is covered in this chapter rather than Chapter 6, where you see the other objects discussed.

As with any JavaScript object, you can create an instance of a `Math` object. However, you often use `Math` without creating an instance of it. For example, you may simply need to add the value of pi to a calculation, in which case you can simply call on the appropriate property. The following list describes the `Math` object properties, all of which are available as static values (without creating an instance):

✔ E: Provides the value of Euler's number, which is approximately 2.718. You can read more about Euler's number at `http://www.mathsisfun.com/numbers/e-eulers-number.html`. (Many people know that this is the number e, which is the base of natural logarithms.)

✔ LN2: Provides the value of the natural logarithm of 2, which is approximately 0.693.

✔ LN10: Provides the value of the natural logarithm of 10, which is approximately 2.302.

✔ LOG2E: Provides the value of the base-2 logarithm of the number e, which is approximately 1.442.

✔ LOG10E: Provides the value of the base-10 logarithm of the number 3, which is approximately 0.434.

✔ PI: Provides the value of pi (also shown as π), which is approximately 3.14.

✔ SQRT1_2: Provides the value of the square root of ½, which is approximately 0.707.

✔ SQRT2: Provides the value of the square root of 2, which is approximately 1.414.

The Math object also provides access to a number of methods. As with the properties, all of these methods are static, which means you can access them without creating a Math instance. The following list describes the Math object methods:

✔ abs(x): Calculates the absolute value of x.

✔ acos(x): Calculates the arccosine of x in radians. You can read more about trigonometric values at http://math2.org/math/algebra/functions/trig/index.htm.

✔ asin(x): Calculates the arcsine of x in radians.

✔ atan(x): Calculates the arctangent of x as a numeric value between $-\pi/2$ and $\pi/2$ radians.

✔ atan2(y, x): Calculates the arctangent of the quotient of y divided by x.

✔ ceil(x): Rounds the value of x up to the nearest integer value.

✔ cos(x): Calculates the cosine of x, where the value of x is in radians.

✔ exp(x): Calculates the value of $e^x$ (e to the power of x).

✔ floor(x): Rounds the value of x down to the nearest integer value.

✔ log(x): Calculates the natural logarithm (base e) of x.

✔ max(x, y, z, ..., n): Determines the number with the highest value and returns that value.

✔ min(x, y, z, ..., n): Determines the number with the lowest value and returns that value.

✔ pow(x, y): Calculates the value of x to the power of y.

✔ random(): Provides a random number between 0 and 1.

✔ round(x): Rounds the value of x to the nearest integer value (either up or down as needed).

✔ sin(x): Calculates the sine of x, where the value of x is in radians.

✔ sqrt(x): Calculates the square root of x.

✔ tan(x): Calculates the tangent of an angle.

# Building Custom Functions

Just about any time you work with JavaScript, you create functions. In fact, if you've typed the code from previous chapters in the book, you've already created a number of functions. However, the following section details why and how you create functions in greater depth. The essential issue to remember is that JavaScript relies heavily on well-crafted functions to perform any significant level of work. (You can find complete code for the examples in the following sections in the \Chapter 07\Functions folder of the download-able code as UsingFunctions.HTML.)

When working through these functions, you may find that you encounter some browser idiosyncrasies. For example, Internet Explorer 10 displays a notice at the bottom of the window asking whether you want to execute the code. You see the message for only a few seconds before it disappears, so you need to quickly tell Internet Explorer 10 that it's acceptable to run the script. Otherwise, the example will fail to work. Always check for browser messages after you load the example to determine whether you need to take additional action to run the example in that particular browser.

## Reducing work using functions

Using functions helps reduce the work you must perform when creating an application. Functions help you reduce your workload in the following ways:

- **Code reuse:** By encapsulating a specific task, you can reuse it as often as needed.

- **Ease of understanding:** Using functions creates a number of black boxes that reduce the complexity of the programming task.

- **Error trapping:** It's usually easier to trap erroneous output from an entire function than it is to check each step within that function for potential problems.

- **Debugging:** When you know that a problem in your application lies in a certain location, it's helpful to get to that point in the application as quickly as possible by bypassing the code you know works.

- **Ease of coding changes:** Cutting and pasting the same code in multiple locations makes it nearly impossible to make changes consistently or completely.

There are other reasons to use functions, but the preceding are the reasons that most developers cite for using them. When you consider the issues that functions resolve, it becomes obvious that they're incredibly useful.

Unfortunately, some developers go overboard and use too many functions, making it harder to understand the code or follow what the developer intends to do. Creating useful functions that actually reduce your workload means thinking through the application process carefully.

The following guidelines help you determine when code should go into a separate function:

✔ Create functions that perform a complete task rather than only part of a task.

✔ Consider creating a new function when the code you've written takes up more than a single page — a function is easier to understand when you can see all of the code on a single screen.

✔ Define new functions with code reusability in mind. Functions should provide enough flexibility to serve a number of callers.

✔ Think of functions as mini-apps — the function should perform one task really well rather than trying to perform multiple tasks poorly.

Never create a new function that replicates the behavior of an existing function or a built-in function. It pays to verify that the function is actually needed before you spend time writing it. Reinventing the wheel will almost certainly cost you time, and you may not even get a superior function for your efforts.

## *Passing parameters to functions*

You pass *parameters* (or arguments) to functions to modify their output in some way. Behavior modification can take many forms, but the idea is to add flexibility to the function in a way that doesn't create a complex environment. The function still performs a single task, but now it can perform that single task in a number of ways or with various data. The following example shows how a function might work with a parameter:

```
function TestParams(param)
{
    // Output the param onscreen.
    document.getElementById("Result").innerHTML =
        "The param is: " + param;
}
```

In this case, the example simply outputs the value of `param`. However, the function could have easily changed `param` in some specific, but consistent, manner. For example, it might have reversed the characters in `param` or performed some other task that isn't already served by a built-in function.

You can call functions that require parameters from other functions or from HTML controls like the one shown here:

```
<input type="button"
       value="Test Param"
       onclick="TestParams('Hello There!')" />
```

In this case, the function receives `Hello There!` as input and outputs the same string to the screen. Notice the use of both double and single quotes in the example. You must enclose strings that you want to pass to the function in either double or single quotes.

## Creating functions with a return value

Many of the built-in functions provide some sort of return value, and you can create functions that provide a return value, too. Use a return value when the function performs a simple task that could be part of a more complex task. For example, when working with a string, you can use the `toUpperCase()` function to change the case of a string that might be manipulated in other ways. Changing the case of a string is a simple, well-defined task, but it could be part of a larger task, and so it provides a return value for that reason. Here's an example of a function with a return value:

```
function TestReturn()
{
    return document.title;
}
```

In this case, the function returns the document's title. The caller may want to do more with the text, so it's returned rather than output directly in some way. In this case, the caller adds some additional text to the output and displays it onscreen, as shown here:

```
function DisplayReturn()
{
    // Output the param onscreen.
    document.getElementById("Result").innerHTML =
        "The return value is: " + TestReturn();
}
```

Using return values lets you nest function calls as deeply as needed to perform complex tasks. When you create an application, break complex tasks down into smaller tasks. If you find that the smaller tasks are still too complicated, break these subtasks down into smaller tasks. It's important to create functions that perform a single task (rather than a part of a task or multiple tasks) but also perform that single task well.

# Creating functions with optional and required arguments

All arguments for a JavaScript function are optional. In fact, the caller can send as many arguments as desired. Of course, if you're expecting only one argument, then you'll process only one argument in most cases. Unfortunately, you might be expecting at least one argument and may not receive any at all. In short, you need some method of dealing with arguments in JavaScript that helps you account for what the caller may or may not send. The following example demonstrates some techniques for working with optional arguments:

```javascript
function OptionalArgument(param)
{
   // Determine whether there were any params passed.
   if (typeof(param) == "undefined")
      param = "Hello There!";

   // Determine whether there are extra params.
   if (typeof(arguments[1]) != "undefined")

      // If so, output the param and optional
      // argument onscreen.
      document.getElementById("Result").innerHTML =
         "The param is: " + param +
         " and the optional argument is: " + arguments[1];

   else
      // Output the param onscreen.
      document.getElementById("Result").innerHTML =
         "The param is: " + param;
}
```

This function requires one argument as input. Of course, the caller might not provide a value for param, which means that param is undefined. You can check for that issue by using the typeof operator. Notice that when param is undefined, the code assigns it a default value. This is the correct way to handle optional named arguments.

JavaScript also provides a special arguments variable. It's an array that contains one element for each argument passed to the function. When someone passes more arguments than you anticipated or your function can accept a variable number of arguments, you can use the arguments variable to work with them. In this case, when the caller passes an additional argument — one not accounted for by param — the application can still display its value onscreen by using a different message from the message it displays when a caller passes zero or one arguments. Normally you use loops to process a variable number of arguments — a topic that appears in Chapter 9.

Sometimes you really do want one and only one parameter. It's a waste of time to complain about too many arguments in most cases, but you can definitely do something about not getting what you need. The following example tests for a specific kind of input to ensure it has what it needs:

```
function RequiredArgument(param)
{
    // Determine whether there were any params passed.
    if (typeof(param) != "string")

        // If not, return to the caller without doing
        // anything.
        return;

    // If so, then display the value onscreen.
    else
        document.getElementById("Result").innerHTML =
            "The param is: " + param;
}
```

In this case, the code checks for a string. When the caller passes something other than a string, the code simply returns without doing anything. Of course, you could pass back a value indicating an error or even display an `alert()` onscreen. How you react to the error is up to you, but you need to keep the single task nature of functions in mind when deciding on a reaction. In this case, doing nothing is the best choice. When the caller does pass a string, the function displays it onscreen.

## Understanding variable scope

Variables have a specific scope in JavaScript. The *scope* of a variable determines where it can be seen. In general, public variables have two possible scopes:

- ✔ **Global:** The variable is visible throughout the entire document. JavaScript doesn't delete the variable from memory until the user closes the document. A global variable is declared outside of any function.

- ✔ **Local:** The variable is visible within a specific function. When that function completes its work, both the function and the variable are deleted from memory. Local variables are defined inside a function and always override a global variable of the same name.

The best way to illustrate local and global variables is to use a short example. The following code shows how to define both a global and local variable and also provides a test for them:

```
// This is a global variable.
var MyNumber = 22;

function TestVariable1()
{
   // This is a local variable.
   var MyNumber = 34;

   // The local variable overrides
   // the global variable.
   document.getElementById("Result").innerHTML =
      "The value of TestVariable is: " + MyNumber;
}

function TestVariable2()
{
   // There is no local variable to
   // override the global variable.
   document.getElementById("Result").innerHTML =
      "The value of TestVariable is: " + MyNumber;
}
```

When the application calls `TestVariable1()`, it outputs the local version of `MyNumber`, which has a value of 34. The local variable overrides the global variable. However, when the application calls `TestVariable2()`, it outputs the global version of `MyNumber`, which has a value of 22.

# Working with Private Properties and Methods

Many developers are under the impression that JavaScript doesn't provide private properties or methods. However, this isn't the case. It's true that JavaScript does lack any specific keyword that designates a particular property or method as private, but the fact remains that it can create and manage private members.

Private members are always created as part of an object's constructor. You can either create properties as a parameter for the constructor or create it within the constructor itself. Private methods are nested within the constructor. The following code shows both private properties and a private method. (You can find complete code for this example in the \Chapter 07\ PrivateData folder of the downloadable code as UsingPrivateData. HTML.)

```
// param is private.
function TestObject(param)
{
   // ThisString is private.
   ThisString = "abc";

   // ChangeString is private.
   function ChangeString(input)
   {
      return input.toUpperCase();
   }
}
```

If you now create a function to test this object, such as `CreateObject()` shown in the following code, you find that the application fails to produce the desired result. In fact, if you're using an editor specifically designed for working with JavaScript, you'll find that `param`, `ThisString`, and `ChangeString()` don't even show up as possible choices. The members are inaccessible.

```
function CreateObject()
{
   var DoTest = new TestObject("def");
   document.getElementById("Result").innerHTML =
      DoTest.ChangeString("def");
}
```

The private members of `TestObject` are also inaccessible to any public methods that you create. Of course, this presents a problem because the object now has private data that's seemingly inaccessible to anything but the constructor. JavaScript has a third level of visibility called *privileged*. Here's a privileged method for `TestObject`:

```
// MeldData is privileged.
this.MeldData = function()
{
   return ChangeString(ThisString + param);
}
```

This function is also defined within the constructor. However, in this case, it's assigned to a public variable, `MeldData`, that acts as a true method. Your editor will display it as a method when you access it. You can pass it data like any other method. However, this method is privileged and has full access to the private data in `TestObject`. If you change `CreateObject()` so it looks like the following example, the application now produces the desired output:

```
function CreateObject()
{
   var DoTest = new TestObject("def");

   // This code won't work.
   //document.getElementById("Result").innerHTML =
   //    DoTest.ChangeString("def");

   // This code will.
   document.getElementById("Result").innerHTML =
      DoTest.MeldData();
}
```

# Chapter 8

# Making Choices in JavaScript

*In This Chapter*

▶ Considering when to make a decision

▶ Using the if structure to make decisions

▶ Using the switch structure to make decisions

*D*ecisions, decisions — life is all about decisions. Because applications mimic real life in many respects, your application needs to make lots of decisions too. However, unlike the impromptu decisions you make, applications require preprogrammed decisions. You decide in advance which decisions the application makes and for what reasons. In addition, you decide under what conditions the application makes the decisions and what happens when a certain decision path is taken. The only variable is the data used to make the decision — you can't easily control the data, which is why you need a decision-making technique in the first place.

Application decisions are expressed as statements. A *statement* consists of a keyword, which is followed by an expression that defines the decision to make. Following the statement is a code block that contains one or more tasks to perform when an expression is true. The combination of the statement and the code block is called a *structure*. Consequently, when you discuss the if statement, you're talking about the combination of keywords and expression that makes the decision. On the other hand, when you discuss the if structure, you mean the combination of the statement and the code block that follows.

This chapter actually helps you discover both the if statement and the switch statement. Each statement fulfills a particular need in JavaScript programming. Yes, you can use either statement for all of your needs, but doing so will make the decision-making process less clear and your code harder to understand. To make the choices you have clearer, the first section of the chapter explores the decision-making process and why you choose one statement or the other to perform specific tasks.

# Understanding the Reasons for Applications to Make Decisions

In a perfect world, the data your application receives would never change, and you would create a precise procedure for handling it that never varies. In such a situation, you'd never need to make a decision because everything would be straightforward and never vary. Unfortunately, real data will change, which means your application must provide a flexible means for dealing with it. Applications commonly make decisions for the following reasons:

✔ Address a go-or-no-go scenario where the data is either inside or outside the expected range

✔ Test whether a condition has occurred

✔ Handle a number of data range selections where each data range requires a different procedure

✔ Enable the user to choose a specific action

✔ Create a menu where the user can choose from a number of actions

✔ Determine when an error has occurred

✔ Handle environmental conditions that are neither good nor bad, but which do require the application to react in specific ways

✔ Provide a randomized environment for training or other purposes

As in life, many application decisions are black and white — either/or situations where you choose one thing or another. The `if` statement is commonly used to make these sorts of decisions. Something is true or it isn't — there's no middle ground. In some cases, the developer needs only to address a situation that's true, such as when an error occurs. In other cases, the developer needs to provide two separate courses of action depending on whether the expression is true or not.

Sometimes a decision isn't black and white. In this case, you can combine `if` statements to create a series of small black-and-white decisions that ultimately end up choosing a shade of gray, or you can use the `switch` statement. The `switch` statement is a kind of menu; based on the data the application receives, it can choose from a number of potential courses of action. The `switch` statement helps your application handle shades of gray situations.

# Deciding When to Use the if Statement

The `if` statement appears a number of times in previous chapters, which should tell you something about working with the `if` statement — you really can't escape using it. The `if` statement is commonly used for testing whether something has happened or not, whether the data is in range or not, or whether the user wants to perform a specific task. The following sections describe the `if` statement in more detail and help you understand the full range of tasks it can perform.

## Creating a simple if statement

One of the most common uses of the `if` statement is to make a simple selection. When the user takes a particular action, something happens. In the following example, when the user clicks OK in the confirm dialog box, the application displays the secret message. (You can find complete code for this example in the `\Chapter 08\IfStatement` folder of the downloadable code as `SimpleIf.HTML`.)

```
// Create an expression that results in true or false.
var Answer = confirm(
    "Do you want to display the secret message?");

// Test the expression using the if statement.
if (Answer)
{
    // Display the secret message when the user
    // clicks OK.
    document.getElementById("Result").innerHTML =
        "This is the secret message!";
}
```

In this case, `Answer` can contain only `true` or `false` because `confirm()` doesn't output any other values. As a consequence, you don't need to perform any sort of value checks on `Answer` — all you need to do is determine the truth value of `Answer` to make the decision.

All decision making expressions that you ever create will have a truth value of some sort — either true or false. Sometimes the truth value is hidden, as when working with the switch structure, but the truth value is there. Computers don't understand anything other than true or false. There are techniques that make it appear that the computer can do something else, but in reality, it all comes down to making a true or false decision as shown here.

## Deciding what else to do

As noted in the previous section, you use the `if` statement in situations when an application needs to do something when the user responds correctly, but ignore the input when the response is incorrect. However, there are times when you must do something when the input is correct and something else when it's incorrect. In this case, you add the `else` clause to the `if` statement as shown in the following example. (You can find complete code for this example in the `\Chapter 08\IfStatement` folder of the downloadable code as `SimpleIfElse.HTML`.)

```
// Create an expression that results in true or false.
var Answer = confirm(
    "Do you want to display the secret message?");

// Test the expression using the if statement.
if (Answer)
{
    // Display the secret message when the user
    // clicks OK.
    document.getElementById("Result").innerHTML =
        "This is the secret message!";
}
else
{
    // Perform an alternative task.
    alert("Click OK next time to see the message!");
}
```

A *clause* is an extension of a structure. In this case, the `else` clause extends the `if` structure to include a second code block that handles the false condition. The example still outputs the secret message when the user clicks OK in the `confirm()` dialog box. However, now the code also displays an `alert()` dialog when the user clicks Cancel. This secondary action helps the user understand how to react to the `confirm()` dialog box to obtain a different output.

## Nesting if statements

There are many reasons why you might *nest* `if` statements — that is, place one `if` statement within another. The following example shows one situation, which leads into the `switch` statement examples later in the chapter. In this case, the user selects an option onscreen, `CheckChoice()` performs a check of that option, and then `CheckChoice()` displays the correct result onscreen. (You can find complete code for this example in the `\Chapter 08\IfStatement` folder of the downloadable code as `NestedIf.HTML`.)

```javascript
function CheckChoice(option)
{
    // Verify that the input is a number.
    if (typeof(option) != "number")
    {
        // Display an error dialog.
        alert("Please provide numeric input!");

        // Return without doing anything more.
        return;
    }

    // Ensure that option is actually an integer.
    var Select = Math.round(option);

    // Verify that the input is in range.
    if ((Select < 1) || (Select > 3))
    {
        // Display an error dialog.
        alert("The value supplied is out of range!");

        // Return without doing anything more.
        return;
    }

    // Make a selection.
    if (Select == 1)
    {
        document.getElementById("Result").innerHTML =
            "You chose Item A.";
    }
    else
    {
        if (Select == 2)
        {
            document.getElementById("Result").innerHTML =
                "You chose Item B.";
        }
        else
        {
            document.getElementById("Result").innerHTML =
                "You chose Item C.";
        }
    }
}
```

This example doesn't rely on a known source of input, so it begins by performing various checks of the data. The first check verifies that the caller has supplied a numeric value. After all, the caller could provide a string or a Boolean value instead. For that matter, the input could be a pointer to another function or anything else that JavaScript supports — you just don't know.

The next step converts the numeric input to an integer. Data conversion is important in JavaScript because it treats both integers and floating point values as numbers. If you want an integer value, using `Math.round()` to get it is the best way to go. This function rounds the input to the nearest integer value, which means you don't end up trying to perform comparisons against values such as `3.5`.

At this point, you know you have a number and that the number is an integer, but you don't know whether the number is in the correct range. A failure to range-check input values is the cause of many woes in JavaScript applications. `CheckChoice()` is expecting integer values in the range of 1 to 3, so the range check looks for these values.

The nested `if` statement is almost anticlimactic at this point. You know that `Select` contains 1, 2, or 3. The first `if` statement checks for a value of 1 and displays a message when it finds that value. When the value is something other than 1, the `else` clause takes over. Within the `else` clause is a nested `if` statement. This `if` statement checks `Select` for a value of 2 and displays the appropriate message when it is. When `Select` is 3, the `else` clause of this second, nested, `if` statement displays the appropriate message. Figure 8-1 shows typical output from this example.

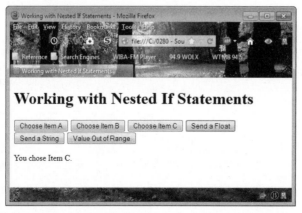

**Figure 8-1:** The example provides a number of buttons to test various conditions.

# Switching Between Choices

Although the `if` statement is commonly used for simple choices, the `switch` statement is used to handle a range of choices. A `switch` provides an elegant way to handle variable data. The following sections describe two forms of `switch` statement. The first provides the means for working with a predefined range of choices, and the second provides the means for working with data that could contain unexpected information. This second form makes the `switch` statement particularly useful because users are unpredictable, and this second form can take such users into account.

# Creating a basic switch

Many developers prefer switch statements over nested if statements because the switch statements are easier to understand. A switch statement also requires less typing to obtain the same result. The following example replicates the example shown in the "Nesting if statements" section, earlier in this chapter. (You can find complete code for this example in the \Chapter 08\SwitchStatement folder of the downloadable code as SimpleSwitch.HTML.)

```javascript
function CheckChoice(option)
{
   // Verify that the input is a number.
   if (typeof(option) != "number")
   {
      // Display an error dialog.
      alert("Please provide numeric input!");

      // Return without doing anything more.
      return;
   }

   // Ensure that option is actually an integer.
   var Select = Math.round(option);

   // Verify that the input is in range.
   if ((Select < 1) || (Select > 3))
   {
      // Display an error dialog.
      alert("The value supplied is out of range!");

      // Return without doing anything more.
      return;
   }

   // Make a selection.
   switch (Select)
   {
      case 1:
         document.getElementById("Result").innerHTML =
            "You chose Item A.";
         break;
      case 2:
         document.getElementById("Result").innerHTML =
            "You chose Item B.";
         break;
      case 3:
         document.getElementById("Result").innerHTML =
            "You chose Item C.";
         break;
   }
}
```

All the logic leading up to the switch statement is the same as before. Whether you use a switch statement or nested if statement, you need to provide logic to ensure that the input is correct, or else your application most likely will fail. In this case, failure equates to the application doing nothing at all, but the concept of failure is the same. Always check your inputs for correct values.

Some people have a hard time understanding where the truth value lies in the switch statement. The switch statement requires a variable, which is Select in this case. Each case clause performs a comparison against the variable. Consequently, you could see the first case clause as saying, case Select == 1.

When working with switch statements, you must also include a break statement at the end of each processing segment. The break statement simply says that the case has been evaluated and handled.

If you leave the break statement out, the code continues with the next executable statement in the next case. This condition is known as *fall-through,* and some developers use it as a programming technique to combine tasks and reduce the amount of code required. Using this technique is dangerous because other developers may not realize that the fall-through is required and therefore may add a break statement for you.

## Using the default option

The switch statement includes another clause, the default clause. The default clause is like the else clause for the if statement. When none of the case clauses are true, the code executes the code in the default clause. The following example uses the default clause to modify the way in which the example in the preceding section works. This version is much easier to understand and use. (You can find complete code for this example in the \Chapter 08\SwitchStatement folder of the downloadable code as DefaultSwitch.HTML.)

```
function MakeAChoice()
{
    // Ask the user to provide input.
    var Selection = prompt("Type a menu option.");

    // Convert the string to a number.
    var IntSelect = parseInt(Selection);

    // Verify the user has provided a number.
    if (isNaN(IntSelect))
```

```
{
    // Display an error dialog.
    alert("Please provide numeric input!");

    // Return without doing anything more.
    return;
}

// Call the selection function.
CheckChoice(IntSelect);
}
```

Instead of providing myriad buttons, this example relies on the `prompt()` dialog box to obtain input from the user. The result is the cleaner interface shown in Figure 8-2. When the user clicks Choose a Menu Item, the application displays a `prompt()` dialog box, where the user can enter a value.

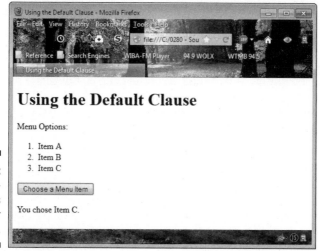

**Figure 8-2:**
This example provides a cleaner interface.

You might think that this is a recipe for disaster, but the application performs the same checks for input validity as before, but it uses a different technique.

In this case, the application uses `partInt()` to verify that the input is a number and to convert the number to an integer value. When the input is incorrect, `IntSelect` is set to Not a Number (`NaN`). The example detects this issue by using the `isNaN()` function. When a user does provide a numeric input, the application calls `CheckChoice()`, which is shown in the following code:

```
function CheckChoice(option)
{
    // Make a selection.
    switch (option)
    {
        case 1:
            document.getElementById("Result").innerHTML =
                "You chose Item A.";
            break;
        case 2:
            document.getElementById("Result").innerHTML =
                "You chose Item B.";
            break;
        case 3:
            document.getElementById("Result").innerHTML =
                "You chose Item C.";
            break;
        default:
            // Display an error dialog.
            alert("The value supplied is out of range!");
            break;
    }
}
```

You may be wondering where the rest of the code is, but this is all you need. The switch statement checks for values of 1, 2, or 3. When the values are outside that range, the code uses the default clause, which contains the out-of-range error message. As you can see, these two functions make the tasks of working with the menu a lot simpler for both developer and user.

# Chapter 9

# Making the Rounds with Loops

*R*epetitive actions appear everywhere in the real world, so they also appear in applications. For example, you don't do a single pushup and stop — you do a number of pushups to achieve a specific fitness goal. You'd be really surprised if an application allowed you to select a single menu item, performed the required task, and then ended so that it couldn't perform any other tasks. Applications repeatedly ask you to select menu or other options to complete a particular goal that consists of many individual tasks. Repetition also appears inside the application. An application downloads individual pieces of a graphic, one piece at a time, until all the pieces appear on the local computer and the application displays them onscreen.

JavaScript supports several kinds of loops: `for`, `while`, `do...while`, and `for...in`. Each loop type has specific advantages in certain situations. For example, the `for` loop offers the advantage of providing a specific start and stop expression. This chapter starts with a discussion of why loops are useful and how to avoid problems when using them. The remaining sections describe each of the loop types in detail and show you how to use them. Most importantly, these sections help you understand when each loop is most useful in an application.

# Discovering Loops

The term *loop* brings up visions of circles. In some respects, when you create a loop in your application, the application goes in circles. It keeps going in circles until you tell it to stop. As it continues to loop, the application performs the tasks that you set for it within the code block defined by the loop structure.

Just as decision structures have a statement that defines an expression used to determine whether the code block executes, loops also rely on the truth value of expressions. A `for` statement defines the terms under which the loop will execute. The associated code block contains the code that the `for` loop executes. The combination of `for` statement and code block is a `for` structure, but most developers call this combination a `for` loop.

Now that you have some idea of what the terminology means, it's time to look at loops in general. The following sections describe why loops are useful and how you can avoid problems when using them.

## Learning why loops are useful

Loops make it possible to perform repetitive tasks easily. There are ways you could re-create the usefulness of a loop, but it would be a painful process. For example, if you knew that you would need to call a function five times, you could place five calls to it in your code. Of course, the result would be a fragile piece of code that would break every time conditions changed even a little. In some cases, such as a situation where you simply don't know how many times to repeat a task, you must have a loop to control the number of repetitions that the code makes.

However, loops do more than simply repeat a list of tasks. You use loops to control the way in which the repetition occurs. For example, you can choose to end a loop early when an error exists, or you might choose to skip a particular sequence of tasks when the conditions warrant (such as not processing strings but instead processing only numbers). In other words, loops are also about controlling a situation in a unique way — by monitoring the data and then reacting to it dynamically.

The ability to end a loop early or to skip a particular loop cycle makes loops uniquely suited to processing arrays and other collections. Because array data changes relatively often in some applications and you can't really depend on an array to maintain a specific length, you must have some sort of loop processing to manage them successfully. This need matches the real-world environment that objects model. For example, your bookcase or music collection grows when you buy new items and shrinks when you give items away, sell them, or throw them out. The real world constantly changes and so do your applications, so loops have an incredibly important role to fulfill.

## Running from the dangers of loops

Loops can run amok. Yes, like some demented robot on an old science fiction movie, a loop can cause all sorts of problems when managed incorrectly. The most common loop-related problems involve the number of cycles that the loop performs. Processing data is a Goldilocks scenario: You want neither too much nor too little — it has to be just right.

The most common problem for loops is the *infinite loop* — one that never ends. All loops have two significant expressions associated with them. The first expression defines when the loop should start, and the second expression defines when the loop should stop. Sometimes a developer thinks that the loop has the right logic defined for both, but the stop expression can prove difficult to create for these reasons:

✔ The loop never reaches the stopping point because the stop expression is wrong.

✔ The loop actually exceeds the stop expression because the stop expression was expecting one result and the loop produced another.

✔ An error causes the loop to malfunction.

The easiest loop-related problem to find is one in which the loop never starts. The developer doesn't see any output, so it's obvious something is wrong. In many cases, an `alert()` that shows the starting state of a variable compared to the start expression for the loop quickly shows the problem. When the start condition is never met, the loop will never start.

The hardest and most subtle loop problem is one in which the loop stops too soon. The loop does some amount of work, and it doesn't get stuck in an infinite loop, but it also doesn't perform the number of cycles you anticipated. The result is often damaged data. The data may look acceptable, but there's something wrong with it. Many applications go into the production environment with subtle loop problems. The worst-case scenario is when the stop expression works sometimes but not in all situations — leading developers to yank out their hair. The next time you see a hairless developer, think about the loop error that the developer was unable to fix.

# Creating for Loops

A `for` loop is best used in situations where you know you want to perform a specific number of cycles. You don't necessarily know the number of cycles when you create the application, but the number of cycles is fixed at runtime, when the user interacts with the application. A `for` loop can be interrupted or told to bypass a specific cycle. However, you can be certain that a properly constructed `for` loop always starts at a specific point and ends at a specific point.

## *Making your first for loop*

The section on creating functions with optional and required arguments in Chapter 7 discusses the need to provide some sort of handling for both optional and required arguments in some functions. There are situations where a function must take a variable number of arguments. You simply don't know how many arguments the caller will send at the outset. The following example demonstrates one technique for creating a function that handles a variable number of arguments. (You can find complete code for this example in the \Chapter 09\ForLoop folder of the downloadable code as SimpleFor.HTML.)

```javascript
function OptionalArgument(param)
{
    // Determine whether there were any params passed.
    if (arguments.length == 0)
    {
        // Display an error message and exit.
        document.getElementById("Result").innerHTML =
            "Nothing Passed!";
        return;
    }

    // Create a string to hold the arguments.
    var Result = new String();

    // Process each of the arguments in turn.
    for (var i = 0; i < arguments.length; i++)
    {
        // Verify that the argument is of the right type.
        if (typeof(arguments[i]) == 'string')
        {
            // Add to the argument string.
            Result += arguments[i] + "<br />";
        }
    }

    // Display the results onscreen.
    document.getElementById("Result").innerHTML = Result;
}
```

The code begins by checking the arguments.length property. When this property is 0, it means that the caller hasn't passed any arguments to the function. The code displays an error message and exits.

The for loop in this example will actually create a string that contains a combination of text and HTML tags in it, so the next step is to create Result as a new String(). After the for loop completes, the application displays the content of Result onscreen.

The `for` statement begins with three expressions. Each of these expressions is separated by a semicolon (`;`). The first expression, `var i = 0`, is the starting point. It creates a variable named `i` and sets its value to 0. The second expression, `i < arguments.length`, tells the `for` loop to continue processing arguments until `i` is equal to or greater than the value of `arguments.length`. In other words, the `for` loop will perform one cycle for each element in `arguments`. The third expression, `i++`, tells the `for` loop how to update `i` after completing each cycle. If you didn't include this expression, the value of `i` would never change, and the loop would never end.

The code block begins by checking the type of variable contained within the current `arguments` element, which is expressed as `arguments[i]`. When this type is a string, the code adds the string, along with an HTML tag, to `Result`. Each loop cycle adds more strings to `Result`, and when the `for` loop ends, `Result` contains every string passed to the `OptionalArgument()` function. Figure 9-1 shows typical output from this example.

**Figure 9-1:**
This example not only shows the for loop but also includes some formatting.

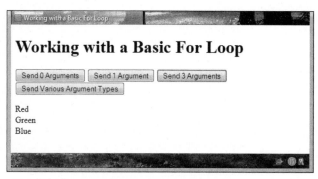

## Using the break statement

The `break` statement lets you stop loop execution, even if the stop expression conditions aren't met. There are many reasons to use the `break` statement. For example, you might want to stop loop execution when the application experiences an error. The following example shows how to use a `break` statement to stop application execution. In this case, processing stops immediately when the application finds data of the incorrect type. (You can find complete code for this example in the `\Chapter 09\ForLoop` folder of the downloadable code as `BreakStatement.HTML`.)

```
function OptionalArgument(param)
{
   // Determine whether there were any params passed.
   if (arguments.length == 0)
   {
      // Display an error message and exit.
      document.getElementById("Result").innerHTML =
         "Nothing Passed!";
      return;
   }

   // Create a string to hold the arguments.
   var Result = new String();

   // Process each of the arguments in turn.
   for (var i = 0; i < arguments.length; i++)
   {
      // Verify that the argument is of the right type.
      if (typeof(arguments[i]) != 'string')
      {
         // When the argument is incorrect, stop
         // loop execution.
         break;
      }

      // Add to the argument string.
      Result += arguments[i] + "<br />";
   }

   // Display the results onscreen.
   document.getElementById("Result").innerHTML = Result;
}
```

In this case, the example stops processing the input arguments immediately after finding an input argument of a type other than string. Consequently, when the application calls OptionalArgument('Red', 'Green', 'Blue'), the application displays all three arguments. However, when the application calls OptionalArgument('Red', 'Green', true, 'Orange'), it displays only Red and Green. Even though Orange is also a correct argument, it appears after true, which is an incorrect argument. Execution stops with true. If the application were to call OptionalArgument(true, 'Red', 'Yellow', 'Orange'), the output would be blank because the first argument is incorrect.

The break statement is used as an exceptional condition. You stop execution because the loop can't continue for some reason. As a consequence, the break statement normally appears as part of an if structure. The if statement defines the exceptional condition. Any loop cleanup you want to perform, such as finalizing a variable's state, must appear before the break statement.

# *Using the continue statement*

The `continue` statement stops processing for the current loop cycle. However, processing continues with the next loop cycle. Although you would generally use a `break` statement to stop loop processing in the event of a non-recoverable error, the `continue` statement lets you create a loop that can recover from errors. In this respect, loops can differentiate between *hard errors* (those that the application can't recover from) and *soft errors* (those that are recoverable).

The `continue` statement is also quite useful for a number of programming techniques, such as filtering. When the loop encounters a situation where an argument, a data item, or an array element is outside the filtering criteria, it can exclude that element by not processing it but continuing on with the next argument, data item, or array element. Filtering is an exceptionally important task for applications to perform because users rarely provide *clean data* — that is, data without erroneous artifacts included.

Because filtering is such an important feature of applications, the following sections review the use of arrays with a `for` loop. The first section reviews the `Array` object properties and methods. The second section shows an example of using a `for` loop to filter an `Array` object to clean up undesirable elements.

## *Working with Array objects in depth*

`Array` objects often require complex handling of data to produce the desired results. For example, the array could contain different data types, and you might need to sort through them to find only the data you need. Fortunately, the `Array` object provides a number of methods and properties to make interacting with them in loops easier. The following list describes the `Array` object properties:

- ✔ `constructor`: Displays a string showing the prototype used to define the object. In this case, you see "function Array() { [native code] }".
- ✔ `length`: Returns the length of the array in elements.
- ✔ `prototype`: Provides the means for adding both properties and methods to an object.

The `Array` object also provides a number of useful methods. You can use these methods to modify the array dynamically during processing and to enhance the ability of the `for` loop to produce useful results. The following list describes each of the `Array` object methods:

- ✔ `concat()`: Creates a single array by joining two or more arrays.
- ✔ `indexOf()`: Locates a specific element within an array and returns the position of that element.

✔ join(): Creates a single string from all of the elements within an array.

✔ lastIndexOf(): Locates the last location of a specific element within an array and returns the position of that element.

✔ pop(): Removes the last element of an array and returns that element.

✔ push(): Adds new elements to the end of an array and returns the new array length.

✔ reverse(): Reverses the order of the elements in an array.

✔ shift(): Removes the first element of an array and returns that element.

✔ slice(): Produces a copy of part of an array and returns that part.

✔ sort(): Sorts the elements of an array.

✔ splice(): Adds or removes elements to or from an array as specified in the arguments.

✔ toString(): Outputs the individual values of each element of an array as a string.

✔ unshift(): Adds new elements to the beginning of an array and returns the new length.

✔ valueOf(): Outputs the native value of each of the elements of an array.

### Interacting with an array

One of the more interesting ways to use the continue statement is as a means for filtering data. When the incoming data doesn't meet some requirement, you filter it out. The following example demonstrates a technique for filtering array data to produce a clean array that you can then process without error. The main reason to perform this task is that you need to use the array repetitively and filtering it each time would prove time consuming, needlessly slowing application performance. (You can find complete code for this example in the \Chapter 09\ForLoop folder of the downloadable code as ContinueStatement.HTML.)

```
function FilterArray()
{
    // Define the original array.
    var OriginalData = new Array(
        "Red", "Orange", "Yellow", 1,
        "Green", true, "Blue");

    // Define an array to receive the filtered data.
    var FilteredData = new Array();

    // Show the original data.
    DisplayArray(OriginalData, "Original");
```

```
        // Filter the data.
    for (var i = 0; i < OriginalData.length; i++)
    {
        // Check for the correct data type.
        if (typeof(OriginalData[i]) != 'string')
        {
            // Go to the next item.
            continue;
        }

        // Add the matching item to the array.
        FilteredData.push(OriginalData[i]);
    }

    // Show the filtered data.
    DisplayArray(FilteredData, "Filtered");
}
```

The example begins by creating an array, `OriginalData`, with some errant data in it. The array is supposed to contain strings, but you can see that it includes both numeric and Boolean data items. The example also creates `FilteredData`, which currently contains nothing but will eventually contain all the useful data from `OriginalData`.

Filtering occurs in the `for` loop. If the current array element isn't of type string, then the code continues to the next loop iteration. However, when the element is of type string, the code uses the `push()` method to add the current array element to `FilteredData`.

Notice the calls to `DisplayArray()`. This is an example of taking code out of a function and placing it in a supplementary function to make the code easier to understand. In addition, it ensures that each function performs a single task. In this case, `DisplayArray()` outputs the array data to a specific location onscreen as shown here:

```
function DisplayArray(TheArray, DisplayID)
{
    // Create an output string.
    var DisplayString = "<ul>"

    // Build the display string.
    for (var i = 0; i < TheArray.length; i++)
    {
        DisplayString += "<li>" + TheArray[i] + "</li>";
    }

    // Complete the list.
    DisplayString += "</ul>";

    // Display the data.
    document.getElementById(DisplayID).innerHTML =
        DisplayString;
}
```

`DisplayArray()` accepts two inputs: an array to process and the identifier of a screen element to receive the data. The usual checks were omitted from this function for the sake of clarity, but if you were creating this function for a production environment, you'd definitely include them.

In this case, `DisplayArray()` used an unordered (bulleted) list to display the data onscreen. So, `DisplayString` receives the starting tag to initialize the string. The array adds list items (`<li>` tags) to `DisplayString` — one for each array element. The ending `<ul>` tag is added after the `for` loop completes, and the item is displayed onscreen in the correct display element. Figure 9-2 shows typical output from this example.

**Figure 9-2:**
Filtering is an important feature of many applications.

# Creating while Loops

Developers commonly use `while` loops when there's no definite ending for a loop. The environment or data must meet a specific condition before the loop stops. With this in mind, it's easier to create an infinite loop with a `while` loop than it is with a `for` loop because you're not always sure about the condition that will end the loop. It's important to plan `while` loops carefully. The following sections discuss how to use the two forms of `while` loops and tell how each `while` loop type is commonly used in applications.

# Using the basic while loop

A basic `while` loop tests for the ending condition immediately. If the ending condition is met, then the loop never executes. This type of loop is useful when you may or may not need to perform processing on some type of variable data. For example, a `while` loop of this sort works perfectly with a function that accepts zero or more optional arguments. The fact that there may not be any arguments to process means that the `while` loop will never execute. The following example shows such a scenario. (You can find complete code for this example in the `\Chapter 09\WhileLoop` folder of the downloadable code as `SimpleWhile.HTML`.)

```
function OptionalArgument(param)
{
   // Display the default output.
   document.getElementById("Result").innerHTML =
      "Nothing Passed!";

   // Create a string to hold the arguments.
   var Result = new String();

   // Process each of the arguments in turn.
   while (param.length > 0)
   {
      // Remove the current argument.
      var Argument = param.shift();

      // Verify that the argument is of the right type.
      if (typeof(Argument) == 'string')
      {
         // Add to the argument string.
         Result += Argument + "<br />";
      }
   }

   // Display the results onscreen.
   document.getElementById("Result").innerHTML = Result;
}
```

In this example, `OptionalArgument()` receives an array as input. When someone sends something other than an array, the function acts as if the user didn't send anything at all. The array can contain any number of elements — the function doesn't care how many or how few.

The `while` loop checks the length of `param`. When `param` contains even a single element, the loop begins processing the data. The call to `shift()` removes the first element from the array, making the array shorter by one element. When this `Argument` is of type string, it's added to `Result`. When the loop ends, the output is displayed onscreen in the same way that the `for` loop example does in the "Making your first for loop" section, earlier in this chapter.

The interesting features of this example are that it's shorter than the `for` loop example and that this version will execute slightly faster because there are fewer comparisons performed during each loop. However, whether it's actually easier to understand depends on how you write applications. Some developers would probably find this form easier to understand as well, but you should use the forms that work best for you as a developer.

## Using the do...while loop

A `do...while` loop works precisely the same as a standard `while` loop except that the ending expression is evaluated at the end of the loop. This means that a `do...while` loop always executes at least once. Developers commonly use `do...while` loops for menus, reading files, and other processes that may require some setup within the loop before the loop can evaluate the expression. The following example shows how you could use a `do...while` loop to create a continuous processing scenario. (You can find complete code for this example in the `\Chapter 09\WhileLoop` folder of the downloadable code as `SimpleDoWhile.HTML`.)

```
function AddItems()
{
    // Create an input variable.
    var Input = new String();

    // Keep accepting input until the user
    // types quit.
    do
    {
        // Obtain new input.
        Input = prompt("Type a new value (quit to exit):");

        // Verify the user hasn't typed quit.
        if (Input.toUpperCase() != 'QUIT')
        {
            // Add the input to the array.
            DataStore.push(Input);

            // Display the result onscreen.
            DisplayArray(DataStore, "Result")
        }
    } while (Input.toUpperCase() != 'QUIT')
}
```

The example relies on a global `Array` named `DataStore` to hold the entries. Obviously, there's no input to process when the application begins, so the user makes a request to add an item. At this point, `Input` has no data, and there's nothing to define whether there's anything to do. The `do...while` loop works perfectly because you don't want `Input` to contain anything until the user puts it there. The user keeps adding items. When the application sees the word *quit* in any form, the data entry stops. This example reuses the `DisplayArray()` function described in the "Interacting with an array" section, earlier in this chapter.

Notice how the application checks for the ending condition in this case. You should always convert input to uppercase or lowercase and then check it against a standardized capitalization. Otherwise, you can't be sure whether the user will type quit, QUIT, Quit, or even qUit. This approach ensures you capture the keyword whatever form the user types it in. (Of course, the user could also click Cancel to stop inputting new values — the code provides a method for exiting the loop by typing a value.)

# Examining Objects Using for/in

Collections, object literals, and classes can prove difficult to process using standard loops because you have to figure out a way to monitor the application's progress through them. Fortunately, JavaScript provides an easier method of dealing with objects of various sorts: the `for/in` loop. Begin with the class description shown in the following code. (You can find complete code for this example in the `\Chapter 09\ForIn` folder of the downloadable code as `SimpleForIn.HTML`.)

```
// Define a customer.
function Customer(FirstName, LastName, Age)
{
   // Add the properties.
   this.FirstName = FirstName;
   this.LastName = LastName;
   this.Age = Age;
}
```

All that this class contains is some properties. You can now iterate through the properties and their associated values using a `for/in` loop as shown here:

```
// Process the customers.
function ProcessCustomer()
{
   // Create a new customer.
   MyCustomer = new Customer("Josh", "Adams", 49);

   // Define a table for output.
   var Output = "<table>";

   // Add a header row.
   Output += "<tr>";

   // Process the headers.
   for (ThisProperty in MyCustomer)
   {
```

```
        Output += "<th>" + ThisProperty + "</th>";
    }

    // End the row.
    Output += "</tr>";

    // Add a data row.
    Output += "<tr>";

    // Process the customer.
    for(ThisProperty in MyCustomer)
    {
        // Add each data element.
        Output += "<td>" + MyCustomer[ThisProperty] +
            "</td>";
    }

    // End the row.
    Output += "</tr>";

    // End the table.
    Output += "</table>";

    // Display the results onscreen.
    document.getElementById("Result").innerHTML =
        Output;
}
```

This example creates an instance of Customer, MyCustomer, and fills it with data. The output in this example is configured as an HTML5 table. The property names are processed as the header using the first for/in loop. Notice that the for/in loop doesn't appear to have either a starting or an ending expression. It's implied that you want to start with the first member of whatever object you process and end with the last member.

When working with an object of the kind shown here, ThisProperty contains the name of a property, not the property value. Therefore, you can obtain the property names directly and display them onscreen as the header using the <th> tag.

Note the difference in the second for/in loop. In this case, ThisProperty is used as an index into the object. The output is the property value, which appears as part of a data row. Figure 9-3 shows typical output from this example.

**Figure 9-3:**
Using the
for/in loop
makes it
possible to
process col-
lections and
classes.

# Nesting Loops

Sometimes you need to nest loops in order to accomplish useful work. For
example, you may need to process a number of items a certain number of
times. A multiplication table is a perfect example of a situation where you'd
need to nest loops. The following example shows one way to perform the
task. (You can find complete code for this example in the \Chapter 09\
ForLoop folder of the downloadable code as NestedLoop.HTML.)

```javascript
<script language="JavaScript">
   // Start the table.
   document.write("<table>");

   // Start a heading row.
   document.write("<tr>");

   // Create a heading.
   for (var i = 0; i <= 10; i++)
   {
      if (i == 0)
      {
         document.write("<th />");
      }
      else
      {
         document.write("<th>" + i + "</th>");
      }
   }

   // End the heading row.
   document.write("</tr>");

   for (var i = 1; i <= 10; i++)
   {
      // Start a data row.
      document.write("<tr>")
```

```
      // Create the row header.
      document.write("<th>" + i + "</th>");

      for (var j = 1; j <= 10; j++)
      {
          // Add each data element.
          document.write("<td>" + i * j + "</td>");
      }

      // End a data row.
      document.write("</tr>")
  }

  // End the table.
  document.write("</table>");
</script>
```

The example begins by creating a header of column values using a simple for loop. Notice the use of an if statement to determine when to display a value and when to keep the cell blank.

The rows are where you need the nested loop. Multiplication is the product of multiplicand and multiplier. The outer for loop provides the row heading and the multiplicand. The inner for loop provides the multiplier and each of the data cells within the table. The product is i * j. Figure 9-4 shows typical output from this example.

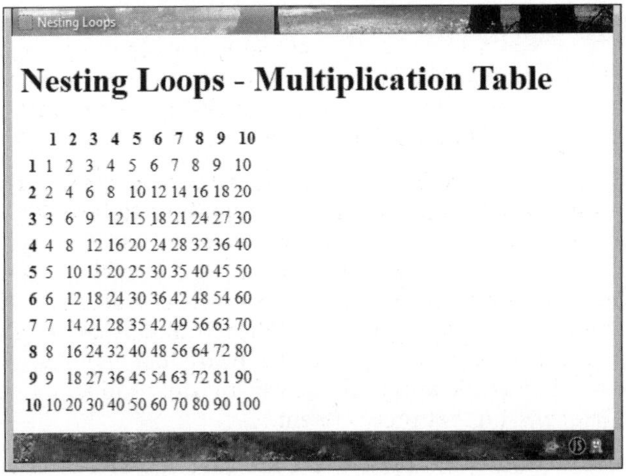

**Figure 9-4:** Multiplication tables are a good example for nested loops.

# Chapter 10

# Performing Error Handling

*N*o one likes errors. However, errors happen. In many cases, you don't even have to do anything wrong to see an error in your code. For example, a user could supply a value that simply doesn't work with the application, or a network error could cause problems. Someone could choose to move a site, or a vendor could change the level of support in a browser. In fact, all sorts of issues can confront the JavaScript developer.

Fortunately, it's also possible to do something about errors. You can use a three-step process to make errors less frightening:

1. **You need to know more about the nature of errors.** Knowing what causes errors in the first place can help you avoid them. Previous chapters in this book provide some examples of how you can avoid errors by doing things like checking the input type of data and validating that the data range falls within the limits you expected.

2. **After you come to understand errors better, you need to know how to *catch* them, which means intercepting them before they become a problem.** After you catch the error, you can do something about it, which means *handling* the error. Catching and handling errors can prevent your application from crashing. You can do something to solve the error before it becomes a problem. When you're proactive about handling errors, the user may not even be aware that an error has occurred. In fact, the best applications are nearly invisible and let the user focus on the information that they present.

3. **You need to understand that there are rare occasions where you can't handle the error.** In this case, you need to tell someone that there's an error. An administrator may need to change settings, or the user may need to check a network connection to make your application work. *Throwing* errors is the act of telling someone that the error has happened. You hope that there's someone there to catch the error you've

thrown so that the application can recover rather than crash. Of course, applications do crash, so it's important that they do so gracefully, without losing data.

Thinking about this process is important because it helps you find errors faster and more completely. The following sections describe these three steps and tell how to use them to diagnose problems in your code.

# Understanding Errors

It's essential to understand the nature of JavaScript errors. You can't overcome something you don't understand. The most important thing to understand is that errors will happen. You can't avoid errors in an application, no matter how hard you try. All developers face some number of errors in every application created because errors reside in every aspect of the computer environment — even within the hardware you use to interact with the application. The following sections help you understand the nature of errors as they apply to JavaScript.

## Defining an error source

Errors don't all happen at the same time and in the same way in JavaScript. The error caused by a developer misplacing a curly brace is different from the error caused by a user providing the wrong sort of input. To understand an error, you must quantify it. One way to define errors and help quantify them is to understand the general error categories for JavaScript:

✔ **Syntax:** Whenever you make a typo of some sort, you create a syntax error. Some JavaScript syntax errors are quite easy to find because the application simply won't run. The editor may even point out the error for you by highlighting a missing curly brace. However, some syntax errors are quite hard to find. JavaScript is case sensitive, so you may use the wrong case for a variable in one place and find that the variable isn't quite working as you thought it would. Finding the one place where you used the wrong capitalization can be quite challenging.

✔ **Interpreted:** You may think that you've typed everything correctly, but the results you receive from the interpreter aren't quite what you expected. For example, if you try to use a `for/in` loop to process an array, what you receive is the array's index value in the variable rather than an individual element from the array. JavaScript is processing the array as intended with the `for/in` loop, but your coding may be assuming that JavaScript has supplied an element as output and the application won't work. These errors are usually obvious because the application won't work. However, you may need to use a debugger to find them because you don't quite understand how JavaScript is working with the code you've created. Yes, the code will run, but it won't run as you thought it would.

✔ **Runtime:** When an error happens as your application runs, it's called a *runtime error.* In most cases, runtime errors come from outside sources — a user may type the wrong thing in a field, the network could go down, a site can move, a browser may not implement the JavaScript code correctly, or some other external problem could occur. In some rare cases, you can even encounter problems where the hardware glitches a specific way just one time (also known as a cosmic hiccup) — the error never occurs again. The whole concept of catching and handling errors comes from a need to deal with runtime errors. The techniques shown in previous chapters for checking data types and data ranges also help keep runtime errors under control. However, be assured that no matter how well you design your defenses, someone will find new ways to create runtime errors for you.

✔ **Semantic:** When you create a loop that executes one too many times, you don't generally receive any sort of error information from the application. The application will happily run because it thinks that it's doing everything correctly, but that one additional loop can cause all sorts of data errors. When you create an error of this sort in your code, it's called a *semantic error.* In many cases, developers also call semantic errors logic errors. The point is that semantic errors occur because the meaning behind a series of steps used to perform a task is wrong — the result is incorrect even though the code apparently runs precisely as it should. Semantic errors are tough to find, and you always need some sort of debugger to find them.

Classifying errors in this way helps you understand how the error happened and possibly when it happened. In some cases, you can even understand why it happened. In most cases, you fix these sorts of errors by modifying your code — you either fix the problem in the code syntax or find new ways to check data sources before you use them.

A developer's most important tool in finding and fixing application errors is patience. You need to carefully observe the application behavior, think about why the error might be happening, and then use the clues you've gathered to examine the code in detail. The process of finding and fixing errors is called *debugging.*

Every serious developer needs a *debugger* (special software that makes finding errors easier) to debug an application. For example, Firefox users often rely on Firebug (`https://getfirebug.com`) to locate errors. Chapter 2 describes the native capabilities of some of the browsers targeted by this book. Getting an add-on such as Firebug enhances the native capabilities to make debugging easier.

The best developers don't let ego get in the way. Other people can often look at your code and find errors in it a lot faster than you can. Other people find the errors faster because the code is unfamiliar to them and they look at the code from a different perspective. These helpers have different skills than you do and experiences that may help them locate the error faster (often because these people have already experienced the error at some point in their careers).

## Defining the error types

JavaScript provides specific error types to make it easier to diagnose the errors that you see in your application. Knowing the error types can make it easier for you to create methods to deal with the error. The following list describes the most common error types found in JavaScript applications:

- ✔ `EvalError`: This error commonly occurs when an application uses the `eval()` function in an incorrect manner.

- ✔ `RangeError`: When an application performs some sort of operation that causes a number to exceed its anticipated range, a function can throw this error. You could also see this error as the result of a math operation gone awry (such as attempted division by zero).

- ✔ `ReferenceError`: Any time you try to use a resource that doesn't exist, you create a reference error. This is the sort of error you might see if you use the wrong capitalization for a variable in part of your application.

- ✔ `SyntaxError`: The interpreter will throw this error to tell you that it has experienced some sort of error parsing your code. There are all sorts of ways in which syntax errors can occur, so it's important to try to locate precisely where the interpreter is experiencing problems parsing your code.

- ✔ `TypeError`: Many of the examples in the book use the `typeof()` operator to check the type of data received by a function. One way to handle the situation where a caller is sending the wrong data to your application is to throw a `TypeError`.

✔ URIError: Uniform Resource Identifier (URI) errors can occur for a number of reasons, including site downtime. The most common reasons you see this particular error is that the `encodeURI()` or `decodeURI()` function is used incorrectly in your application. However, it pays to look for other sources of this particular error.

Some of these error types can prove tricky to figure out — especially when you check your code and determine that it's correct. One of the areas you should look at is whether you've defined the `<script>` tag correctly. Some browsers are quite picky about this tag and won't provide a desired level of support unless you create it correctly. For example, when you want to use JavaScript 1.7 features in your code, you must tell certain browsers that you want to use this support by creating your `<script>` tag like this:

```
<script type="application/javascript;version=1.7">
... Your Application ...
</script>
```

Notice that the tag must specifically include a `version=1.7` attribute. Otherwise, the browser will assume you want to use an older version of JavaScript that is defined by the vendor somewhere in the vendor's documentation. The source of your syntax error might be the level of support the browser provides rather than an actual error in your code.

When looking for errors in your code, you may see a place where you want to specifically stop. The `debugger` keyword is understood by most debuggers, even the native support provided as part of your browser. Simply include the `debugger` keyword immediately before the line of code you suspect is causing problems in the application. When the interpreter sees this keyword, it stops execution and turns control over to the debugger so that you can see what the application is doing at that point. The debugger will provide some means of restarting the application so that you can continue execution as before.

A lot of developers also rely on the use of the `alert()` dialog box to display debugging messages during the debugging process. Yes, the advanced features of products such as Firebug make use of the `alert()` less necessary, but using the dialog box for a quick check of variable values works quite well.

# Catching Errors

The basic idea behind error trapping is to try one or more tasks to determine whether they'll work as anticipated.

## Using the try...catch block

When a line of code generates an error, the code catches the error, examines it, and attempts to fix the problem (or at least fail gracefully). The combination of error trapping and catching is called *error handling*. To handle errors, you use the `try...catch` block shown in the following code. (You can find complete code for this example in the `\Chapter 10` folder of the downloadable code as `HandleErrors.html`.)

```
<script language="JavaScript">
   try
   {
      // Generate an error.
      allert("Display a message");
   }
   catch(Err)
   {
      // Write the error information onscreen.
      document.write("<p>The Error Type is: " +
         Err.name + "</p>");
      document.write("<p>The Error Message is: " +
         Err.message + "</p>");
   }
</script>
```

In this case, the developer has made a typo that causes the program to access a nonexistent function, `allert()`. The `try` part of the block attempts to execute the function, but because the function doesn't exist, the `try` block fails.

At this point, the `catch` block takes over. Notice that the `catch` block accepts a single parameter, which is always going to be an `Error` object. The capabilities of the `Error` object vary by browser because each vendor has implemented it in a slightly different way. However, you always receive an error type and message. You can use these two features to diagnose the error type and possibly recover from it. Figure 10-1 shows typical output from this example.

**Figure 10-1:**
Browsers always provide you with an error type and message.

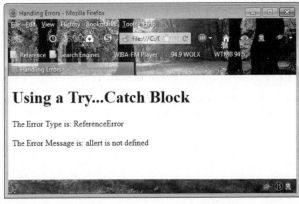

As you can see from Figure 10-1, the error trapping is extremely accurate in this case. It tells you precisely what is wrong with the code. You can't always depend on the error handling to work this well. A good guideline is to make the try block as small as possible when working with code to ensure you can find the error with greater ease and also to obtain better error information.

## Understanding the Error object

The `Error` object, like every other JavaScript object, supports some basic properties and methods that work across all browsers. Your specific browser may support special `Error` object features that aren't discussed in this book, but you can find documented by the vendor.

Although it's safe to use generic properties and methods in your production application, use vendor-specific properties and methods only as an aid for debugging the application. The following list describes the generic `Error` object properties:

- ✔ `constructor`: Displays a string showing the prototype used to define the object. In this case, you see "function Error() { [native code] }".

- ✔ `message`: Provides a message that describes the error. The quality of the message depends on which browser you use and the kind of error generated.

- ✔ `name`: Provides the name of an error type that you can use to narrow down the area in which the error occurred. The "Defining the error types" section, earlier in this chapter, describes the error type names in more detail.

- ✔ `prototype`: Provides the means for adding both properties and methods to an object.

The `Error` object also provides a number of standard methods. As with properties, vendors provide a number of non-standard methods you can employ during the debugging phase of your application. The following list describes the standard methods provided by the `Error` object:

- ✔ `toSource()`: Outputs the source of an error as a string that you can use when re-throwing an error.

- ✔ `toString()`: Outputs a string that describes the `Error` object.

- ✔ `valueOf()`: Outputs the native value of the error, normally the error message.

# *Throwing Errors*

There are times when you can't handle an error or you can't handle it in the location where the error occurs. *Throwing* an error means creating a new `Error` object that a `try...catch` block can handle. JavaScript doesn't provide any sort of default error handling. It won't tell the user something is wrong either. When working with JavaScript, you must provide the complete error-handling package. (You can find complete code for this example in the `\Chapter 10` folder of the downloadable code as `ThrowingErrors.HTML`.)

```javascript
function OptionalArgument(param)
{
    try
    {
        // Determine whether there were any params passed.
        if (arguments.length == 0)
        {
            // Throw an error.
            throw new ReferenceError("No Data Supplied");
        }

        // Create a string to hold the arguments.
        var Result = new String();

        // Process each of the arguments in turn.
        for (var i = 0; i < arguments.length; i++)
        {
            // Verify that the argument is of the right type.
            if (typeof(arguments[i]) != 'string')
            {
                throw TypeError(
                    "Incorrect Data Supplied, type:" +
                    typeof(arguments[i]) + " value: " +
                    arguments[i]);
            }

            // Add to the argument string.
            Result += arguments[i] + "<br />";
        }
    }
    catch(Err)
    {
        // Display the error onscreen and return.
        document.getElementById("Result").innerHTML =
            Err.name + "<br />" + Err.message;
        return;
    }

    // Display the results onscreen.
    document.getElementById("Result").innerHTML = Result;
}
```

The `OptionalArgument()` function example from Chapter 9 is now reworked to use error-trapping techniques. In this case, the example throws specific error types to make it possible for a developer using the function to find problems with input quickly. When the caller doesn't provide a value or the value is of the incorrect type, the application throws a specific kind of error that tells the caller precisely what went wrong. Figure 10-2 shows typical output from this example.

**Figure 10-2:** Throwing errors can make it easier to locate specific problems.

Notice that the names of the classes used in the source code precisely match those found in the "Defining the error types" section of this chapter. Always use specific errors when you can. However, you may encounter situations when none of the standard error types meet your needs. In this case, you can create a custom error type. The article at `https://developer.mozilla.org/docs/JavaScript/Reference/Global_Objects/Error` describes how to create custom error types. You also find some additional information about the standard error types as part of that article.

# Part IV
# Interacting with Users and HTML

## *Form Event Support in JavaScript*

| Event | Support | Description |
|-------|---------|-------------|
| onblur | `<form>` | Occurs when a form loses focus. This event is often used to provide support for features such as asking the user whether to save changes the user has made to form content. |
| onchange | `<input>`, `<select>`, and `<textarea>` | Occurs when the content of a form element, the control content selection, or the control's checked state have changed. You use this to perform tasks such as detecting invalid data. |
| onfocus | `<label>`, `<input>`, `<select>`, `<textarea>`, and `<button>` | Occurs when an element receives focus. Developers use this event to provide special effects, such as displaying a drop-down list of valid options that the user can choose. |
| onreset | `<form>` | Occurs when a user requests a form reset. Resetting the form returns the content to its default state. Users request a reset when the form data has become invalid or unmanageable. |
| onselect | `<input>` and `<textarea>` | Occurs when a user selects text within the element that has focus. Developers can use this event to present options such as formatting the selected content or performing tasks such as looking up the word in a dictionary. |
| onsubmit | `<form>` | Occurs when the user submits the form. Developers use this event to perform the task of transmitting the data to the server or to perform validations tasks. |

Find a step-by-step process you can use for creating CSS in an easier and faster manner at http://www.dummies.com/extras/html5programmingwithjavascript.

# In this part . . .

✔ Discover how you use the Document Object Model (DOM) to interact with users through JavaScript.

✔ Understand how events make it possible to react to user and environment changes programmatically.

✔ Use Cascading Style Sheets (CSS) to create an interesting and flexible interface for the user.

✔ See special HTML5 features you can use to create more exciting applications with special functionality using less code.

✔ Recognize how windows make it possible to separate information and make it easier for the user to work with.

# Chapter 11

# Understanding the Document Object Model

## In This Chapter

▶ Understanding the Document Object Model (DOM)

▶ Interacting with various HTML elements

▶ Using events to your advantage

▶ Changing the page appearance with styles

▶ Creating and using nodes to affect structure

*T*he Document Object Model (DOM) is the means of interaction between JavaScript and HTML5. While HTML5 provides the user interface, JavaScript provides the back-end logic used to make that interface react to user input. The two can't work well without each other. In fact, many of the examples in this book already rely on the DOM in order to provide basic output. You can't interact directly with an HTML5 tag, change the structure of a page, or modify the appearance of the content without interacting with the DOM in some way.

The DOM has multiple levels that you'll encounter in this chapter. The deepest layer is content in the form of text or objects. There are the tags (HTML) that define the interpretation of certain kinds of content. Then there are the core objects that define the actual structure (nodes) of the document. Of course, the final level is the browser itself, which interprets the tags and the structure that contains them to present information to the user onscreen. The section on using JavaScript objects in Chapter 5 presents an overview of some of this information, especially the browser objects, but this chapter goes into far greater detail so that you can better use the DOM to create exciting presentations for your users.

Interacting with the DOM isn't a single-step process either. There are ways to view the DOM and the way it affects the presentation of content. For example, you use styles to define the physical appearance of the page. You may decide to use a particular font in one location and rely on a specific color in another area. There are also events to consider. A user may hover the mouse pointer over a particular area, which creates a change in the appearance of the page that's controlled by JavaScript. This chapter presents a good overview of many of these special changes. However, you'll want to review Chapter 12 for more details about events and Chapter 13 for more details about Cascading Style Sheets (CSS). Part V of this book is where you'll see the most spectacular special effects — the purpose of this chapter is to build the basis on which you create those special effects.

# Introducing the Document Object Model (DOM)

JavaScript provides support for a number of DOM object types. The kind of DOM objects that you need to consider for this section are the HTML DOM objects — those that affect the appearance of a page onscreen. The HTML DOM objects encase the content you provide and define how the browser presents that information to the viewer.

The following list provides an overview of the most common HTML DOM objects that you use when working with JavaScript:

- ✔ **Document:** Provides access to all the elements of an entire page. Every page loaded into a browser becomes a `Document` object that you access using the `document` keyword.
- ✔ **Event:** Allows interaction with the events and event handlers associated with a page. Each element type has specific events associated with it, such as the `click` event associated with the `Button` object.
- ✔ **HTMLElement:** Provides a base class from which all HTML elements are derived. This base class defines the properties and methods that all HTML elements provide.
- ✔ **Anchor:** Represents an HTML hyperlink.
- ✔ **Area:** Defines the area within an HTML image map that's used to create clickable regions for a graphic element.
- ✔ **Base:** Specifies the default address or a default target for all links on a page.
- ✔ **Body:** Represents the `<body>` tag portion of a page, including all of the elements contained within that tag.
- ✔ **Button:** Represents a button on a page. This object is specifically associated with the `<button>` tag, rather than the `<input>` tag form of button.
- ✔ **Form:** Represents a form and includes all of the elements within that form.

✔ **Frame and IFrame:** Represents a frame (the `<frame>` tag) or inline frame (the `<iframe>` tag) and all the elements within that tag.

✔ **Frameset:** Provides access to a frameset that contains two or more frames. This object specifies only the number of rows and columns used to hold the associated frames.

✔ **Image:** Represents an embedded image.

✔ **Input Button:** Represents an `<input>` tag of type button used for building a form.

✔ **Input Checkbox:** Represents an `<input>` tag of type checkbox used for building a form.

✔ **Input File:** Represents an `<input>` tag of type file upload used for building a form. When the user clicks the button, the browser presents a browse dialog box used to locate the file.

✔ **Input Hidden:** Represents an `<input>` tag of type hidden. A hidden element is used to send data to the server but is invisible to the end user.

✔ **Input Password:** Represents an `<input>` tag of type text used for building a form. This particular form of text control displays asterisks instead of the characters the user has typed to keep passwords and other secret information hidden.

✔ **Input Radio:** Represents an `<input>` tag of type radio button used for building a form.

✔ **Input Reset:** Represents an `<input>` tag of type button used for building a form. This button type is used to reset the form to its original state.

✔ **Input Submit:** Represents an `<input>` tag of type button used for building a form. This button type is used to send data to the server.

✔ **Input Text:** Represents an `<input>` tag of type text used for building a form.

✔ **Link:** Creates an HTML link on the page.

✔ **Meta:** Defines meta data used to describe page content, automatically refresh content, or perform other tasks.

✔ **Object:** Creates a generic object used to hold non-text data such as pictures, controls, and audio.

✔ **Option:** Represents a drop-down list where the user can choose a single entry.

✔ **Select:** Represents a drop-down list where the user can choose one or more entries.

✔ **Style:** Specifies the appearance of other elements on the page.

✔ **Table:** Creates a table on the page and contains both row and cell elements used to hold content.

✔ **td and th:** Represents a data cell within a table. The `<td>` tag is used for general data items, while the `<th>` tag defines headings.

✔ **tr:** Represents a row of data cells within a table.

✔ **Textarea:** Represents a multi-row text element on the page.

This list contains objects. Most of these objects are accessed using the document object. For example, you access the `Form` objects on a page using the `document.forms` property. The object provides the means for manipulating the characteristics of the items you access using the collection stored in the property. The `document` object also provides access to some elements that aren't stored as objects, such as the `title` property. You change the document's title by assigning a new value to the `title` property.

You should also note that there's a `Body` object for the `<body>` tag within the document, but apparently not a `Head` object to access the information in the `<head>` tag. Working with the `<head>` tag can become a bit interesting at times because it involves interacting with the server — a topic discussed in Chapter 17. When accessing items in the `<head>` tag, you access the individual tags described in the following list as properties of the `document` object:

✔ `baseURI`: Specifies the base URI for a page that's found in the `<base>` tag. This property gets or sets the content of the `href` attribute.

✔ `bgSound`: Provides a means for adding a background sound to the page.

✔ `link`: Provides the means for linking external content, such as a `.CSS` file, to the current page.

✔ `meta`: Allows reading, writing, and creation of meta tags used to describe a document.

✔ `script`: Provides access to existing scripts and allows creation of new scripts on a page. If you don't provide a value for the `type` property, the browser assumes that the script relies on the JavaScript language, which is the default for all current browsers.

✔ `styleSheets`: Allows reading, writing, and creation of style information used to format the content of a document.

✔ `title`: Provides access to the `<title>` tag of a document.

It's important to note that you can access all of these elements as objects within your code by assigning the tag an `id` attribute. Using this approach often provides access to additional information about the tag. For example, if you start with a tag like this:

```
<meta id="contentType"
      http-equiv="content-type"
      content="text/html;charset=UTF-8" />
```

you can access a number of individual properties associated with the tag using code like this:

```
var Meta = document.getElementById("contentType");

document.write("<p>http-equiv: " +
               Meta.httpEquiv + "<p />");

document.write("<p>content: <br />");
var Content = Meta.content.split(";");
for (var i = 0; i < Content.length; i++)
{
    document.write(Content[i] + "<br />");
}
document.write("</p>");
```

This chapter can't discuss absolutely every aspect of the HTML DOM interface that's accessible to JavaScript. You can find an outstanding pictorial view of all the interfaces at `http://help.dottoro.com/lagstsiq.php`. This site also tells you which browsers support a particular interface — a tricky support question that all developers must answer at some point.

# Accessing Individual HTML Elements

Whether you want to change content, presentation, or interaction, you must gain access to an individual HTML element to do it. For example, if you want to change the caption on a button, you must have access to the button first. No matter what the change is, it requires that you first obtain access to the required element. The following sections discuss the techniques you use to access and interact with individual HTML elements using the HTML DOM objects, properties, and methods described earlier in the "Introducing the Document Object Model (DOM)" section.

## Modifying the output stream

Think of a physical stream when considering streams in a computer system. In a physical stream, individual atoms of water flow from one location to other along a specific path. Likewise, in a computer stream, individual bits of data flow from one location to another along a specific path. Modifying the output stream means to change the flow of data in the path. You can dam the flow by closing the stream, add a new flow by writing to it, or allow the data flow by opening the stream. The following list describes the functions associated with the output stream:

✔ `close()`: Closes an output stream that was opened using the `open()` method.

✔ `open()`: Opens a new output stream to receive content from either the `write()` or `writeln()` function.

By default, the open stream is the current document. When you use the `write()` or `writeln()` function without specifically opening a stream, the output goes to the document that's currently loaded into the browser.

✔ `write()`: Outputs the text you provide to the currently opened stream.

✔ `writeln()`: Outputs the text you provide to the currently opened stream and ends the output with a newline character, which makes the output easier to see when viewing the page source in a browser.

These four functions make it possible to modify the output stream. In fact, the `write()` function is used in quite a few examples in earlier chapters. Here's an example that combines stream modification with a few of the other concepts discussed to this point in the chapter. (You can find complete code for this example in the `\Chapter 11\HTML` folder of the downloadable code as `OutputStream.HTML`.)

```
<script language="JavaScript">
    // Get the first stylesheet associated with
    // this document.
    var Sheets = document.styleSheets[0];

    // Obtain the rules on that sheet.
    var Rules = Sheets.cssRules;

    // Display each of the rules onscreen.
    for (var i = 0; i < Rules.length; i++)
    {
        // Obtain a single rule and write the name
        // of that rule onscreen.
        var Rule = Rules[i];
        document.write("<p>" + Rule.selectorText +
                    "<br />");

        // Obtain a list of styles for the rule.
        var Styles = Rule.style;

        // Display each of the styles onscreen.
        for (var j=0; j < Styles.length; j++)
        {
            // Obtain the name of a property.
            var PropertyName = Styles[j];

            // Use the property name to locate its value
            // and display both name and value.
```

```
        document.write(PropertyName + " : " +
            Styles.getPropertyValue(PropertyName) +
            "<br />");
    }

    // End the document rule printout.
    document.write("</p>");
  }
</script>
```

The example document includes a `<style>` tag that defines the formatting for various elements. Of course, it would be nice to know how the page is formatted. Each `<style>` tag associated with a page is one item in the `styleSheets` property, which you can access using an index. This page has only one `<style>` tag so the code accesses it using the `styleSheets[0]` index. Each CSS style has one or more rules defined for it, which you can access using the `cssRules` property.

At this point, the example relies on a nested `for` loop to determine the rule name and each of the styles defined within the rule. A style property consists of a style name and a style value. You must use the style property name to access the value using the `getPropertyValue()` method. Figure 11-1 shows the output from this example.

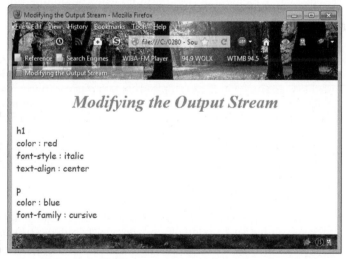

**Figure 11-1:**
Use the CSS-related properties and objects to learn about page formatting.

You can use the various methods and properties associated with the `styleSheets` property and its children to modify styles as well as read them. You can see an example of adding styles to tags in the "Working with Styles" section, later in this chapter. Chapter 13 provides additional examples of interacting with CSS by using JavaScript.

## Affecting HTML content

The whole reason to display a page is to provide content to the viewer. It may seem as if pages are all about formatting, graphics, design elements, and so on, but these items are window dressing for the main event — the content that the page provides. The following example shows some simple techniques for changing content on a page. (You can find the complete code for this example in the \Chapter 11\HTML folder of the downloadable code as ChangeContent.HTML.)

```
function ChangeContent()
{
    // Modify the <p> tag.
    document.getElementById("Change1").innerHTML =
    "Changed!";

    // Modify the <input> tag.
    document.getElementById("btnChange")
    .setAttribute("value", "Clicked");
}
```

Even though this example looks simple, it contains everything needed to change content in almost every situation. When working with an HTML element, such as the <p> tag, you use the innerHTML property to make changes. The kind of element is unimportant — this technique works equally well on <div>, <span>, and <h1> tags.

When working with a control, however, you often need to work with the value attribute instead of the innerHTML property. For example, when working with a button type <input> tag, you must change the button's caption using the value attribute, as shown in the example. This difference between elements and controls seems to confuse a lot of people. The easy way to remember what to do is to look at the appearance of the item onscreen. When an item has a graphic appearance, such as a control, you use the value attribute.

## Changing attributes

Every HTML tag can include two forms of information: content that appears between the beginning and ending of the tag and attributes. The content normally takes the form of text, but it can also include an object, such as a picture, a link to a video, or a sound. Most attributes require specific information. For example, an attribute associated with formatting requires information that describes how to format content. You can generally divide attributes into the following categories:

✔ **Content:** Defines the information that appears onscreen to the viewer.

✔ **Formatting:** Modifies the way that the information appears onscreen. For example, it could add special colors or change the appearance of the font used to display text.

✔ **Control:** Specifies the way in which a user can interact with the content. For example, you can decide that a text box will allow the viewer only to read the content rather than read and write it.

✔ **Identification:** Provides a description or other identifier to other controls or to JavaScript, so that these other entities can uniquely identify the host control.

✔ **Event:** Determines the function used to handle the specific event, such as a user click or the change of content.

JavaScript doesn't place any limitations on the sorts of changes you can make to attributes. However, you need to exercise caution because some changes will have unexpected results. For example, you can't modify the way that the controls on a page work and expect the user to make any sense of your application. The following example shows how to modify various attributes of a page. (You can find complete code for this example in the \Chapter 11\HTML folder of the downloadable code as ChangeAttributes.HTML.)

```
function EnableButton()
{
   // Reconfigure btnSecond.
   var Button2 = document.getElementById("btnSecond");
   Button2.removeAttribute("disabled");
   Button2.setAttribute("value", "Change Content");
}

function ChangeP1()
{
   // Now that the second button is enabled, use
   // it to change the <p> tag style.
   var P1 = document.getElementById("p1");
   P1.setAttribute("class", "special");
}
```

This example has two buttons. At the outset, the first button is disabled. The user can see the button, but the button isn't functional. To make the button functional, the user clicks the first button, which calls EnableButton(). To enable the button, the code removes the disabled attribute. The caption for the second button is incorrect at this point. It currently says Disabled, so the code also changes the value attribute to Change Content.

Now that the second button is enabled and has the right caption, the user can click it. The <p> tag currently uses the default CSS style for that tag. To change the text style, the code adds a `class` attribute using `set Attribute()` and sets the value to `special`. Adding the `class` attribute automatically changes the text form. Figure 11-2 shows typical output from this example.

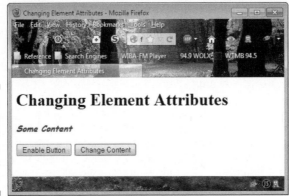

# Considering Events

It's helpful to associate events with actions. The action need not be on the user's part. In some cases, some other entity will perform the action. For example, a network failure or the completion of a file download could initiate an event. That said, Table 11-1 describes events that are associated with the HTML interface.

| Table 11-1 | Events Associated with the HTML Interface | |
|---|---|---|
| **Event** | **Type** | **Description** |
| onabort | Frame and object | The user or other entity caused the page or an individual object, such as a picture, to stop downloading. |
| onblur | Form | A form element has lost focus. This event normally occurs with the <label>, <input>, <select>, <textarea>, and <button> tags. |

| Event | Type | Description |
|-------|------|-------------|
| onchange | Form | A form element, the selection, or the checked state have changed. This event normally occurs with the `<input>`, `<select>`, and `<textarea>` tags. |
| onclick | Mouse | The user has clicked on an element. |
| ondblclick | Mouse | The user has double-clicked on an element. |
| onerror | Frame and object | An error of some type has occurred, such as the failure of a picture to load correctly. This event normally occurs with the `<object>`, `<body>`, and `<frameset>` tags. |
| onfocus | Form | A form element has received focus. This event normally occurs with the `<label>`, `<input>`, `<select>`, `<textarea>`, and `<button>` tags. |
| onkeydown | Keyboard | The user has pressed a key. |
| onkeypress | Keyboard | The user has pressed and released a key. (The event is actually fired during the key press.) |
| onkeyup | Keyboard | The user has released a key. |
| onload | Frame and object | The browser has loaded a document, a frameset, or an object. |
| onmousedown | Mouse | The user has pressed a mouse button down while pointing at a document element. |
| onmousemove | Mouse | The mouse pointer is passing over a particular document element. |
| onmouseout | Mouse | The mouse pointer has moved outside a particular document element. |
| onmouseover | Mouse | The mouse pointer has moved into the space used to hold a document element. |
| onmouseup | Mouse | The user has released a mouse button while pointing at a document element. |

*(continued)*

**Table 11-1** *(continued)*

| Event | Type | Description |
|-------|------|-------------|
| onreset | Form | The user has reset the form. |
| onresize | Frame and object | The document view has changed in size. |
| onscroll | Frame and object | The document view has scrolled. |
| onselect | Form | The user has selected some text. This event normally occurs with the `<input>` and `<textarea>` tags. Some browsers may also support this event for object selection (such as when a user selects a picture). |
| onsubmit | Form | The user has submitted the form. |
| onunload | Frame and object | The browser has unloaded a document, a frameset, or an object. |

As you can see from Table 11-1, all HTML events have one thing in common; their names begin with the word *on*. An event doesn't have to use the word *on*. This is simply a convention used to make it easier to determine that a particular control attribute is an event and requires the name of an event handler, rather than content or formatting.

One of the more interesting effects that you find on sites is the change that occurs in controls and elements when the mouse pointer hovers over them. The following example shows one way to create a mouseover effect (there are many). Developers commonly use the mouseover effect to draw the viewer's attention to an active area of the page. (You can find complete code for this example in the \Chapter 11\Events folder of the downloadable code as Mouseover.HTML.)

```
function ChangeDisplay(Id, Class)
{
    // Change the class of the specified
    // element or control to a new value.
    document.getElementById(Id).setAttribute(
        "class", Class);
}
```

All that you need to do to create a mouseover effect is change the class attribute of the control to a different style. In addition, you need to define the styles needed to make the change. However, you need to tell the control when to change its appearance. That means adding the correct event entries to the tag. Here's the `<input>` tag used for this example.

```
<input id="btnClick"
       class="Normal"
       type="button"
       value="ClickMe"
       onmouseover="ChangeDisplay('btnClick', 'Selected')"
       onmouseout="ChangeDisplay('btnClick', 'Normal')";
       onclick="SayHello()" />
```

The onmouseover event is fired when the user hovers the mouse over the button. The example changes the button's style to Selected. The onmouseout event is fired when the user moves the mouse cursor outside of the area occupied by the button. In this case, the code changes the style back to Normal. The effect is to show when the button is selected and the user can click it. It's a nice visual effect that can really help people with special visual requirements.

# Working with Styles

Styles are important because they help dress up otherwise drab pages and help viewers focus on specific content. Using the correct styles makes a page easier to read and can draw the viewer's attention to different areas as needed. The following example shows one technique for programmatically changing the styles on a page. (You can find complete code for this example in the \Chapter 11\Styles folder of the downloadable code as AddingStyles.HTML.)

```
<script language="JavaScript">
   function ChangeStyles()
   {
      // Modify the <p> tag style.
      var PTag = document.getElementById("MyPTag");
      PTag.style.fontFamily = "cursive";
      PTag.style.color = "blue";
      PTag.style.textAlign = "center";
      PTag.style.border = "medium double green";
   }
</script>
```

It's possible to change the style of any individual element by accessing that element's style property as shown. When you have access to it, you can change any style feature that you could normally change using CSS. Figure 11-3 shows typical output from this example.

CSS is a big topic, and there's no way that a part of a chapter can even hope to discuss the topic. Chapter 13 provides some additional information on CSS, but if you really want some good information on CSS itself, try the tutorial on the W3Schools.com site at `http://www.w3schools.com/css`.

# Working with Nodes

The core DOM objects deal with the structure of a page. Each page comprises various types of nodes. The section on using JavaScript objects in Chapter 5 provides you with a description of built-in objects that JavaScript supports for working directly with HMTL5 nodes. In fact, that same section has a short example showing how to use a few of these objects. The following sections provide a more detailed description of working with nodes, along with a couple additional examples on how to interact with nodes directly.

## Creating new elements

Pages comprise nodes. The entire chapter has dealt with nodes of particular types. For example, you've worked with various elements and controls, their elements, and content. All of this information is stored in a page as a series of hierarchical nodes. The hardest part of working with nodes is discovering the techniques required to access a particular node. When you understand the structure of the nodes and how to access them, you can dynamically modify pages to meet any need.

The following example shows a simple technique for adding a new element to a page. Later chapters refine these techniques, but for now, focus on just the idea that nodes appear in a hierarchical order on the page. (You can find complete code for this example in the \Chapter 11\Nodes folder of the downloadable code as ModifyNodes.HTML.)

```
function AddNodes()
{
   // Create a new <p> tag and assign values
   // to it.
   var P2 = document.createElement("p");
   P2.setAttribute("id", "p2");
   P2.innerHTML = "New Content";

   // Insert this new <p> tag before the existing
   // button.
   document.body.insertBefore(P2,
      document.getElementById("btnFirst"));

   // Create a new button and assign values to it.
   var Button2 = document.createElement("input");
   Button2.setAttribute("id", "btnSecond");
   Button2.setAttribute("type", "button");
   Button2.setAttribute("value", "Remove Nodes");
   Button2.setAttribute("onclick", "RemoveNodes()");

   // Add this new button after the existing
   // button.
   document.body.appendChild(Button2);
}
```

Using the techniques shown here and a little careful construction of your page, you can insert an element of any type anywhere you need it on the page at any time. This code adds two nodes: a <p> tag and a new button. You create both by calling createElement() with the correct tag type. After you have the new element, you can assign values to it as needed. The example shows both an element and a control. Working with other elements and controls is much the same as shown here.

The tricky part is getting the new item in the right place. In this case, the code uses insertBefore() to place the new <p> tag before the existing button on the page. This means that the button must have the id attribute defined to make it easier to locate the button on the page. You supply both the new element and the existing button as input to the call.

Adding a new element to the end is much easier. You call appendChild() with the new element. Figure 11-4 shows a typical example of the output from this application.

**Figure 11-4:**
It's possible
to change
the appear-
ance of a
page by
adding new
elements.

## Removing existing elements

This section adds onto the example shown in the preceding section. The page now has a new <p> tag and a new button. The button actually works after you add the following function to the example. (You can find complete code for this example in the \Chapter 11\Nodes folder of the download-able code as ModifyNodes.HTML.)

```
function RemoveNodes()
{
   // Remove the new <p> node that we just added.
   document.body.removeChild(
      document.getElementById("p2"));

   // Remove the new button.
   document.body.removeChild(
      document.getElementById("btnSecond"));
}
```

In both cases, the code removes the elements by calling removeChild() with the element you want to remove. To make this code work easily, you really do need to define the id attribute for each element and control on the page. Otherwise, finding the specific item you want to remove becomes difficult.

# Chapter 12

# Handling Events

· · · · · · · · · · · · · · · · · · · · · · · · · · · · · · · · · · · · · · · · · ·

· · · · · · · · · · · · · · · · · · · · · · · · · · · · · · · · · · · · · · · · · ·

*A* lot of developers make a big deal out of events and feel that they're just a bit confusing. However, all that an event really says is that something has happened. Something happens, and then your application reacts to it. There's a bit more to it than that, but if you want to avoid becoming confused about events, always think about them as saying something has happened.

This chapter examines events in detail because events are the action portion of an application — the part that a user actually sees when interacting with the application. Previous chapters show you how to perform some basic tasks when reacting to events, such as displaying a dialog box or information onscreen when a user clicks a button. This chapter goes into more detail about events and helps you see how they can make your applications easier and more exciting to use.

Most HTML controls provide sufficient events to support most user needs. In some cases, you may decide to add a custom event to your code. This chapter also provides an overview of the process for creating custom events. Using custom events can help you extend JavaScript's functionality in new ways. For example, you can use custom events to react to special features on your server or to provide the viewer with notification that certain tasks have completed. Events are useful for a broad range of tasks that the originators of JavaScript never envisioned and for which you may not find a third-party library.

# Introducing Events

Events actually occur in three parts — just as events in real life do. First, someone must proclaim the event. A tree falls in the woods. That's the event. Second, someone must be listening for the event. You're standing in the woods and hear the tree fall. In this case, you're the listener — the one who has heard the event. Third, someone must react to the event. You decide to get your axe, cut up the tree, and use it for firewood this winter. In this case, you've handled the event in a specific way. Someone else may handle the event in another way. Events, listeners, and handlers appear as part of JavaScript applications as well. The following sections describe events in greater detail.

## Performing basic event tasks

All the events that come built into JavaScript work with HTML controls in some way. You can create custom events that work with code, but that's an advanced programming technique you won't use often (except for special circumstances). In most cases, developers group the events into one of a number of categories:

- ✔ **Mouse:** Most people interact with a page by using a mouse. By adding specific mouse-related events, your application can provide visual cues, such as a mouseover, or perform tasks, such as reacting to a click.

- ✔ **Keyboard:** Almost any time you have forms on a page, you'll need to provide keyboard support through events. Simple forms may not require such support, but larger forms do. Many people keep their hands on the keyboard in the interest of efficiency, so the keyboard support you add will make your application significantly easier to use.

- ✔ **Frame or object:** Loading a document into the browser creates a frame that holds the document. In addition, you can split up a page into segments by using inline-frames (IFrames) that make it possible to load multiple documents to create a cohesive view. Whenever you load a document or an object, such as a picture, associated with a document, you need to load resources and other items the document requires at the right time. The browser generates events to tell you when it's safe to load specific resources.

- ✔ **Form:** Most sites have special pages that contain forms. For example, you may need help with a product or want to contact the company for other forms of support. Using a form makes it possible for people to communicate in a manner that supports a level of automation (so that the server can handle the information, rather than relying on human input). Form-based events make it possible to perform tasks such as submitting a form or reacting to user input when creating form content.

No matter which event you choose to handle, the event itself has an action name, such as `click`, and the listener has a name that includes the event name and the word *on,* such as `onclick`. Event handlers don't have a specific naming convention. Most developers give the event handler a practical name that reflects the task the event handler performs, such as `DisplayString()` when the event handler displays a string onscreen as the result of a mouse click. Choose names for events, listeners, and handlers carefully so that you can remember what tasks these elements perform and others can better understand your code.

Now that you have a better idea of how events are put together, it's time to discover the individual events. The following sections describe each event category and the listeners associated with that category. The listeners are important because you assign your event handler function to the listener. In JavaScript terms, the event handler subscribes to the listener.

### Understanding the mouse events

Almost every page you encounter has some sort of mouse event associated with it. Any time you see a special effect that occurs when the mouse is moved, such as dropping down a menu, the special effect is the result of handling a mouse event. The following list describes the built-in mouse events that JavaScript supports:

- ✔ `onclick`: Occurs whenever a user clicks on the element. The `onclick` and `ondblclick` events normally signify that the user wants to perform a task of some type. The associated event handlers perform a specific task-related action. An `onclick` event signifies that the user wants to perform the default action.

- ✔ `ondblclick`: Occurs whenever a user double-clicks on the element. Most developers use `ondblclick` to signify a special task-related action, such as selecting data.

- ✔ `onmousedown`: Occurs whenever a user presses the mouse button down and holds it when over the element. The `onmousedown`, `onmousemove`, and `onmouseup` events are normally used with dragging objects or other positional tasks. The drag begins with an `onmousedown`, continues with `onmousemove`, and completes with `onmouseup`.

- ✔ `onmousemove`: Occurs whenever the mouse cursor moves over the element.

- ✔ `onmouseover`: Occurs whenever the mouse cursor moves into the space occupied by the element. The `onmouseover` and `onmouseout` events are normally associated with special effects. For example, you can show a special effect on the face of a button when the user moves the mouse over it. These two events also make it possible to perform tasks such as displaying hidden menus.

✔ onmouseout: Occurs whenever the mouse cursor moves out of the space occupied by the element.

✔ onmouseup: Occurs whenever a user releases the mouse button when the pointer is over the element.

## Understanding the keyboard events

Keyboard events are seldom used by developers, which is a pity because adding keyboard support to your application makes the application significantly easier to use. *Keyboardists* — people who tend not to use the mouse for anything — gain significant speed advantages when an application sports keyboard event handling. However, keyboard support helps a broad range of other people, too. For example, many people with special accessibility needs rely heavily on keyboard support when they're unable to work well with a mouse.

The following list describes each of the built-in keyboard events that JavaScript supports:

✔ onkeydown: Occurs when the user presses a key. The onkeydown, onkeypress, and onkeyup events can work together to make it possible to use control key combinations, such as Alt+P to print. The onkeydown event indicates the control key press, the onkeypress event indicates which standard key is pressed, and the onkeyup indicates the completion of the control key sequence.

✔ onkeypress: Occurs when the user presses and then releases a key. The event actually occurs when the user presses the key.

✔ onkeyup: Occurs when the user releases a key.

## Understanding the frame or object events

Proper handling of document and object loading and unloading is essential when creating a well-behaved site. Many sites behave poorly because the application doesn't handle events such as onabort, which means the user must wait for something to finish loading before regaining control over the page. Users normally respond by closing the browser and not returning to the site. Table 12-1 describes each of the built-in frame or object events that JavaScript supports.

**Table 12-1    Frame and Object Event Support in JavaScript**

| *Event* | *Support* | *Description* |
|---|---|---|
| onabort | `<object>` | Occurs when a resource, such as a picture, has stopped loading before it has completed. This event normally occurs as the result of user action. It could signify that the user is tired of waiting for the page to load. |
| onerror | `<object>`, `<body>`, and `<frameset>` | Occurs when a resource, such as a picture, hasn't loaded correctly. This event normally indicates that there's a problem with the application code, browser connection, or resource storage. You should provide code to handle the error. |
| onload | `<object>` | Occurs when a browser completes loading a document, frameset, or other object. Developers often use this event to load supplementary resources or perform automatic tasks, such as displaying a picture. |
| onresize | `<object>`, `<body>`, and `<frameset>` | Occurs when the document is resized. This event normally occurs as the result of a user action, such as changing the browser window size. You can use this event to rearrange content for better appearance within the new display space. |
| onscroll | `<object>`, `<body>`, and `<frameset>` | Occurs when a document is scrolled. This event normally occurs as a result of user action. |
| onunload | `<body>` and `<frameset>` | Occurs when a browser unloads a document, frameset, or other object. Developers often use this event to ensure data is saved and resources are deallocated. |

### Understanding the form events

Some form events are quite practical. The user must have a means of submitting the form, so handling the `onsubmit` event is essential. Other form events are nice, but not absolutely essential. For example, the `onblur` event lets you perform tasks such as asking the user about saving form data as needed. Table 12-2 describes the built-in form events that JavaScript supports.

| Table 12-2 | Form Event Support in JavaScript | |
|---|---|---|
| *Event* | *Support* | *Description* |
| onblur | `<form>` | Occurs when a form loses focus. This event is often used to provide support for features such as asking the user whether to save changes the user has made to form content. |
| onchange | `<input>`, `<select>`, and `<textarea>` | Occurs when the content of a form element, the control content selection, or the control's checked state have changed. You use this to perform tasks such as detecting invalid data. |
| onfocus | `<label>`, `<input>`, `<select>`, `<textarea>`, and `<button>` | Occurs when an element receives focus. Developers use this event to provide special effects, such as displaying a drop-down list of valid options that the user can choose. |
| onreset | `<form>` | Occurs when a user requests a form reset. Resetting the form returns the content to its default state. Users request a reset when the form data has become invalid or unmanageable. |
| onselect | `<input>` and `<textarea>` | Occurs when a user selects text within the element that has focus. Developers can use this event to present options such as formatting the selected content or performing tasks such as looking up the word in a dictionary. |
| onsubmit | `<form>` | Occurs when the user submits the form. Developers use this event to perform the task of transmitting the data to the server or to perform validations tasks. |

*Focus* is the condition where an element of any type receives user input and attention. For example, when a text box has the focus, anything the user types will appear in that text box.

## *Working with attributes*

All the examples so far in the book have assigned a handler directly to a listener within a tag. For example, when you have a tag that contains the following code

```
    <input id="btnChange"
           type="button"
           value="Change the Styles"
           onclick="ChangeStyles()" />
```

the `ChangeStyles()` function subscribes to the `click` event through the `onclick` listener. This is a direct assignment. Your application requests the subscription as part of creating the initial tag.

However, there's another way to subscribe to events. Instead of subscribing as part of the tag, you can subscribe within your application code by interacting directly with HTML attributes. This example begins with two buttons — one that has an event handler assigned to it and another that doesn't, as shown here. (You can find complete code for this example in the \Chapter 12\ EventBasics folder of the downloadable code as UsingAttributes.HTML.)

```
<input id="btnAssign"
       type="button"
       value="Assign the Event Handler"
       onclick="AssignHandler()" />
<input id="btnClickMe"
       type="button"
       value="Click Me" />
```

In this case, clicking `btnAssign` calls the `AssignHandler()` function. On the other hand, clicking `btnClickMe` does nothing. The button depresses, but the user doesn't see anything as a result because there's nothing assigned to the `onclick` event.

To have anything happen when the user clicks `btnClickMe`, you must assign a function to the `onclick` event. The following code performs this task:

```
function AssignHandler()
{
    // Subscribe to the click event.
    document.getElementById(
        "btnClickMe").onclick=SayHello;

    // Display a subscription message.
    alert("Button Assigned");
}

function SayHello()
{
    // Display a message.
    alert("Hello There");
}
```

Notice that the code assigns `SayHello` to `onclick`. To make the assignment, you provide the name of the event handler without any parentheses. In addition, the name appears without quotes — you assign the function itself, not the name of the function.

JavaScript has a limitation in this case. You can't pass any data to the event handler except an `Event` object, which is described in the "Working with the Event object" section, later in this chapter. This makes working with events different in this situation than when working with tags. A tag allows the use of arguments, but this approach doesn't.

# Clicking to Create an Event

The `click` event is the most commonly employed event. Users click to execute tasks, to choose options, and to see details. It's important to understand that the `click` event is something that users understand well and that you must address in most cases in order to create a functional application. The following sections provide some details about event handlers as a whole and then demonstrate how to employ these details as part of a `click` event handler.

## Understanding the objects at your disposal

The examples to date haven't considered the objects that you can access while handling an event. These objects are important because they provide additional information about the event. As your applications grow in complexity, you find that you need additional information in order to process the event correctly. For example, you may subscribe a single event handler to multiple events. When this happens, the event handler code needs to detect which event it's servicing and act appropriately.

It's always an error to create a one-size-fits-all event handler. As with any function, your event handler should perform a single task well rather than multiple tasks in a mediocre manner. Some developers make the mistake of trying to cram too much functionality into a single function. When in doubt, create functions for each event your application must handle. Use multiple assignments to a single event handler only when such an assignment makes sense. The following sections describe the event-related objects in further detail.

### Working with the Event object

Any event handler can receive an `Event` object that describes the event. Even when you programmatically assign an event handler to an event, the event handler still has access to the `Event` object. The `Event` object can tell you a number of things about the application. It provides access to constants, properties, and methods.

The three constants deal with how your application works with a particular browser. When two elements, a parent and a child, both target the same event handler, the browser must choose which element should be serviced by the event handler first. There are two completely different strategies for accomplishing this task: capturing and bubbling. The strategy that your application sees depends on the browser you're working with. A discussion of the details of these strategies is complex, and you should write your code without any thought of a particular element-processing order in mind. Because of the esoteric nature of this topic, it isn't discussed in this book. You can read more about these strategies at `http://www.quirksmode.org/js/events_order.html`.

The following list describes the `Event` object constants:

- ✔ `CAPTURING_PHASE`: The browser is using the capturing method, and the parent element is serviced first.

- ✔ `AT_TARGET`: The current event is being serviced by the event handler. This constant applies to every browser no matter which strategy the browser applies.

- ✔ `BUBBLING_PHASE`: The browser is using the bubbling method, where the child element is serviced first.

The properties that the `Event` object provides can tell you some interesting facts about the event, such as which element is calling and when it called the event handler. Discovering details about the elements that have called the event handler can help the event handler provide better processing. The following list describes the properties associated with the `Event` object:

- ✔ `bubbles`: Returns `true` when there's a bubbling event taking place.

- ✔ `cancelable`: Returns `true` when the application can cancel an event, so that its default action can't occur. There are many reasons to cancel an event, but most of them involve error conditions of some sort. For example, a user might not enter data correctly, so submitting the data would result in an error, and the application can cancel the submission.

- ✔ `currentTarget`: Provides access to an object that defines the element that called the event handler. In this case, the focus is on the event listeners rather than directly on the element.

✔ `eventPhase`: Specifies the current event phase as a numeric value. You use the `Event` object constants to perform a comparison in this case.

✔ `target`: Provides access to an object that defines the element that called the event handler. In this case, the focus is directly on the element rather than any event listeners associated with it.

✔ `timeStamp`: Defines the time at which the event occurred in milliseconds. You must use one of the `Date` object methods to convert the output of this property into a human-readable form.

Even though the standard says that `timeStamp` should contain the number of milliseconds since January 1, 1970, many browsers provide other values, such as the number of milliseconds since the browser first started. Consequently, you can't use this value to obtain a specific time unless the browser and platform support this feature. However, you can always use this property to determine the time between events.

✔ `type`: Provides the name of the event. For example, if the user clicks a button and the `onclick` listener calls the event handler, you see click as output.

The `Event` object methods tend to change the way in which the application processes the event. For example, an application may choose to cancel an event if the conditions for completing it are unacceptable. The following list describes each of the `Event` object methods in more detail:

✔ `initEvent()`: Defines specifics about an event:

- Event type

- The event's ability to bubble

- Whether the application can cancel the event's default action

✔ `preventDefault()`: Cancels the event's default action. In other words, the actions that normally take place by default won't take place.

✔ `stopPropagation()`: Stops further propagation of the event. Generally, this means that the application won't call any additional event handlers. You can use this feature when an event handler has answered all of the event's needs and there's no additional processing required.

### Working with the Document event object

The `Document` event object is unique in that it lets you create other events. You use the `createEvent()` method to create an event that could simulate something like a mouse click. Even though this object provides just one method, it's a powerful method. The only way to really understand this particular object is to see it in action. The following example performs three tasks:

✔ Provides a means of generating a simulated click

✔ Adds an event handler that prevents the default action of simulating the click

✔ Removes the event handler that prevents the default action of simulating the click

This is a somewhat advanced example, but it's also incredibly useful code because you can use it to add automation to your applications that will prove helpful to less skilled users. (You can find complete code for this example in the \Chapter 12\EventBasics folder of the downloadable code as SimulateClick.HTML.)

```
function SimulateClick()
{
   // Create the event.
   var ClickEvent = document.createEvent("MouseEvents");

   // Configure the event.
   ClickEvent.initMouseEvent(
      "click", // Event type
      true,    // Can use the bubble technique?
      true,    // Is this event cancelable?
      window,  // View, should always be window.
      0,       // Number of mouse clicks.
      0,       // Screen X coordinate
      0,       // Screen Y coordinate
      0,       // Client X coordinate
      0,       // Client Y coordinate
      false,   // Ctrl Key Pressed?
      false,   // Alt Key Pressed?
      false,   // Shift Key Pressed?
      false,   // Meta Key Pressed?
      0,       // Number of button clicked.
      null);   // Related target

   // Obtain a reference to the object.
   var TestCheck = document.getElementById("chkTest");

   // Perform the click and record whether the click
   // was cancelled by another handler.
   var Succeeded = TestCheck.dispatchEvent(ClickEvent);

   // Display the result of the simulation onscreen.
   if (Succeeded)
   {
      alert("The click succeeded!");
   }
   else
   {
      alert("The click was cancelled!");
   }
}
```

The code begins by obtaining a reference to the target event object, which is MouseEvents in this case. The initMouseEvent() function takes a host of arguments — all of which are required to make the example work. You already know the purpose of most of those arguments. However, you can read more about them at https://developer.mozilla.org/docs/DOM/event.initMouseEvent. The next section of this chapter provides additional documentation about this particular event object.

After the code creates an event, it's time to obtain a reference to the control that will use the event. In this case, the example uses a check box named chkTest. To issue the event, the application calls dispatchEvent() with the event, ClickEvent, as the argument. This act *fires* (issues) the event. The return value determines whether the event succeeded. When using the default listener and handler, the check box is either selected or deselected, depending on its previous state.

The code ends by determining the return status of Succeeded. If nothing prevents the event from succeeding, Succeeded is true, and the first alert() displays onscreen. Otherwise, you see the second alert() message. Of course, the question now is how to prevent the default action from occurring. The following code performs this task:

```
function PreventDefault(event)
{
   // Prevent the default action.
   event.preventDefault();
}

function AddHandler()
{
   // Obtain an object reference.
   var TestCheck = document.getElementById("chkTest");

   // Add the event handler.
   TestCheck.addEventListener(
      "click",           // Type of event
      PreventDefault,    // Name of the event listener.
      false);            // Use the capture technique?
}

function RemoveHandler()
{
   // Obtain an object reference.
   var TestCheck = document.getElementById("chkTest");

   // Add the event handler.
   TestCheck.removeEventListener(
      "click",           // Type of event
      PreventDefault,    // Name of the event listener.
      false);            // Use the capture technique?
}
```

When the `PreventDefault()` function is active, it accepts an `Event` object (see the preceding section) as input. This event handler automatically stops the default action from happening by calling `preventDefault()`. The check box isn't selected, and `Succeeded` is set to `false` when this happens.

However, the `PreventDefault()` function isn't active at the outset. To make it active, the application calls `AddHandler()`, which adds an event listener using the `addEventListener()` function to the check box, `chkTest`. Compare this approach with the technique discussed in the "Working with attributes" section, earlier in the chapter, and you find both methods work equally well, but this approach lets you determine whether the browser can use the capture technique for working with multiple event handlers. To remove the event handler, the application calls `RemoveHandler()`, which reverses the process by calling `removeEventListener()` with the same arguments as before.

### *Working with the Mouse and Keyboard event objects*

The `Mouse` and `Keyboard` event objects are essentially the same. They provide the same properties and methods. The only difference is that you use one with a mouse and the other with the keyboard. The initialization technique also differs. The preceding section shows an example of using the mouse form of this object. The following list describes the properties used by both objects:

- ✔ `altKey`: Returns `true` when the user pressed the Alt key at the time the event was triggered.

- ✔ `button`: Specifies which mouse button was pressed by the user. JavaScript recognizes up to three standard buttons as follows:

  - 0: Left mouse button (Internet Explorer 8 and earlier return a value of 1 for this button; newer versions of Internet Explorer return 0 as expected)

  - 1: Middle mouse button (Internet Explorer 8 and earlier return a value of 4 for this button; newer versions of Internet Explorer return 1 as expected)

  - 2: Right mouse button

  When working with a left-handed mouse, the parameter values are reversed, which means that the left button now returns a value of 2, and the right button now returns a value of 0. You would need to provide some sort of configuration screen and store user values as part of a cookie in order to support a left-handed mouse because the mouse doesn't provide any sort of identification that JavaScript can capture.

- ✔ `clientX`: Provides the horizontal pixel value of the mouse pointer, relative to the current window, when an event was triggered.

- ✔ `clientY`: Provides the vertical pixel value of the mouse pointer, relative to the current window, when an event was triggered.

✔ ctrlKey: Returns true when the user pressed the Ctrl key at the time the event was triggered.

✔ keyIdentifier: Provides a numeric identifier of the key the user pressed.

✔ keyLocation: Provides a numeric identifier of the physical location of the key that the user pressed on the keyboard. This information may seem useless at first. However, you can use this information to perform tasks such as detecting whether the right or left Alt key is pressed.

✔ metaKey: Returns true when the user pressed the meta key when the event was triggered.

The meta key is browser- and platform-specific. When working with the Macintosh, the meta key is commonly the Mac (Command) key with either Firefox or Safari. A few people have reported that pressing the diamond key on MIT keyboards also triggers the meta key. You can find out more about the meta key for Linux systems at http://askubuntu.com/questions/19558/what-are-the-meta-super-and-hyper-keys. Apparently, pressing the Windows key on a Windows system doesn't trigger this property with any browser. The recommendation is to avoid using this particular property because it works randomly or not at all.

✔ relatedTarget: Specifies whether there's an element related to the element that triggered the event. For example, when working with a mouseover event (see the "Understanding the mouse events" section, earlier in the chapter, for details), this property contains the identifier of the element that the mouse just exited. Normally, this property contains null to indicate that there's no related target.

✔ screenX: Provides the horizontal pixel value of the mouse pointer, relative to the screen as a whole, when an event was triggered.

✔ screenY: Provides the vertical pixel value of the mouse pointer, relative to the screen as a whole, when an event was triggered.

✔ shiftKey: Returns true when the user pressed the Shift key when the event was triggered.

Not every browser supports every JavaScript feature. Some browsers don't support the mouse and keyboard event objects. It's essential that you test your application on the platforms your clients will use with the browsers that you anticipate the client using.

## Passing parameters to the event handler function

Under certain conditions, JavaScript automatically assigns an Event object to an event handler. The main conditions are that you must assign the event handler programmatically and the event handler must provide a parameter to receive the Event object. Therefore, this example begins with an <input> tag, coupled with a script to assign the event handler as shown here. (You can find complete code for this example in the \Chapter 12\EventBasics folder of the downloadable code as PassingParameters.HTML.)

```
<input id="btnClickMe"
       type="button"
       value="Click Me" />
<script language="JavaScript">
   // Subscribe to the click event.
   document.getElementById(
      "btnClickMe").onclick=CheckEvent;
</script>
```

In this case, the code simply assigns CheckEvent to the click event for btn-ClickMe. Notice that you don't specify any sort of argument as part of the assignment.

The event handler does define an event parameter. In addition, because this event handler contains code to track the time differential between clicks, it also requires a global variable to hold the last event time. Here's the code you need to test the use of the Event object in this case:

```
// Create a global variable to hold the event time.
var LastEvent = 0;

function CheckEvent(event)
{
   // Obtain an event time value.
   var EventDifference;
   if (LastEvent == 0)
   {
      EventDifference = "First Click";
   }
   else
   {
      EventDifference = event.timeStamp - LastEvent;
   }

   // Save the last event time.
   LastEvent = event.timeStamp;

   // Display statistics about the event.
   document.getElementById("Output").innerHTML =
      "Bubbles? " + event.bubbles +
      "<br />Cancelable? " + event.cancelable +
      "<br />ID: " + event.currentTarget.id +
      "<br />Time: " + EventDifference +
      "<br />Event Type: " + event.type;
}
```

The code shows the kind of information available to you when processing an event. For example, you can determine all the relevant facts about the event source, including the kind of event that occurred. Depending on the sort of event that called the event handler, you can also obtain information about which key the user pressed or the current position of the mouse.

Notice that the example is careful to treat the `timeStamp` property as a time differential, not an absolute time. Testing shows that results vary when using the `timeStamp` property, so you need to assume that you can determine only a time differential from it. Figure 12-1 shows typical output from this example.

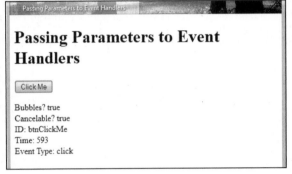

**Figure 12-1:**
The Event object provides all sorts of information to your application.

# Pressing a Key

One of the big obstacles for keyboardists is performing tasks quickly with browser-based applications. A keyboardist makes efficient use of a computer by using the keyboard and eschewing the mouse. To access different fields on a form, a keyboardist relies on Alt+Key keystrokes. With this in mind, you could create a form that accommodates the keyboardist. Here's the partial form that's used for this example. (You can find complete code for this example in the `\Chapter 12\EventObjects` folder of the downloadable code as `PressingKey.HTML`.)

```
<form id="TestForm"
      onkeypress="CheckStrokes(event)">
   <h1>Processing Keystrokes</h1>
   <div>
      <label>(N)ame: </label>
      <input id="txtName"
             type="text" />
   </div>
   <div>
      <label>(A)dress: </label>
      <input id="txtAddress"
             type="text" />
   </div>
   <div>
```

```
            <label>(C)ity: </label>
            <input id="txtCity"
                   type="text" />
    </div>
</form>
<script language="JavaScript">
    document.getElementById("txtName").focus();
</script>
```

Whenever a user presses a key combination in this form, the application calls
`CheckStrokes()` to determine which keys are pressed. Notice the inclusion
of the special `event` keyword here to pass the `Event` object to the event
handler. The short script at the end of the form simply sets the focus on the
first field in the form, which is the Name field. The parentheses around each
of the characters in the `<label>` element tell the user which Alt+Key combination to use to access that field.

You don't want *speed key* processing (the act of looking for Alt key combinations) to slow the application, so the `CheckStrokes()` function has to be as
short as possible. The following code performs the required task quickly and
efficiently:

```
Function CheckStrokes(event)
{
    // Check for an Alt key press.
    if (event.altKey)
    {
        // Determine which character the user pressed
        // and perform the required focus change.
        switch
          (String.fromCharCode(event.charCode).toUpperCase())
        {
            case "A":
                document.getElementById("txtAddress").focus();
                break;
            case "C":
                document.getElementById("txtCity").focus();
                break;
            case "N":
                document.getElementById("txtName").focus();
                break;
        }
    }
}
```

The first task is to determine whether the user has pressed the Alt key. If so,
`event.altKey` is `true`. The second task is to convert `event.charCode`
from a numeric value that reflects the Unicode number of a character, to
an actual character by calling `fromCharCode()`. To ensure consistent
handling of the keystrokes, the result is converted to uppercase by calling
`toUpperCase()`. The code then uses a simple `switch` statement to choose
which control should receive focus.

# Creating Custom Events

The standard events provided with JavaScript perform well for most common tasks. For example, you must have a method of performing a click, and JavaScript provides a standard event to handle this need. However, there are times when you need to pass information that the makers of JavaScript can't foresee. In this case, you must create a custom event. The following sections discuss how to work with custom events.

## Working with the CustomEvent object

The CustomEvent object provides the means for creating a new event — one that isn't part of JavaScript by default. The CustomEvent object is deceptively simple. All it contains are the two properties described in the following list:

✔ **Event name:** A string containing the name that you want to use for the event. The name can be anything you want, but it can't contain any whitespace characters, such as the space. Use an underscore (_), if desired, to separate words.

✔ **Event data:** An object literal that contains the data you want to pass as part of the event. This part of a custom event can become quite complex because you can pass any amount of data in any form you want, as long as the data fulfills the object literal format. The event data comes in two forms:

- *Standard data:* You can provide information for any of the properties supported by the standard Event object described in the "Working with the Event object" section, earlier in this chapter. Most developers define the bubbles and cancelable properties as a minimum.

- *Custom data:* A custom event can contain custom data in any form. You must avoid using the names of any standard properties. For example, you can't give a custom property the name bubbles. Many developers use the detail property to contain details about the custom event, but this is only a convention, and you're free to use any form you see fit.

## Creating the custom event code

JavaScript makes it quite easy to create custom events of your own. These events could be anything. For example, you might want to provide some means of handling user input on a page that posts the information on the company's site, as well as sending it to administrators by using e-mail. There are many uses for custom events, but they all follow the same pattern. This example begins the global custom event object shown here. (You can find complete code for this example in the \Chapter 12\CustomEvent folder of the downloadable code as CreateEvent.HTML.)

```
// Define a new event.
var SpecialEvent = new CustomEvent(
   "SpecialMessage",
   {
      detail:
      {
         message: "Hello There",
         time: new Date()
      },
      bubbles: true,
      cancelable: true
   });
```

Notice that this event relies on a form of object literal. (See the section on working with object literals in Chapter 5 for details.) However, notice how detail is actually a nested object literal. You can nest information as many levels deep as needed. If you later want to change some feature of the event, you can do so. For example, to change the message, you would use code similar to this:

```
SpecialEvent.detail.message = "A new message!";
```

Now that you have a custom event to use, you need to go through three phases to implement it. First, you must assign the event to a control. The example uses a label and tells the application to make the assignment as part of the form loading process using: <body onload="AssignEvent()">. Here's the code you need to assign the event to the label:

```
function AssignEvent()
{
   // Obtain the object reference.
   var Label = document.getElementById("CustomLabel");

   // Assign an event to the object.
   Label.addEventListener(
      "SpecialMessage", HandleEvent, false);
}
```

The "Working with the Document event object" section of this chapter shows this same technique used for a standard click event. Here you see it used for the SpecialMessage custom event. Whether you assign a standard or custom event, the technique is the same.

The second phase of implementing a custom event is firing the event. This example relies on a button to perform the task, but any action could fire the event. All you need is an action where you can attach code to perform the task of firing the event. Here's the event firing code used for this example:

```
function FireEvent()
{
    // Obtain the object reference.
    var Label = document.getElementById("CustomLabel");

    // Fire the event.
    Label.dispatchEvent(SpecialEvent);
}
```

The `dispatchEvent()` function performs the actual work. Notice that you fire the event using the event object you created earlier. If you had wanted, you could assign values to any of the content found in the custom event. For that matter, you could create new content as needed as long as the recipient knows how to work with the new content.

The third phase of implementing a custom event is providing the event handler. The event handler receives the custom event from the control that's assigned to the event handler. Here's the event handler used in this case:

```
function HandleEvent(event)
{
    // Display the event information.
    document.getElementById("CustomLabel").innerHTML =
        "Control: " + event.currentTarget.id +
        "<br />Message: " + event.detail.message +
        "<br />Time sent: " +
        event.detail.time.toTimeString();
}
```

All that this event handler does is display the custom event information onscreen. Figure 12-2 shows typical output from this example.

**Figure 12-2:**
Custom events can contain any information needed to perform a task.

Creating a Custom Event

# Creating a Custom Event

Control: CustomLabel
Message: Hello There
Time sent: 14:05:49 GMT-0600 (Central Standard Time)

Fire Custom Event

# Chapter 13

# Connecting with Style: JavaScript and CSS

### In This Chapter

▶ Interacting with HTML-based formatting

▶ Creating HTML style elements dynamically

▶ Moving and positioning HTML elements

▶ Developing a JavaScript-based menu

*A*t one time, HTML pages were plain or used inconsistent tags for formatting content, such as the outdated `<center>` tag. Many of these tags are deprecated (no longer available) in HTML5. For example, the `<center>` tag is no longer available. (See `http://www.w3schools.com/tags/tag_center.asp` for details.) Cascading Style Sheets (CSS) provide a means for formatting HTML content in a consistent manner that works well with all newer browsers. Using CSS makes the job of the page designer and application developer easier while providing significantly more flexibility in formatting options. You can provide CSS in these ways:

✔ As part of HTML tags

✔ Within the current page

✔ As an external file

Using CSS also makes it possible to support special user needs. A user can simply substitute a CSS file to meet any special requirements, such as larger fonts. In short, CSS is a big win for anyone working with HTML documents. This chapter doesn't describe CSS in detail — that would require an entire book of its own. However, you can find a great CSS tutorial on the W3Schools site at `http://www.w3schools.com/css/` if you need a refresher. Using a CSS generator can also help. You can find these applications in a number of locations online, such as `http://www.css3.me/` and `http://css3 generator.com/`. To gain a fuller understanding of how CSS works with HTML, you can read *HTML, XHTML & CSS For Dummies,* 7th Edition by Ed Tittel and Jeff Noble (Wiley).

This chapter does describe how you can programmatically interact with CSS, modify it as needed, or even create new styles dynamically. You also discover how to produce some special effects by using CSS. Many developers work with external files when interacting with CSS. You can do that with JavaScript, but in the interest of making the examples clear, this chapter will work with CSS as part of HTML tags or within the header of the current page.

# Changing HTML Elements

The focus of CSS is on the HTML element. CSS answers the question of how a <p> tag appears to the viewer. The following sections discuss two methods of working with HTML elements statically: as part of the individual tag and within a header that defines a style for all tags of the same type.

It's a mistake to assume that all browsers render CSS precisely the same. Two browsers on the same system running the same operating system often offer slightly different presentations. In addition, it's an error to think that a browser will provide a consistent appearance on all platforms it supports. For example, Firefox presents slightly different displays when using Mac OS X, Linux, and Windows. A browser can also show the page differently when device constraints demand. A page shown on a smartphone screen differs from the same page shown on a PC. Think of CSS as more of a guideline than an absolute requirement.

## Working with HTML tags

One of the options for configuring the HTML tags on a page is to grab all the tags of a certain type and format them as part of a loop. That's what the following example does. (You can find complete code for this example in the \Chapter 13\HTMLElements folder of the downloadable code as Tags.HTML.)

```
function ChangeStyles()
{
    // Modify the <h1> tag style.
    var Header = document.getElementsByTagName("h1")
    for (var i = 0; i < Header.length; i++)
    {
        Header[i].style.fontFamily = "Arial";
        Header[i].style.fontSize = "45px";
        Header[i].style.fontWeight = "bold";
        Header[i].style.color = "green";
        Header[i].style.textAlign = "center";

        Header[i].style.marginLeft = "20px";
        Header[i].style.marginRight = "20px";
        Header[i].style.border = "medium double green";
    }
```

```
// Modify the <p> tag style.
var Para = document.getElementsByTagName("p");
for (var i= 0; i < Para.length; i++)
{
    Para[i].style.fontFamily = "serif";
    Para[i].style.fontStyle = "italic";
    Para[i].style.fontSize = "1em";
    Para[i].style.color = "blue";
}
}
```

In this case, the example uses `getElementsByTagName()` to obtain an array of all of the elements of a particular type on a page. The example formats both the `<h1>` and `<p>` tags on the page. When you have a list of these elements, you can format each element in turn by using a `for` loop as shown. (Chapter 9 discusses loops in detail.) The example shows a number of common formatting tasks, including setting the margins for an element.

When you're working with graphic additions, such as a border, it helps to have an understanding of where the various styles fit into the picture. For example, the *margin* affects the distance between the edge of the screen and the border, and *padding* affects the distance between the border and the content it encloses. You can find a good discussion of this topic at `http://www.w3.org/TR/CSS2/box.html`.

You should notice a few features in this example. A `fontFamily` property can contain a family name, such as Arial, or a generic name, such as serif. The font size can appear in pixels (px) or ems (one em is equal to 16 px), amongst other value types. You can also use relative measures for the font size, such as small. Figure 13-1 shows typical output from this example.

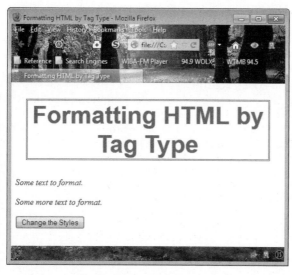

**Figure 13-1:** Formatting elements as a group means you don't need to know specific element identifiers.

## Working with heading styles

Most developers are used to working with a `<style>` tag that appears in the `<head>` element of a page. JavaScript is able to construct a `<style>` tag for you programmatically as shown in the following example. (You can find complete code for this example in the `\Chapter 13\HTMLElements` folder of the downloadable code as `HeadingTag.HTML`.)

```
function ChangeStyles()
{
    // Obtain access to the header.
    Head = document.getElementsByTagName("head")[0];

    // Create a <style> tag.
    StyleTag = document.createElement("style");

    // Set the <style> tag type.
    StyleTag.type = "text/css";

    // Create a variable to hold the style information.
    var Styles =
        "h1 {font-family:Arial;font-size:45px;" +
        "font-weight:bold;color:green;text-align:center;" +
        "margin-left:20px;margin-right:20px;" +
        "border:medium double green;}" +
        "p {font-family:serif;font-style:italic;" +
        "font-size:1em;color:blue}";

    // Add the style to the <style> tag.
    StyleTag.appendChild(document.createTextNode(Styles));

    // Add the <style> tag to the heading.
    Head.appendChild(StyleTag);
}
```

The results from this example are precisely the same as the example in the preceding section. The difference is that the formatting information appears in the `<style>` tag rather than with each element individually. To make this example work, you construct the `<style>` tag content as a string. The application then uses the `createTextNode()` function to turn the string into a text node and inserts it as content for the `<style>` tag, `StyleTag`, using `appendChild()`. To add the `<style>` tag to the `<head>` element, the code calls the `appendChild()` function a second time.

## Working with IDs

The techniques shown in the two preceding sections of the chapter work well when you want to modify the appearance of a group of tags. To change the appearance of specific tags, you must work with specific IDs as shown in the following example. (You can find complete code for this example in the `\Chapter 13\HTMLElements` folder of the downloadable code as `ElementID.HTML`.)

```
function ChangeStyles()
{
   // Modify the <h1> tag style.
   var Header = document.getElementById("Header");
   Header.style.fontFamily = "Arial";
   Header.style.fontSize = "45px";
   Header.style.fontWeight = "bold";
   Header.style.color = "green";
   Header.style.textAlign = "center";
   Header.style.marginLeft = "20px";
   Header.style.marginRight = "20px";
   Header.style.border = "medium double green";

   // Modify the <p> tag style.
   var Para = document.getElementById("Paragraph");
   Para.style.fontFamily = "serif";
   Para.style.fontStyle = "italic";
   Para.style.fontSize = "1em";
   Para.style.color = "blue";
}
```

In this case, only the elements with the specific identifiers provided by the code to the `getElementById()` function are modified in appearance. For example, when the code calls `document.getElementById("Header")`, `Header` receives a reference to the object with an `id` of `Header`, and the changes that follow only affect that particular object. The output is similar to the other two examples except the second paragraph remains unchanged.

# Building Dynamic HTML Elements

One of the building blocks for creating special effects for any page is the ability to make dynamic changes to the page. For example, you may want to create a special effect for the selected element as shown in the following example. (You can find complete code for this example in the `\Chapter 13\Dynamic` folder of the downloadable code as `Dynamic.HTML`.)

```
function ChangeStyles(event)
{
   // Obtain a reference to the element.
   var ThisElement = document.getElementById(
      event.currentTarget.id);

   // Check the event type.
   if (event.type == "mouseover")
   {
      // Change the target element's CSS class.
      ThisElement.setAttribute("class", "Selected");
   }
   else
   {
      ThisElement.setAttribute("class", "Normal");
   }
}
```

This code accepts an event as input. The code obtains a reference to the
element provided by the Event object. It then checks the event.type property to determine what type of event has happened (either a mouseover or
a mouseout). The type of event determines what sort of formatting the element uses.

Of course, it would be handy to provide some sort of automation for assigning an event handler for the onmouseover and onmouseout events. The following code performs this task for you:

```
<script language="JavaScript">
   // Obtain a list of elements that use the <p> tag.
   var ElementList = document.getElementsByTagName("p");

   // Process each of these tags in turn.
   for(var i = 0; i < ElementList.length; i++)
   {
      // Add handlers for the mouseover and mouseout
      // events.
      ElementList[i].onmouseover = ChangeStyles;
      ElementList[i].onmouseout = ChangeStyles;
   }
</script>
```

This is another variant of interacting with a group of elements that use
the same tag — the <p> tag in this case. The code obtains an array of
these elements by calling getElementsByTagName(). It then assigns the
ChangeStyles() function to the onmouseover and onmouseout properties of each element. The result is that each <p> tag on the page reacts when
you hover the mouse over it.

# Animating and Positioning HTML Elements

It's interesting to see what sorts of things you can do with a combination of CSS and JavaScript. For example, you could create an application that makes it possible for the user to drag and drop items around on the display. The following example is a little simpler than that. In this case, the code moves a button in response to a click. (You can find complete code for this example in the \Chapter 13\Dynamic folder of the downloadable code as Programmatic.HTML.)

```
function ChangeStyles()
{
   // Obtain a reference to the button.
   var ThisButton = document.getElementById("btnChange");

   // Change its absolute position onscreen.
   ThisButton.style.position = "absolute";
   ThisButton.style.left = "150px";
   ThisButton.style.top = "250px";
}
```

The code works by obtaining a reference to the button element, btnChange. It then sets the positioning for that element to absolute and makes changes to both the left and top properties. The result is that the control moves onscreen.

# Creating JavaScript-Based Menus

All of the previous examples in this chapter prepare you in some way for this final example — a simple menu system that relies on a combination of CSS and JavaScript. The concept is straightforward. When you hover a mouse pointer over a menu, it opens any submenu and lets you choose one of the options on the submenu, if desired. Moving the mouse to a different menu closes the first submenu and opens another (assuming there's one to open). The following sections take a three-phase approach to creating the menu:

✔ Define the HTML used to display the menu elements.

✔ Create the CSS required to make stylistic changes to the elements.

✔ Design code to make the menus open and close as needed.

The URLs used for this example aren't meant to be functional. If they actually end up taking you anywhere, it's purely coincidental. (You can find complete code for this example in the \Chapter 13\Menus folder of the downloadable code as JavaScriptMenu.HTML.)

# Designing the HTML

This example is based on heavily formatted lists. There are many other ways to create menus, but this approach works quite well. Theoretically, you could easily store the menus on disk or in a database and use JavaScript to construct the required list code for you. However, for now, concentrate on the fact that this menu system is static and provides specific options as shown in the following code:

```html
<ul id="menu">
   <li id="Item1">
      <a href="http://www.somewhere.com"
         onmouseover="CloseMenu()">Home</a>
   </li>
   <li id="Item2">
      <a href="http://www.somewhere.com"
         onmouseover="OpenMenu('Item2Submenu')">Events</a>
      <ul id="Item2Submenu"
          onmouseover="KeepSubmenu()"
          onmouseout="CloseMenu()">
         <a href="http://www.somewhere.com">Event 1</a>
         <a href="http://www.somewhere.com">Event 2</a>
         <a href="http://www.somewhere.com">Event 3</a>
      </ul>
   </li>
   <li id="Item3">
      <a href="http://www.somewhere.com"
         onmouseover="OpenMenu('Item3Submenu')">
            Contact Us
      </a>
      <ul id="Item3Submenu"
          onmouseover="KeepSubmenu()"
          onmouseout="CloseMenu()">
         <a href="http://www.somewhere.com">Telephone</a>
         <a href="http://www.somewhere.com">Mail</a>
         <a href="http://www.somewhere.com">E-mail</a>
      </ul>
   </li>
</ul>
```

There are three main menu options: Home, Events, and Contact Us. The Home menu lacks submenus. The Events menu does have a submenu consisting of Event 1, Event 2, and Event 3. The Contact menu provides Telephone, Mail, and E-mail as submenus. Figure 13-2 shows how the formatted menu will eventually appear.

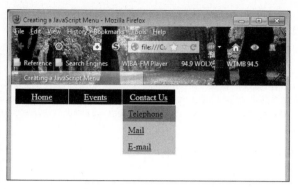

## Defining the styles

The lists that you created in the preceding section won't look much like a
menu at the outset. The secret is the formatting provided by the CSS that
follows:

```css
<style type="text/css">
    #menu
    {
        margin: 0;
        padding: 0;
    }
    #menu li
    {
        margin: 0;
        padding: 0;
        list-style: none;
        float: left;
    }
    #menu li a
    {
        display: block;
        margin: 0 1px 0 0;
        padding: 4px 10px;
        width: 80px;
        background: black;
        color: white;
        text-align: center;
    }
    #menu li a:hover
    {
        background: green;
    }
    #menu ul
```

```
    {
        position: absolute;
        visibility: hidden;
        margin: 0;
        padding: 0;
        background: grey;
        border: 1px solid white;
    }
    #menu ul a
    {
        position: relative;
        display: block;
        margin: 0;
        padding: 5px 10px;
        width: 80px;
        text-align: left;
        background: lightgrey;
        color: black;
    }
    #menu ul a:hover
    {
        background: #7f7fff;
    }
</style>
```

This CSS code is presented in the order of detail. The #menu formatting is
for the topmost <ul id="menu"> tag. The main menu items are formatting
in turn by the #menu li and #menu li a styles. When a user hovers the
mouse over a main menu item, the #menu li a:hover style changes the
background color to green. The submenu formatting is accomplished by the
#menu ul and #menu ul a styles. Again, when the user hovers the mouse
over a submenu item, the #menu ul a:hover style defines a color change
for that menu item.

The reason the example uses this approach for producing the special effects
for this menu system is to demonstrate that it's possible. You always have
options when creating special effects. When you find that one approach isn't
working well, try another approach and you may find it works better.

## Creating the JavaScript functions

The JavaScript functions have to perform four tasks. The first task is to track
the status of the menu system and ensure that the menu remains stable. The
following code performs that task:

```
// Holds the current open menu item.
var Item;

// Holds the timeout value.
var Timer;

// Hide the menu after clicking outside it.
document.onclick = CloseMenu;
```

The Item variable contains the current menu item. Timer holds a value that determines when a submenu will close automatically. If you don't provide this value, the menu behaves quite erratically, and users may find it difficult to select items. Finally, the code must provide a means to automatically close menu items when a user clicks outside the menu system, which is what the document.onclick = CloseMenu assignment does.

The second task is to provide a means for opening the submenus, which are hidden at the outset. Making the submenu visible allows access to the entries it provides. The following code shows a technique for opening the submenus:

```
function OpenMenu(Menu)
{
   // If there is an item that is open, close it.
   if (Item)
   {
      Item.style.visibility = "hidden";
   }

   // Obtain an item reference for the new menu.
   Item = document.getElementById(Menu);

   // Make it visible.
   Item.style.visibility = "visible";
}
```

Notice that the code first checks to ensure that the previous submenu is actually closed. Otherwise, the user could see two open submenus, which would definitely be confusing. After the code makes the previous submenu hidden, it makes the current submenu visible. In both cases, the example relies on the visibility property to perform the task.

The third task is to provide a method for closing a menu. This particular feature is a little tricky because you don't necessarily want the menu to close immediately. Otherwise, the user won't have time to select a submenu item before it closes. The following code shows how to perform this task with a time delay in place:

```
function CloseMenu()
{
    // Set a timer for closing the menu.
    Timer = window.setTimeout(PerformClose, 500);
}

function PerformClose()
{
    // If the item is still open.
    if (Item)
    {
        // Close it.
        Item.style.visibility = "hidden";
    }
}
```

When the application requests that a submenu close, the code creates a 500 millisecond delay, after which the `window` automatically calls `PerformClose()`. When an item exists, `PerformClose()` sets its `visibility` property to hidden to hide the submenu from view.

There are three ways in which a submenu can close. A submenu can close when a user selects another main menu item, when the user moves the mouse cursor off of the submenu, or when the user clicks on a main or submenu item. When a user is hovering the mouse over a submenu item, the code must keep the submenu open. That's the fourth task the application must perform using the following code:

```
function KeepSubmenu()
{
    // Reset the timer.
    window.clearTimeout(Timer);
}
```

As long as the user hovers the mouse over the submenu, it will remain open because the timer is constantly reset. The moment the user moves the mouse off the submenu or clicks one of the submenu items, the timer restarts, and the submenu closes.

# Chapter 14

# Enhancing HTML5 Forms with JavaScript

............................................................

## In This Chapter

▶ Reviewing special HTML5 form features

▶ Interacting with form elements

▶ Performing validation checks on forms

............................................................

**S**o far the book has discussed forms in general. The form examples rely on the modern features that JavaScript supports, but they could have been any form from any of the newer versions of HTML. This chapter is different. Instead of looking at forms in general, you encounter forms specifically designed for use in an HTML5 environment.

Many people think newer is better. However, that isn't always the case. This chapter presents a tradeoff. Yes, you get to use the new features that HTML5 provides to create robust applications that require less coding on your part. The new features that HTML5 supports make it easier to create applications that work consistently across platforms and browsers. The tradeoff is that these applications won't run on older browsers that don't support HTML5 (many of these older browsers don't even support the version of HTML in existence at the time they were created). The applications may look like they'll work for a while, but eventually they'll fail. When you have a lot of users that rely on older browsers and are unlikely to upgrade, you risk alienating them in order to take advantage of new technology. It's also important to note that HTML5 is still in the process of becoming a standard, so you may still see changes in how it works.

The first section of this chapter is a must read because it helps you understand the new features that HTML5 brings for forms. Previous chapters help you understand forms as they exist for the majority of browsers today. These new features are specific to HTML5, and you can use them only with HTML5 applications. To use the new features, you must know that they exist and understand why they're so important.

The rest of the chapter provides specific examples of how HTML5 can make your development experience much better and improve the user's experience as well. You discover how HTML5 provides greater flexibility, enhances security, creates a reliable environment, and defines better consistency. All these elements are essential given the heavy reliance on browser-based applications today.

# Revisiting the HTML5 Form Features

Before you can begin using the new form features of HTML5, you need to know what they are. HTML5 strives to make the user experience better by creating a more flexible environment. The addition of controls that make input requirements more specific reduce user frustration with inputting incorrect data. In addition, these changes make the environment more secure by making it harder to input unexpected data, and they make the environment more consistent because the controls help developers create robust applications without resorting to odd coding techniques. The following sections provide you with an overview of the various HTML5 changes.

## Working with the new elements

HTML5 provides a number of new elements that make it easier to write applications. The following list provides an overview of these elements:

- `<article>`: Defines standalone text that makes sense on its own. Even though the text appears as part of a larger page, you could move the text somewhere else and still find it readable. Potential sources of articles include:
  - How-to post
  - Forum post
  - Blog post
  - Commentary or opinion piece
  - News story
  - Comment
- `<aside>`: Provides material that's related to the rest of the material on a page, but is in addition to it and not actually part of that material. Many people refer to such material as a sidebar. The main content of the page should read well without the aside in place.
- `<audio>`: Specifies the source and playing conditions for audio presented on a page.
- `<bdi>`: Provides the means of placing text that may be formatted in an alternative direction in isolation from the text surrounding it. For example, if you wanted to place a Chinese quote on an English language page, you could use the Bi-Directional Isolation (BDI), `<bdi>`, tag to do it.

## Out with the old tags

HTML5 lacks support for a number of older tags. This means you can't mix these older controls with the newer controls that HTML5 does support. Here's a list of common tags that HTML5 doesn't support: `<acronym>` (use the `<abbr>` tag instead), `<applet>` (use the `<object>` tag instead), `<basefont>` (use Cascading Style Sheet, CSS, instead), `<big>` (use CSS instead), `<center>` (use CSS instead), `<dir>` (use CSS instead), `<font>` (use CSS instead), `<frame>`, `<frameset>`, `<noframes>`, `<strike>` (use the `<del>` tag instead), and `<tt>` (use CSS instead). There isn't a direct replacement for frames in HTML5. The main problem with frames is that they cause accessibility, usability, and security issues. The recommendation is to use a combination of CSS and inline-frames (IFrames) to mimic frames when you need them. You can find an excellent article on the topic at `http://www.peachpit.com/blogs/blog.aspx?uk=Frames-are-Dead-Long-Live-Iframes`.

It's also important to note that some attributes are also gone. For example, the `align` attribute used with the `<input>` tag is no longer available. In this case, you use CSS as a replacement.

---

✔ `<canvas>`: Allows dynamic drawing of graphics on the page using a language such as JavaScript. The canvas acts as a container for the drawing — the developer must still provide code to perform the actual drawing.

✔ `<embed>`: Allows inclusion of an external application or interactive content (such as a plug-in).

✔ `<figcaption>`: Defines a caption for a figure that's placed within a `<figure>` tag.

✔ `<figure>`: Creates a container for holding self-contained material such as images, diagrams, and code listings.

✔ `<footer>`: Contains information about the container element in which it appears. This tag is normally used to provide descriptive information about the container's content.

✔ `<header>`: Provides a heading or navigational aids for the container in which it appears.

✔ `<hgroup>`: Defines a group of headings used together to create content. For example, you could use this feature to create an outline on pages with complex content.

✔ `<mark>`: Specifies that the affected content is highlighted in some way.

✔ `<nav>`: Creates a blog of navigational links. This tag is used for major link blocks rather than individual links that appear in other areas of a document.

✔ `<rp>`: Specifies how a browser should react if it doesn't support ruby annotations. This tag is used with the `<rt>` and `<ruby>` tags to provide a complete solution for ruby annotations.

A *ruby annotation* is a short run of text that appears alongside the baseline text that's used to show pronunciation or to provide a short annotation. This feature is normally used with East Asian languages. You can read more about ruby annotations at `http://www.w3.org/TR/ruby`. The demonstration at `http://www.alanflavell.org.uk/www/umusalu.html` shows ruby annotations in use.

✔ `<rt>`: Provides an explanation or annotation of pronunciation of text. This tag is used with the `<rp>` and `<ruby>` tags to provide a complete solution for ruby annotations.

✔ `<ruby>`: Defines a ruby annotation. This tag is used with the `<rp>` and `<rt>` tags to provide a complete solution for ruby annotations.

✔ `<section>`: Creates a document section. A document section can include chapters, headings, footers, or other sectional content.

✔ `<source>`: Links the document to external multimedia resources such as audio or video files.

✔ `<video>`: Specifies the source and playing conditions for video presented on a page.

This list is incomplete for a good reason (you can find a complete list at `http://www.w3schools.com/tags/default.asp`). Some of the tags are poor choices for creating applications, so the book doesn't discuss them. You may be tempted to use tags that aren't supported well by other browsers, but you must consider the ramifications of doing so. For example, the `<command>` tag doesn't appear in this list because it's poorly supported by browsers. Only Internet Explorer version 9 and above support the tag, so you'd need to be sure that application users have this browser installed. Likewise, Internet Explorer doesn't support the `<datalist>` or `<keygen>` tags (although a majority of other browsers do support them). When you build an application for use in an organization with specific criteria, tags such as `<details>` could prove useful; but again, the `<details>` tag works on the Mac only, and the user must use either the Chrome or Safari browsers. At least one tag, `<time>`, is also read by all browsers, but they don't render it in any way, making the tag pretty much useless.

## Working with the new controls

Forms are hard to put together at times. Part of the problem is that the real world has more data types than HTML was originally designed to accommodate. It's no wonder, then, that each new version of HTML has included a few new `<input>` tags to make form creation simpler. Table 14-1 describes the `<input>` tag additions for HTML5.

**Table 14-1**

## New Controls Available with HTML5

| Control | Supported Browsers | Description |
|---------|-------------------|-------------|
| `<input type="color">` | Chrome and Opera | Displays as a color picker dialog box on browsers that support it. Browsers that don't support this control often display it as a text box where the user can enter a color name or other valid color input. |
| `<input type="date">` | Chrome, Safari, and Opera | Displays a date picker dialog box on browsers that support it. Browsers that don't support this control often display it as a text box where the user can enter a valid date. |
| `<input type="datetime">` | Safari and Opera | Displays a date and time picker dialog box on browsers that support it. Input includes a time zone. Browsers that don't support this control often display it as a text box where the user can enter a valid date. |
| `<input type="datetime-local">` | Safari and Opera | Displays a date and time picker dialog box on browsers that support it. Input relies on the local time zone. Browsers that don't support this control often display it as a text box where the user can enter a valid date. |
| `<input type="email">` | Firefox, Chrome, and Opera | Renders as a standard text box for inputting an e-mail address. However, using a specific control helps the user understand the kind of content you want. In addition, mobile devices often provide a context-specific keyboard for inputting the information. |
| `<input type="month">` | Chrome, Safari, and Opera | Renders as a standard text box for inputting the month and year. However, using a specific control helps the user understand the kind of content you want. In addition, mobile devices often provide a context-specific keyboard for inputting the information. |
| `<input type="number">` | Chrome, Safari, and Opera | Creates a text box and spinner combination for inputting a number on browsers that support it. Browsers that don't support this control often display it as a text box where the user can enter a valid number. |

*(continued)*

**Table 14-1 (continued)**

| Control | Supported Browsers | Description |
|---|---|---|
| `<input type="range">` | Chrome, Safari, and Opera | Displays a slider where a user can choose from a range of input values on browsers that support this control. Browsers that don't support this control often display it as a text box where the user can enter a valid value (usually numeric). |
| `<input type="search">` | Chrome and Safari | Renders as a standard text box for inputting a search term. The text box does include a clear button on browsers that support it. Using a specific control helps the user understand the kind of content you want. |
| `<input type="tel">` | N/A | No browsers currently support this control. However, when support becomes available, the control renders as a standard text box for inputting a telephone number. Using a specific control helps the user understand the kind of content you want. In addition, mobile devices often provide a context-specific keyboard for inputting the information. |
| `<input type="time">` | Chrome, Safari, and Opera | Creates a specialized segmented text box and spinner combination for inputting the time on browsers that support it. The hours, minutes, seconds, and milliseconds each have a separate entry area in the text box. Browsers that don't support this control often display it as a text box where the user can enter a valid time. |
| `<input type="url">` | Firefox, Chrome, and Opera | Renders as a standard text box for inputting a URL. However, using a specific control helps the user understand the kind of content you want. In addition, mobile devices often provide a context-specific keyboard for inputting the information. |
| `<input type="week">` | Chrome, Safari, and Opera | Renders as a standard text box for inputting the week (as a numeric value) and year. However, using a specific control helps the user understand the kind of content you want. In addition, mobile devices often provide a context-specific keyboard for inputting the information. |

It's important to note that none of the tags in Table 14-1 enjoys support from all the browsers and platforms on the market today; you need to choose these additional tags carefully. You can find demonstrations of most of these controls at `http://dev.opera.com/articles/view/new-form-features-in-html5`. Because these tags are so useful, expect to see better support for them in future versions of most browsers.

## Understanding the new attributes

HTML5 provides access to a number of useful new attributes. There are only two new form-specific attributes: `autocomplete` and `novalidate`. The `autocomplete` attribute determines whether the browser turns autocomplete on or off for a form as a whole. Every browser on the market supports the `autocomplete` attribute. The `novalidate` attribute is true when the browser should avoid validating form input. Only Firefox, Chrome, and Opera support the `novalidate` attribute, which means you must use it with care.

The `<input>` tag also has a number of new attributes associated with it. Of the new attributes, Internet Explorer supports only the `height` and `width` attributes. Table 14-2 provides an overview of the attributes and tells you which browsers support them. In most cases, most browsers, with the exception of Internet Explorer, support the new attributes.

| Table 14-2 | `<input>` Tag Attribute Additions in HTML5 | |
|---|---|---|
| **Attribute** | **Supported Browsers** | **Description** |
| auto complete | Firefox, Chrome, Safari, and Opera | Determines whether the browser turns autocomplete on or off for a specific control. It's possible to change the form-level setting independently from the control-level setting. The control-level setting always takes precedence. |
| autofocus | Firefox, Chrome, Safari, and Opera | Determines that the element should automatically receive the focus when the page loads when set to true. |
| form | Firefox, Chrome, Safari, and Opera | Specifies that an element belongs to one or more forms. You can create a single element to appear on multiple forms by providing a comma-separated list of forms. |
| form action | Firefox, Chrome, Safari, and Opera | Defines the name of an application file that will process the input when the form is submitted to the server. |

*(continued)*

### Table 4-2 *(continued)*

| Attribute | Supported Browsers | Description |
|---|---|---|
| `form enctype` | Firefox, Chrome, Safari, and Opera | Specifies the kind of encoding that the browser should use when submitting the input to the server. |
| `formmethod` | Firefox, Chrome, Safari, and Opera | Controls the method that the browser will use for submitting the input to the server. For example, you can choose to submit the data by using the post method. |
| `formno validate` | Firefox, Chrome, and Opera | Specifies that the affected input isn't validated prior to submitting it to the server when set to `true`. |
| `formtarget` | Firefox, Chrome, Safari, and Opera | Defines a target that should receive output (the result) from the server after submitting the form. Each input can have a different target for multiple outputs. |
| `height` and `width` | Internet Explorer, Firefox, Chrome, Safari, and Opera | Control the height and width of any element. It's essential to set both height and width when loading graphics to ensure consistent and error-free browser operation. |
| `list` | Firefox, Chrome, and Opera | Specifies which `<datalist>` tag to use as input for a list of items. |
| `min` and `max` | Chrome and Opera | Determine the minimum and maximum values that an input element can accept. |
| `multiple` | Firefox, Chrome, Safari, and Opera | Allows the user to enter more than one value in an input element when set to true. |
| `pattern` `(regexp)` | Firefox, Chrome, and Opera | Provides a regular expression that's used to validate the input element's data when the user submits it. Even if your JavaScript editor lets you use this attribute with all (or most) input controls, browsers only check it with the `text`, `search`, `url`, `tel`, `email`, and `password` `<input>` types. |

| Attribute | Supported Browsers | Description |
|-----------|--------------------|-------------|
| place holder | Firefox, Chrome, Safari, and Opera | Allows the developer to provide a hint or short piece of text to describe the expected input value for an input element. The text appears grayed out and disappears when the user starts inputting data. |
| required | Firefox, Chrome, and Opera | Ensures that the user provides a value for the input element, but doesn't ensure that the input is correct (or even feasible) when set to `true`. Even if your JavaScript editor lets you use this attribute with all (or most) input controls, browsers check it with only the `text`, `search`, `url`, `tel`, `email`, `password`, date pickers, `number`, `checkbox`, `radio`, and `file` `<input>` types. |
| step | Firefox, Chrome, and Opera | Define an input interval for the `number`, `range`, `date`, `datetime`, `datetime-local`, `month`, `time`, and `week` `<input>` types. This attribute determines the interval between values, such as 3, 6, 9, 12, and 15 when using a `step="3"` attribute value. |

# Accessing Form Elements

As with any other HTML elements, you can interact directly with HTML5 elements. The trick is to ensure that the elements you choose will work with the browsers and platforms you need to support. In this example, you see how to use the `<figure>` and `<figcaption>` tags as part of a solution that loads an image from disk and stores it in an `<img>` tag. The following code shows the HTML you use to perform the task. (You can find complete code for this example in the `\Chapter 14` folder of the downloadable code as `ImageLoad.HTML`.)

```
<figure onclick="Clicked()">
   <img id="Image"
        src=""
        alt=""
        height="200px"
        width="200px">
   <figcaption id="Caption" />
</figure>
```

The `<figure>` tag acts as a container that holds the tags `<img>` and `<figcaption>`. The use of a container like this means that you can perform tasks such as formatting both image and caption at the same time. Events are also handled jointly. In this case, it doesn't matter whether the user clicks the image or the caption, the application calls `Clicked()`. In this case, all that `Clicked()` does is display a message to the user as shown here:

```
function Clicked()
{
   // Display a message.
   alert("You clicked the image.");
}
```

JavaScript is fully capable of accessing these elements. In this case, the `<img>` tag is empty when the form loads. Clicking a button displays the image onscreen by changing the `<img>` tag content. Here's the code needed to load the image:

```
function LoadImage()
{
   // Specify the image.
   var Image = document.getElementById("Image");
   Image.alt = "This is a test image.";
   Image.src = "TestImage.png";

   // Set the caption.
   var Caption = document.getElementById("Caption");
   Caption.innerHTML = "A Test Image";
}
```

When working with the `<img>` tag, you access the `src` (image source) and `alt` (image alternative text description) attributes directly. Set the `<figcaption>` content using the `innerHTML` property. Figure 14-1 shows typical output from this example.

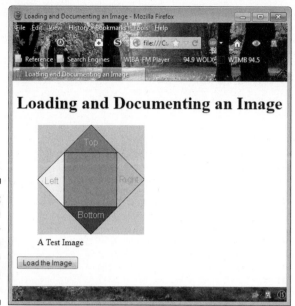

**Figure 14-1:**
Use the
<figure>
tag to make
it easier to
work with
media.

# Validating Forms

Validation is an important part of working with forms. Unfortunately, not every browser provides support for the validation features of HTML5. The example in this section won't work with Internet Explorer because Internet Explorer fails to support any of the HTML5 validation features. In order to validate input for Internet Explorer, you need to use the techniques described in previous chapters. For example, Chapter 9 shows techniques for validating optional arguments that you could also use to validate form data.

A large part of validating data in HTML5 is creating the right type of form. The following code shows a simple form with a name, telephone number, and two password fields (an original and a confirmation). (You can find complete code for this example in the \Chapter 14 folder of the downloadable code as ValidateData.HTML.)

```
<form action="#" method="post"
      enctype="multipart/form-data">
   <fieldset>
      <div>
         <label>Name:</label>
         <input id="Name"
                type="text"
                placeholder="Type Your Name"
                maxlength="100"
```

```
                        required
                        x-moz-errormessage="Type Your Name"/>
            </div>
            <div>
                <label>Telephone:</label>
                <input id="Telephone"
                        type="tel"
                        placeholder="Type Your Number"
                        pattern="\d\d\d \d\d\d \d\d\d\d"
                        required
                        x-moz-errormessage=
                            "Type Your Number as XXX XXX XXXX"/>
            </div>
            <div>
                <label>Password:</label>
                <input id="P1"
                        type="password"
                        placeholder="Password" />
            </div>
            <div>
                <label>Confirm Password:</label>
                <input id="P2"
                        type="password"
                        placeholder="Password"
                        onfocus="ValidatePassword(
                            document.getElementById('P1'), this);"
                        oninput="ValidatePassword(
                            document.getElementById('P1'), this);"/>
            </div>
        </fieldset>
        <fieldset>
            <div>
                <input id="Submit"
                        type="submit"
                        value="Submit Data" />
            </div>
        </fieldset>
</form>
```

The first two fields use automatic validation as supplied by HTML5. Notice the use of the `required` attribute in both cases, which means the user must type a value (not necessarily a correct value). In addition, the `placeholder` attribute provides a clue as to what the user needs to type, which is always a good first step in obtaining information. The `maxlength` attribute prevents users from trying to type too much or someone inputting a script instead of content. Likewise, the `pattern` attribute looks for specific information from the user.

The generic error messages that HMTL5 provides are acceptable, but hardly enlightening. This example shows how to use the `x-moz-errormessage` attribute in order to create a custom error message. Many browsers don't support this attribute, so users may still see the generic error message, but there's at least a chance that users will see something that's a little more targeted toward providing helpful information.

The two password fields can't rely on standard HTML5 validation. In this case, you must use JavaScript to confirm that the user has entered the same password in both fields and that the fields do, in fact, contain a password. Here's the `ValidatePassword()` function used to perform the validation:

```
function ValidatePassword(P1, P2)
{
   if (P1.value != P2.value ||
       P1.value == "" ||
       P2.value == "")
   {
      P2.setCustomValidity(
         "The Password Is Incorrect");
   }
   else
   {
      P2.setCustomValidity("");
   }
}
```

The example verifies that both password fields contain an entry and that the entry is the same in both fields. Of course, your password check could do more. Figure 14-2 shows a typical validation error message for this example. The error message appears as a pop-up. Notice how each field contains a helpful hint on what to type.

**Figure 14-2:**
Validation is an important part of any application.

# Chapter 15

# Interacting with Windows

• • • • • • • • • • • • • • • • • • • • • • • • • • • • • • • • • • • • • • • • • •

• • • • • • • • • • • • • • • • • • • • • • • • • • • • • • • • • • • • • • • • • •

*A* browser presents a window to the Internet. The view a user sees depends on the location of that window at any given time. Many people think of houses when they think of windows. However, the window to the Internet is more like the window of a car. You travel to a location and see a particular view based on that location.

Browsers provide the means to interact with the `window` object so that it's possible to change the view in various ways. The glass used to create the window is known as the `screen` object. Sometimes you want to view something you saw recently, in which case you can call on the `history` object to provide an instant replay. When moving to a new location, you rely on the `navigator` object. The `location` object tells you about your current location. Taken together, all these objects represent the Browser Object Model (BOM), which is the focus of this chapter.

You are introduced to the BOM in the section on using JavaScript objects in Chapter 5. This chapter provides a more intense view of the BOM so that you can use it to perform specific tasks within the browser. As part of working with these objects, you're also introduced to special tasks you can perform, such as creating customized dialog boxes. In short, this chapter is the next step in working with browser objects.

# *Working with Windows*

The `window` object is the container for everything else in your browser. You use the `window` object to determine how the browser reacts to the Internet and then perform tasks with the content the Internet provides. The `window` object actually contains the other objects you use to perform tasks with the browser, including the `screen`, `history`, `navigator`, and `location` objects. The following sections describe how to work with the `window` object in more detail.

## *Determining window characteristics*

The window characteristics determine many of the things you can do with your application. For example, the window width and height determine how much information you can display. In most cases, you use this information as part of a larger application, but sometimes it's helpful to see what's available. The `window.innerHeight` and `window.innerWidth` properties are useful for placing information onscreen. Figure 15-1 shows some of the statistics you can obtain for the `window` object. (You can find complete code for this example in the `\Chapter 15\Windows` folder of the downloadable code as `WindowCharacteristics.HTML`.) It's important to note that some features that used to be available are no longer accessible due to security concerns. For example, it used to be possible to set the status bar information directly using script. However, some scripts used this feature to spoof site information — making the user's system vulnerable to viruses or opening the door for phishing attacks.

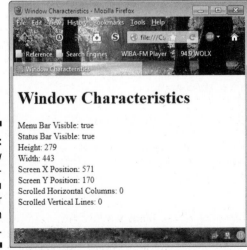

**Figure 15-1:**
The window characteristics help you adjust your application output.

Consequently, you can obtain some information about the status bar, but you can't change the status bar content. A few browsers, such as Internet Explorer, don't allow any sort of status bar access or even access to information about it.

# Changing window attributes

The `window` object contains a number of interesting methods you can use to change window characteristics or perform tasks such as displaying a dialog box. The methods that you can use with a particular window depend on a number of criteria:

✔ Security settings of the current platform

✔ Security features of the browser

✔ Browser settings modified by the user

✔ State of the browser

In general, you can't assume the user will allow you to do anything. You can certainly try to perform tasks, but the platform, browser, or user could prevent it. In addition, some tasks are simply impossible when the browser is in a certain state. For example, you'll likely find that you can't move or resize the browser when it's maximized. In fact, you can't ever resize or move the browser window when working with the Windows 8 version of Internet Explorer (the one that you access from the Start screen, also known as Metro). With this in mind, the following code may or may not work with your browser. (You can find complete code for this example in the `\Chapter 15\ Windows` folder of the downloadable code as `SetSizePosition.HTML`.)

```
function ChangeSizePosition()
{
    // Open a new blank window.
    var NewWindow = window.open("", "New Window",
        "width=300,height=300");

    // Wait to resize the window.
    NewWindow.window.alert(
        "Click OK to Move and Resize the Window");

    // Move and resize the new window.
    NewWindow.resizeTo(600, 600);
    NewWindow.moveTo(20, 20);
}
```

This function begins by creating a new blank window (the first argument normally contains the URL of the page you want to open). It then performs an absolute resize and move of that window. You can also perform a relative resize and move by using the `resizeBy()` and `resizeTo()` methods. This particular technique comes in handy when you want to ensure information is presented in a certain way. For example, you may open a custom window for displaying product details on your site and want to ensure that the window matches the original design concept.

Notice the technique used to access content within the new window. You can use this approach to create interesting effects within the new window while controlling it from the existing window.

If you find that the script doesn't work at all, make sure you don't have the browser maximized. In addition, many browsers let you turn off the ability to resize and move the window. For example, when using Firefox, you open the Options dialog box and select the content tab. Click Advanced in the JavaScript option and you see a list of options for enabling or disabling the ability to resize and move the window. Make sure these options are selected.

# Accessing the Screen

The screen object tells you about the user's system — the screen used to create the window to the Internet. By knowing the screen information, you can better determine what's possible with the user's system. For example, you can determine the number of available colors or the actual size of the screen. Figure 15-2 shows statistics that developers commonly need to create platform-friendly applications. (You can find complete code for this example in the `\Chapter 15\Screen` folder of the downloadable code as `ScreenFeatures.HTML`.)

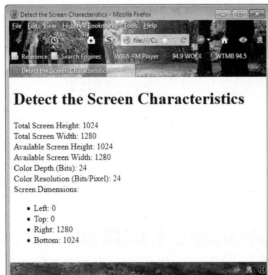

**Figure 15-2:**
Use the screen charac-teristics to create platform-friendly applications.

# Finding a Location

Knowing where you're at is an important part of working with applications in a browser environment. The `location` object makes it possible to determine the current location that the user is viewing. In fact, you can take the location information apart so that you can work with just the part you need. The following sections describe how to work with location information and provide one technique for modifying the location.

Although you can run most examples in this book directly from your hard drive, this is one situation where running the example from your Web server is really helpful because otherwise you won't see the full list of elements. The output from these examples also uses a somewhat contrived URL of `http://localhost/GetLocation.html?Make a Query`. The query portion isn't actually functioning, but it does provide additional output.

## Determining the current location

The location object provides access to a number of properties that let you interact with the complete URL or dissect it into its components. The `href` property displays the entire URL. Properties such as `search` and `port` provide access to URL components. Figure 15-3 shows the example URL when displayed on the test server. Notice that the Port field is blank because the server is using the default port of 80. If you were using a special port, you'd see it listed in the Port field. (You can find complete code for this example in the `\Chapter 15\Location` folder of the downloadable code as `GetLocation.HTML`.)

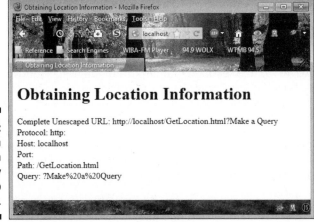

**Figure 15-3:**
The location information is easily divided into components.

The `location` properties always provide the escaped version of the URL. To see the human-readable version, you must use the `unescape()` function. The first line in the output in Figure 15-3 shows the result of using the `unescape()` function on the `href` property. Meanwhile, the last line shows the escaped version of the `search` property.

## Changing the location

Navigating to a new page is an important part of browser-based application design. Of course, you can always add links to an application and let the user make any location changes. However, there are times when you want to programmatically change location. The following functions show how to use the three methods the `location` object provides for changing location. (You can find complete code for this example in the `\Chapter 15\Location` folder of the downloadable code as `SetLocation.HTML`.)

```
function AssignURL()
{
    location.assign("GetLocation.html?Make a Query");
}

function ReplaceURL()
{
    location.replace("GetLocation.html?Make a Query");
}

function ReloadURL()
{
    location.reload();
}
```

The `assign()` method assigns a new URL to the current page. What you see is the page provided as input to the method. In this case, you see the same page as shown in Figure 15-3.

The `replace()` method seemingly performs the same task as the `assign()` method. However, there's a subtle, but important, difference between the two methods. When a browser replaces the current page, rather than assigning it, the back button is no longer functional on most browsers. The new page actually does replace the current page. This is an important difference because shopping cart applications often require that the user not click the back button. Designers make the mistake of assigning the page, rather than replacing it. When you create an application where the back button should be disabled, make sure you use the `replace()` method.

The `reload()` method performs the same task as the reload button on the browser. However, there's an important difference in this case. If you call `reload(true)`, the page doesn't load from the local cache. Instead, the page is loaded from the server. You can use this behavior to fix problems with an application when a network error has caused a fault in the page. Reloading from the server (something the user can't do easily) restores the content to the form that you originally intended.

# Searching History

The `history` object is probably the least well documented feature of the BOM. In addition, there are many differences between browsers and platforms. Some features that seem like they should work don't end up working consistently. There's an interesting article entitled, "Manipulating History for Fun & Profit" at `http://diveintohtml5.info/history.html` that describes a few of these features, but you honestly shouldn't consider using them in a production application.

Fortunately, there are some features that you can use consistently. For example, you can use the `history.length` property to determine the current number of entries in the history list. Unfortunately, you can't view the content of those entries to determine the URLs that the browser has stored or even obtain a list of page titles. The `history` object also includes these methods, which do seem to work on every browser and platform:

- `back()`: Navigates to the previous URL in the history list. The current item isn't removed from the history list, so you can go back to it by calling `forward()`.

- `forward()`: Navigates to the next URL in the history list.

- `go()`: Moves to a specific URL in the history list. You can provide a numeric input to move forward (using positive numbers) or backward (using negative numbers) a specific number of places in the list. It's also possible to provide a specific URL that appears in the list.

# Working with Navigator

The navigator object provides support for a number of interesting properties and methods. All of these properties and methods tell you something about the browser used to access the page. Here's a list of the most commonly supported properties for this object:

✔ `appCodeName`: Provides the vendor's codename for the product.

✔ `appName`: Returns that commercial (released) name of the product. Unfortunately, the value returned is wrong in most cases.

✔ `appVersion`: Theoretically returns the version number of the browser, but this information is incorrect in some situations.

✔ `cookieEnabled`: Specifies whether the browser has cookie support enabled.

✔ `onLine`: Specifies whether the browser is online. This is the setting for working offline rather than actually connecting to the network. In other words, the browser might not have a network connection and this property will still return `true`.

✔ `platform`: Provides information about the platform for which the browser is compiled. This property doesn't reflect the platform the browser's currently executing on.

✔ `userAgent`: Returns a specially formatted header that the browser returns to the server when making a request. This information may not actually reflect the browser functionality, but rather it may reflect how the browser wants to appear to the server.

This string is complicated to read and use. That's why the browser detection example in Chapter 2 uses the jQuery library, rather than parse the information in the user agent string. The explanation at `http://www.howtogeek.com/114937/htg-explains-whats-a-browser-user-agent` is helpful in discovering precisely how this string's formatted.

The methods are equally useful. You can use them to detect browser support for certain functionality. In most cases, the browser offers the required feature, but the user may have turned it off. Here are the methods of interest:

✔ `javaEnabled()`: Specifies whether the browser has Java support enabled.

✔ `taintEnabled()`: Specifies whether the browser has data tainting enabled.

*Data tainting* is a technique originally introduced by Netscape Navigator 3 — it allows one window to see the properties in another window. The idea is that the two windows can share data and developers can create more interesting applications. However, data tainting proved to be a huge security risk, and many people have it turned off even if their browser supports the feature (which isn't likely in newer browsers). The TechRepublic article at `http://www.techrepublic.com/article/javascript-security-is-making-strides/5034711` discusses data tainting, and other security issues, in greater depth.

Many browsers support other properties and methods that help you find out more about the browser and its functionality. These lists represent the commonly used properties and methods. Figure 15-4 shows typical output from each of the properties and methods described in the lists. (You can find complete code for this example in the \Chapter 15\Navigator folder of the downloadable code as CheckBrowser.HTML.)

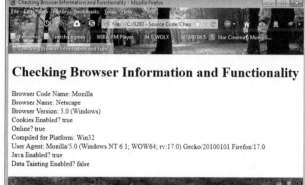

**Figure 15-4:**
Use the navigator object to detect browser information.

# Creating a Pop-Up

JavaScript provides access to three kinds of dialog boxes: alert(), confirm(), and prompt(). You can see each of these dialog boxes in action in previous chapters. In fact, you initially meet the alert() function in the section in Chapter 1 on understanding the alert() function. The first instance of the confirm() dialog box appears in the section on using JavaScript objects in Chapter 5, and the section on the default option in Chapter 8 demonstrates the prompt() function. The following sections add to the information you already know. For example, you discover how to make information appear on multiple lines in these dialog boxes. You also discover how to move beyond these three basic dialog boxes by creating dialog boxes of your own.

## Controlling line breaks

Sometimes you need to divide content on multiple lines. To perform this task, you add an escape character to the string. An *escape character* is a special signal to JavaScript to perform some special processing on a string. It's actually two characters, the backslash (\) followed by another character. Here's a list of the escape characters that JavaScript understands:

✔ \': single quote

✔ \": double quote

✔ \\: backslash

✔ \n: new line

✔ \r: carriage return

✔ \t: tab

✔ \b: backspace

✔ \f: form feed

You can add these escape characters into strings to perform special tasks, such as displaying content on multiple lines. The following example shows how to perform this task. (You can find complete code for this example in the \Chapter 15\DialogBox folder of the downloadable code as MultipleLines.HTML.)

```
<input id="btnShow"
       type="button"
       value="Display the Dialog"
       onclick="alert('This is a really long message,' +
           '\r\nso you need to split it on multiple ' +
           'lines');" />
```

If you were to display this message, without the escape characters, it would display as a single long line. Unfortunately, a single long line may not work on some devices, and it would appear unwieldy on most others. The code adds a \r (carriage return), which moves the cursor back to the beginning of the line, and a \n (newline), which places the cursor on the next line. As a consequence, the output from the alert() appears on two lines, as shown in Figure 15-5.

## Creating a modal dialog box

The three dialog boxes that JavaScript provides by default are helpful, but they aren't everything that a typical developer requires to create a robust application. There are times when you need a custom dialog box in order to focus the user's attention on a specific need or requirement.

You can find a number of methods for creating a custom dialog box online, some of which rely on special libraries and produce some dazzling results. The example in this section relies on the overlay method — a simple technique for creating a usable dialog box. The following code shows how you create an overlay using a <div> as part of your page. (You can find complete code for this example in the \Chapter 15\DialogBox folder of the downloadable code as ModalDialog.HTML.)

```
<div id="Overlay">
   <div>
      <p id="DlgContent">Content Goes Here</p>
      <input id="btnYes"
             type="button"
             value="Yes"
             onclick="DlgHide('Yes')" />
      <input id="btnNo"
             type="button"
             value="No"
             onclick="DlgHide('No')" />
   </div>
</div>
```

These tags produce a dialog box that contains a message and two buttons
labeled Yes and No. You must change the message, but have the option of
changing the buttons as needed. For that matter, you need not stick to just
two buttons — you can modify the overlay to meet any formatting requirements needed. The overlay can also have any number of inputs desired. In
short, this is a simplification that you can extend quite easily to meet any
requirement.

Having just the tags would mean that the viewer could see the overlay at all
times. In addition, there would be nothing to distinguish the overlay from the
regular information onscreen. With this in mind, you need to create some
CSS to differentiate the overlay and to keep it hidden until needed. Here's one
way to approach the task:

```
#Overlay
{
    visibility: hidden;
    position: absolute;
    left: 90px;
    top: 120px;
    width:200px;
    height:90px;
    text-align:center;
    border: solid;
    background-color: lightgray;
}
```

As with the overlay tags, the CSS is fully configurable using JavaScript code. For example, you could add code to center the overlay by changing the `left` and `top` values. The example keeps things simple, but it's important to realize that all of these values are fully configurable.

The dialog box appears when a user clicks a button. To make that happen, you need an `onclick` event handler (Chapter 12 describes event handlers in greater detail). The following code performs the basic tasks required to interact with the dialog box:

```
function DlgShow(Message)
{
    // Change the message.
    var Msg = document.getElementById("DlgContent");
    Msg.innerHTML = Message;

    // Display the dialog box.
    var Dlg = document.getElementById("Overlay");
    Dlg.style.visibility = "visible";
}
```

The example provides a configurable message, which is passed to `DlgShow()` through `Message`. All you need to do is change the `Msg.innerHTML` value to change the message. The dialog box is displayed when the code changes the `visibility` property value to `"visible"`.

Now that the dialog box is visible, you need a way to make it go away again. When the user clicks either Yes or No, the buttons call `DlgHide()` with an appropriate `Result`. The following code shows the technique used to make the dialog box disappear:

```
function DlgHide(Result)
{
    // Display the result onscreen.
    var Output = document.getElementById("Result");
    Output.innerHTML = "You clicked: " + Result;

    // Hide the dialog box.
    var Dlg = document.getElementById("Overlay");
    Dlg.style.visibility = "hidden";
}
```

In this case, the application also displays the result onscreen. You could return the value for further processing if desired. Figure 15-6 shows a typical dialog box produced by this example.

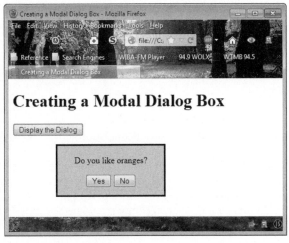

**Figure 15-6:**
Using an overlay helps you create a usable custom dialog box.

# Using Cookies

*Cookies* store application information on the user's drive. When a user visits a site, the application can use a cookie to store information for future use. Some cookies are quite simple and store the user's name or the date of the user's last visit. Other cookies are quite complex and could store information about application state. A cookie could put a user back to where the user was the last time the application was active. No matter how simple or complex a cookie is, the basic techniques for working with cookies are the same. The following sections describe how to set, get, and check a cookie. (You can find complete code for this example in the `\Chapter 15\Cookies` folder of the downloadable code as `UseCookies.HTML`.)

## Setting a cookie

It pays to create functions that will set and get cookies so that you don't have to write the same code repeatedly. The following example accepts three inputs: the name of the cookie, the value of the cookie, and the number of days until it expires:

```
function SetCookie(Name, Value, Expiration)
{
    // Create a date variable that contains
    // the expiration date.
    var ExpDate = new Date();
    if (Expiration != null)
        ExpDate.setDate(ExpDate.getDate() +
                        Expiration);

    // Encode the data for storage.
    var CookieValue = escape(Value) +
        "; expires=" + ExpDate.toUTCString();

    // Store the cookie.
    document.cookie = Name + "=" + CookieValue;
}
```

Normally, you'd add data input checks to a function that you plan to use in a variety of situations. This example leaves them out for the sake of clarity.

The code begins by calculating the expiration date. It begins by creating a new `Date` object, `ExpDate`, and adding the number of days until the cookie expires to it. Always think of the expiration date as more of a suggestion than an absolute. A user can configure the browser to remove cookies each time the browser is shut down, or the user can remove the cookies manually at any time.

To store a cookie value, you must *escape* it — that is, remove any whitespace characters from it. The example removes the space characters and then adds the expiration date. Suppose you want to store a cookie, `Username`, with a value of `John`. What you end up with is a string that contains the username and expiration date: `John; expires=Sun, 08 Dec 2013 21:43:52 GMT`. The cookie's actually stored in the `document.cookie` property as `Username=John; expires=Sun, 08 Dec 2013 21:43:52 GMT`.

## Getting a cookie

Assuming the user has saved the cookies your application created, you need to retrieve them before you can make use of the data they contain. The values are stored on disk as name/value pairs. The data is escaped, which makes it easy to store but impossible to read. The following code shows how to retrieve all the cookies, search for a specific cookie, and then make the data readable:

```
function GetCookie(Name)
{
    // Obtain all of the cookies and split
    // them into individual cookies.
    var Cookies=document.cookie.split(";");

    // Process each cookie in turn.
    for (var i=0; i<Cookies.length; i++)
    {
        // Obtain the name of the cookie.
        var CName = Cookies[i].substr(0,
            Cookies[i].indexOf("="));

        // Obtain the value of the cookie.
        var CValue = Cookies[i].substr(
            Cookies[i].indexOf("=") + 1);

        // Replace any escaped characters.
        CName = CName.replace(/^\s+|\s+$/g, "");

        // If the name of the cookie matches the
        // name that was passed by the caller, return
        // the associated cookie.
        if (Name == CName)
        {
            return unescape(CValue);
        }
    }

    // Return a null value when the cookie isn't found.
    return null;
}
```

The cookies are stored as one long string where each cookie is separated from the next by a semicolon (;). The example uses the split() function to turn this string into an array of individual cookies. At this point, the code can process the cookies one at a time.

Each cookie is stored as a name/value pair. The code begins by retrieving the name, and then the value, using string manipulation functions. Another way to perform the same task is to use the split() function again with equals (=) as the delimiter. You would then find the name in the first array element and the value in the second array element.

You now have an escaped name and value. The code removes the escape characters in the cookie name so that it can perform a direct comparison with the name that was passed to the function. When the names match, the code returns the value to the caller.

## Checking a cookie

The GetCookie() and SetCookie() functions make it easy to work with cookies by using JavaScript. This example tracks the user's name. When the system doesn't have the user's name stored, the application asks for it and stores it for later use as shown in the following example:

```
function CheckName()
{
    // Obtain the user's name.
    var UserName = GetCookie("Username");

    // Check for a user name.
    if ((UserName == null) || (UserName == ""))
    {
        // Obtain a username from the user.
        UserName = prompt("Please type your name: ");

        // Set a cookie for the username that will
        // expire in one year.
        SetCookie("Username", UserName, 365);
    }
    else
    {
        // Otherwise, extend the message.
        UserName = "Back " + UserName;
    }

    // Display the user's name onscreen.
    var SetName = document.getElementById("Name");
    SetName.innerHTML = UserName;
}
```

The function begins by attempting to get the stored cookie. When there's no cookie to get, the function returns null. A user could also choose to simply press Enter when asked for a name. This would result in a blank value. The code also checks for a blank and asks the user to enter a name again.

When there's a name stored on the drive, the code modifies the message onscreen to reflect this fact. So, if this is a new user, the message says Welcome Name, but if this is a returning user, it says Welcome Back Name. The point is that you have a simple method for detecting returns versus new entries.

# Part V
# Extending JavaScript Further

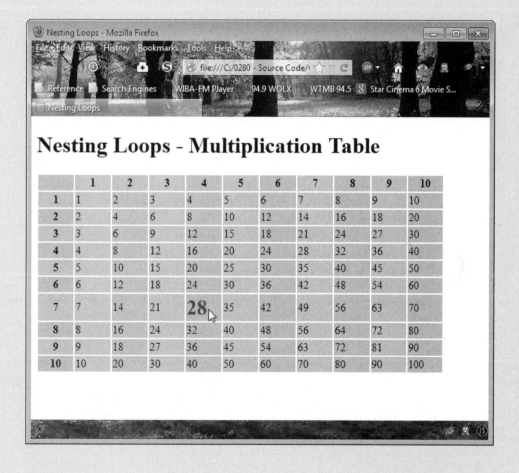

# In this part . . .

- ✔ Discover how to use XML to store all sorts of data.

- ✔ Devise applications that rely on Asynchronous JavaScript and XML (AJAX) to make partial page updates that are more efficient.

- ✔ Use third-party libraries, such as jQuery, to create applications faster and easier.

- ✔ Rely on jQuery to make AJAX even easier to use.

- ✔ Create applications that use animation and special effects to enhance the user experience and add a little pizzazz to your site.

# Chapter 16

# Working with XML in JavaScript

*T*he eXtensible Markup Language (XML) is a means of storing data complete with context in a way that's transferrable to every platform and usable by every browser. That's a tall order. However, XML is now used for a broad range of storage tasks, even when the storage is on a local system. You also find XML used for everything from application configuration to Web service interactions. Even though XML isn't a perfect solution for every need, it's an extremely flexible method for working with data of all sorts.

This chapter begins with a basic overview of XML and provides you with resources for further study, should you want more information. XML is so flexible that entire books are written about the topic that hardly scratch the surface of what you can do. The first section of this chapter focuses on how you work with XML in this book, along with a few basics you need to know.

One of the more important requirements for working with XML is to find a way to validate the information you receive. Validating the data is important because you need to know that the information you're using is correct. The validation process ensures only that the data is in the right format and of the right type. Unfortunately, computers still have no way of ascertaining the truth value of data — determining whether the content is correct. Someone could enter a name on a form, but the name might not be correct.

The remainder of the chapter provides some examples of how to combine JavaScript and HTML5 to interact with XML data. You won't do anything too fancy in this chapter, but future chapters extend the information you obtain here to perform some interesting tasks. This chapter focuses on accessing, navigating, and displaying the data in XML files so that you get a feel for how this process works.

# Introducing XML

XML is an important technology because it makes it possible to transfer data anywhere in a form that every computer can understand. Previous data storage technologies were often proprietary and worked only on the platform on which they were created. The only way to transfer data in many cases was to rely on text formats that lost the context of the data. You could transfer a list of usernames to another computer, but not the fact that they were usernames. Context is incredibly important because it defines how the data is used and modifies the data meaning in subtle ways. XML solves this problem by providing a means to transfer both the data and its context. The following sections provide a brief overview of XML you can use to work through the examples that appear in later chapters of the book.

## Gaining an overview of XML

XML is a markup language like HTML. You use tags to define the data context. For example, if you see `<name>Joe Smith</name>` in an XML file, you know that the data, `Joe Smith`, is a name. Unlike HTML, there are no predefined tags in XML — you define the tags you need based on the contextual requirements of the data. What XML provides is a structured method for storing the data so that a *parser,* software designed to interpret XML, will be able to interact with it.

An XML file contains data and contextual information about the data. It doesn't provide a method for displaying the information onscreen, nor does it provide any means of validating the structure of the data. Yes, the XML file will present the data in a structured manner, but you later discover that the structure itself may be incorrect unless it's validated in some way. The "Validating XML" section, later in this chapter, discusses the issue of ensuring the data structure is correct so that software can interpret and use the data.

There are some basic rules for XML files. For example, all opening tags must have a closing tag. Having just an opening tag is invalid, and the parser will raise an error if it sees an opening tag without a corresponding closing tag. You can create a shortcut for both opening and closing tags. When a tag doesn't contain any data, just context, you can present it as a single entity. For example, if a user didn't enter a name, the name tag could appear as `<name />`. The ending slash signifies the closing of the tag.

All XML files have a required processing instruction. The processing instruction tells the parser that the file is an XML file. It also provides some basic information about the XML file, such as the XML version. Many texts call this particular processing instruction the XML declaration. Here's a basic XML processing instruction:

```
<?xml version="1.0" encoding="UTF-8"?>
```

In this case, the XML file is based on version 1.0 of the specification. It's also encoded using the Uniform Transformation Format 8-bit (UTF-8) standard (which you can read about at `http://www.utf-8.com`). XML files can use a number of different encoding standards, but UTF-8 is one of the most common standards. In this case, *encoding* reflects the way the characters are stored on disk.

An XML file can contain more than one processing instruction. For example, if you want to use a particular file to validate the XML, you use a processing instruction to tell the parser to use that file. Later parts of this chapter describe the various processing instructions that you encounter most often.

## Understanding elements

An XML element is the combination of an opening tag, optionally some data, and a closing tag. A name element might look like this: `<name>Joe Smith </name>`. The basis of an XML file is the elements it contains.

You can create elements with any name you desire. The name should reflect the kind of data contained within the element, but XML doesn't actually care what name you use. It does have some rules for working with elements.

Every XML document is a tree structure that begins with a root node. A node is a single element and all it contains. There's only one root node in any XML tree, and the tree must contain at least one root node. In looking at a tree structure like this one:

```
<Customers>
    <Customer>
        <Name>Joe Smith</Name>
        <Age>42</Age>
        <FavoriteColor>Blue</FavoriteColor>
    </Customer>
</Customers>
```

the `<Customers>` element is the root node for the document. It contains all the other elements. The `<Customers>` root node consists of multiple `<Customer>` nodes, elements that contain information about individual customers. The `<Customers>` node is the parent of the `<Customer>` nodes, and the `<Customer>` nodes are the children of the `<Customers>` node.

The names you use for elements are case sensitive. A node named `<customer>` is different from a node named `<Customer>`. In addition, element names have these requirements:

✔ Can contain letters, numbers, and other characters

✔ Can't start with a number or punctuation character

✔ Can't start with the letters *xml* (or any capitalization of XML)

✔ Can't contain spaces, but you can use the underscore (_) to simulate a space

When creating an XML structure, the tags must be properly nested. For example, `<b><i>Emphasized Text</b></i>` might work in an HTML document, but it won't work in XML because the tags are nested incorrectly. The correct ordering of the tags is `<b><i>Emphasized Text</i></b>`, so that the `<b>` tag properly encapsulates the `<i>` tag.

Because of the way in which XML works, you can't use certain characters within the data. For example, `<Comparison>x < y</Comparison>` will generate an error because you've used the less-than (<) symbol in the data. This element should instead appear as `<Comparison>x &lt; y</Comparison>`, where `&lt;` represents the less-than symbol. Table 16-1 shows a list of character replacements you should use within the XML data.

| Table 16-1 | XML Character Replacements | |
|---|---|---|
| *Character* | *Replacement* | *Description* |
| & | &amp; | Ampersand |
| ' | &apos; | Apostrophe |
| > | &gt; | Greater than |
| < | &lt; | Less than |
| " | &quot; | Quotation mark |

 As you work through the structure of an XML file, you may want to make notes to yourself. An XML file can have comments in it. You simply place the comment within a starting `<!--` and ending `-->` character set and place your comment between. For example,

```
<!-- This is a comment. -->
```

contains an XML comment. The parser ignores anything you place inside the comment.

## *Understanding attributes*

Elements contain major data concepts and structure the data to make it easy to work with. Developers tend to use attributes as a means of further describing the data. An *attribute* is a name/value pair that appears within an element. For example, here's an attribute for a `<Customer>` node:

```
<Customer LastUpdated="01/15/2013">
    <Name>Joe Smith</Name>
    <Age>42</Age>
    <FavoriteColor>Blue</FavoriteColor>
</Customer>
```

In this case, the time the information was last updated is supplementary — it doesn't affect the overall data. The overall data — the customer information — would still be usable without the attribute. There's some overlap between element and attribute data, and some developers have different viewpoints of precisely when to use one or the other. In fact, some developers never use attributes. XML doesn't require that you use them. There are some rules for using attributes:

- ✔ An attribute must always appear as part of an element.

- ✔ It must always contain a name and value pair separated by the equals sign (=).

- ✔ The value must always appear in quotes.

- ✔ Attributes can use either single or double quotes, but the beginning and ending quote must be the same.

- ✔ Use the character replacements shown in Table 16-1 when using certain characters in your attribute.

Be careful in using attributes too heavily in your data. Attributes present a number of potential problems that make some developers avoid them.

- ✔ An attribute can contain only one piece of data, not multiple pieces like an element can.

- ✔ Attributes can't contain tree structures, so you can't vary the information easily.

- ✔ It isn't easy to expand attributes because the software that's used to read them will expect a certain number of attributes that contain specific data.

Attributes do serve well as a means of providing amplifying data. Just be careful to use them correctly. You should never end up with elements that look like this:

```
<Customer LastUpdated="01/15/2013"
         Name="Joe Smith"
         Age="42"
         FavoriteColor="Blue" />
```

## Working through a basic file

This chapter uses some simple customer information for example purposes. Of course, XML data can become quite complex. For example, when working with a Web service, you see many layers of data contained in a highly nested tree structure. However, for the purposes of explanation, this file is just fine. (You can find complete code for this example in the \Chapter 16 folder of the downloadable code as Customers.XML.)

```
<?xml version="1.0" encoding="UTF-8"?>
<Customers>
    <Customer LastUpdated="01/15/2013">
        <Name>Joe Smith</Name>
        <Age>42</Age>
        <FavoriteColor>Blue</FavoriteColor>
    </Customer>
    <Customer LastUpdated="01/21/2013">
        <Name>Amy Wang</Name>
        <Age>33</Age>
        <FavoriteColor>Orange</FavoriteColor>
    </Customer>
</Customers>
```

The file contains the XML declaration, which is a kind of processing instruction. The root node, <Customers>, contains two <Customer> nodes, each with the same tree structure. Each <Customer> element contains a single attribute, LastUpdated, which shows the date that the information contained with the node was last updated.

Trying to visualize the data by looking at just the code can be difficult, especially when you're using a simple text editor to create it. Fortunately, you have another alternative. Simply open the XML file in your browser, and you generally see a color-coded alternative view like the one shown in Figure 16-1. The minus signs next to some lines of code let you collapse those lines so you see just an overview of the data.

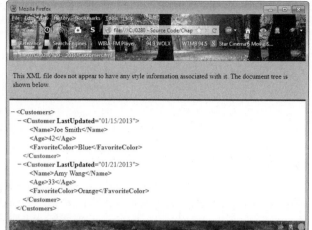

**Figure 16-1:**
Most browsers make it easy to view the content of XML files.

# Displaying XML Using XSLT

XML is a great way to store data. However, it isn't the easiest way to see the data. All of the tags tend to hide the data rather than make it easy to understand. A generated XML file tends to lack whitespace, which makes viewing it even more difficult. Although this book focuses on viewing XML by using JavaScript on an HTML5 page, you need to know that there are other ways to view XML.

Some developers use a Cascading Style Sheet (CSS) method (you can read about this method at `http://www.htmlgoodies.com/beyond/css/displaying-xml-files-using-css.html`), but most developers prefer to use XML Stylesheet Language for Transformations (XSLT). Using XSLT has some significant advantages in flexibility and the ability to work with complex data over CSS, but XSLT is also a little harder to learn. You can see an XSLT tutorial at `http://www.w3schools.com/xsl`.

Nothing works quite so well as a quick example to demonstrate how XSLT works. To use XSLT with an XML file, you need to add a processing instruction to the XML file. The following processing instruction tells the browser displaying the `Customer2.XML` file to use the `CustomerOut.XSLT` file to format the information. (You can find complete code for this example in the `\Chapter 16` folder of the downloadable code as `Customers2.XML` and `CustomerOut.XSLT`.) This is the only difference between the `Customers2.XML` file and the `Customers.XML` file described in the preceding section of the chapter.

```
<?xml-stylesheet type="text/xsl" href="CustomerOut.xslt"?>
```

To transform an XML document into a document you can see, you build an HTML document from it. The following code provides a typical example of XSLT code that you might use for transformation purposes:

```xml
<?xml version="1.0" encoding="UTF-8"?>
<xsl:stylesheet
    xmlns:xsl="http://www.w3.org/1999/XSL/Transform"
    version="1.0">
  <xsl:template match="/">
    <html>
      <body>
        <h1>Customer Listing</h1>
        <table border="1">
          <tr>
            <th>Name</th>
            <th>Age</th>
            <th>Favorite Color</th>
          </tr>
          <xsl:for-each select="Customers/Customer">
            <tr>
              <td>
                <xsl:value-of select="Name" />
              </td>
              <td>
                <xsl:value-of select="Age" />
              </td>
              <td>
                <xsl:value-of
                    select="FavoriteColor" />
              </td>
            </tr>
          </xsl:for-each>
        </table>
      </body>
    </html>
  </xsl:template>
</xsl:stylesheet>
```

That's right: XSLT is actually another form of XML, so it starts out with the XML declaration. The `<xsl:stylesheet>` root node defines the document as providing XSLT support. It includes a namespace attribute that tells the browser where to find information on how to interpret XSLT. You can find out more about namespaces at `http://www.w3schools.com/xml/xml_namespaces.asp`.

The `<xsl:template>` tag tells the browser what information to retrieve from the XML file for display purposes. This document retrieves everything in the XML file.

The next steps begin creating the HTML document, complete with the tags required to do so. This is an abbreviated page. Normally, you'd include all the required tags. The page includes a heading and the start of a table.

The `<xsl:for-each>` tag processes each of the `<Customer>` entries in the file. The file then builds the rows and data cells for the table. The `<xsl:value-of>` tag retrieves the data values of the `<Name>`, `<Age>`, and `<FavoriteColor>` elements. Figure 16-2 shows typical output from this example.

**Figure 16-2:**
The formatted customer data is much easier to see.

Some browsers encounter problems using the example from the local drive. For example, Chrome displays a blank page when you access `Customers2.XML` from the local drive. To test this technique in a way that works for most browsers, copy the files to your Web server and then access the XML file from the Web server. Using the setup described in Chapter 2, you should be able to use `http://localhost/Customers2.xml` as the URL and see the results in Figure 16-2 using all three of the test browsers.

# Validating XML

One of the strengths of XML is that it presents data in a highly structured manner that makes the context of the data clear and understandable. However, one of the weaknesses of XML is that it doesn't tolerate errors well. When a parser encounters an error in your XML file, it typically stops at that point and doesn't perform any additional processing. With this in mind, the following sections provide a brief overview of what you can do to validate the XML used in your applications.

## Understanding the concept of well-formed

Before you can use an XML document in any capacity, it must be well-formed. A *well-formed* XML document contains all of the features described so far in the chapter. It follows the rules specified in the various sections of the chapter. The problem is that most developers don't speak XML, and you won't use production data to gain experience working with XML in most cases. The files you create for experimentation purposes must be well-formed too.

Fortunately, you don't have to invest in fancy software to check your work or rely on someone else's eyes to find the mistakes you've made. A number of sites provide XML validators you can use for checking your work. Two such sites are

- **<?xml?>:** `http://www.xmlvalidation.com`
- **W3Schools:** `http://www.w3schools.com/xml/xml_validator.asp`

In both cases, you simply copy and paste your XML into the window provided and click a button, and the application tells you about any errors in your file. Both sites also provide a means for working with complete files, rather than using the cutting and pasting approach.

## Discovering XSD

The fact that an XML document is well-formed doesn't say much. It's easy to create a well-formed XML document that won't work because the structure is incorrect. For example, the data might not include a required node, or the node might use the wrong capitalization or be misspelled. All sorts of errors can creep into data files that aren't validated in some way. The use of XML Schema Definition (XSD) files makes it possible to check the precise structure of a file and display a list of errors in it.

A complete discussion of XSD would consume several chapters, and you won't actually use this strategy in the examples in this book. However, using XSD is an important technique in situations where data errors of any sort could be catastrophic. (Think about banking or medical records.) You can gain a better understanding of XSD through the excellent W3Schools tutorial at `http://www.w3schools.com/schema/default.asp`. The CodeGuru tutorial at `http://www.codeguru.com/java/article.php/c13529/XSD-Tutorial-XML-Schemas-For-Beginners.htm` is shorter but provides helpful information on this technique as well.

# Loading XML with JavaScript

So far, this chapter has helped you explore XML as a storage technology, methods to display it, and methods to validate it. All of this preliminary information is helpful in using XML with JavaScript. Now that the preliminaries are out of the way, it's time to view an example of how you can interact with XML files using a combination of JavaScript and HTML5.

The example in this section shows how you could parse an XML document by using JavaScript and display its content onscreen. What you need to consider in reviewing this example is that you gain substantial flexibility using JavaScript and that the example shows only the tip of the iceberg when it comes to the things you can do. (You can find complete code for this example in the \Chapter 16 folder of the downloadable code as Navigate.HTML.)

```javascript
<script language="JavaScript">
   // Create a connection to the file.
   var Connect = new XMLHttpRequest();

   // Define which file to open and
   // send the request.
   Connect.open("GET", "Customers.xml", false);
   Connect.setRequestHeader("Content-Type", "text/xml");
   Connect.send(null);

   // Place the response in an XML document.
   var TheDocument = Connect.responseXML;

   // Place the root node in an element.
   var Customers = TheDocument.childNodes[0];

   // Retrieve each customer in turn.
   for (var i = 0; i < Customers.children.length; i++)
   {
       var Customer = Customers.children[i];

       // Access each of the data values.
       var Name = Customer.getElementsByTagName("Name");
       var Age = Customer.getElementsByTagName("Age");
       var Color = Customer.getElementsByTagName(
           "FavoriteColor");

       // Write the data to the page.
       document.write("<tr><td>");
       document.write(Name[0].textContent.toString());
       document.write("</td><td>");
       document.write(Age[0].textContent.toString());
       document.write("</td><td>");
       document.write(Color[0].textContent.toString());
       document.write("</td></tr>");
   }
</script>
```

All modern browsers support the XMLHttpRequest object. You can use this object to create a connection to any server and request resources from it. In this case, the application is using the XMLHttpRequest to request the Customers.XML file, but you can use it for any resource. You can find out more about this object at http://www.w3.org/TR/XMLHttpRequest.

To request data, you must first define the information you need. In this case, the code uses the open() function to specify that it wants to use the GET method of obtaining the data, that the data is located in Customers.XML, and that it wants to make a synchronous request. A *synchronous request* is one in which the browser waits for the data and processes it immediately. You can also create asynchronous requests by using a callback function. The code also sets the request header to the kind of data that the application is requesting. The send() function sends the information to the server.

On return from the send() function call, the responseXML property contains an XML document. There are other response properties you use for data of other types. For example, if you requested a text file, you use the responseText property instead.

The XML document contains the root node, Customers, at element 0. It places this data in Customers. The Customers.children property contains two Customer child nodes — one for each customer in the file. A for loop processes each of these Customer nodes. Because each Customer child node has a unique name, you can use the getElementsByTagName() function to retrieve the data they contain.

The resulting variables — Name, Age, and Color — are then used to add data to the table on the page. Notice that you must use the textContent property and then convert this property to a string by calling toString(). Otherwise, the table will display an object name, rather than the actual data. Figure 16-3 shows typical output from this example.

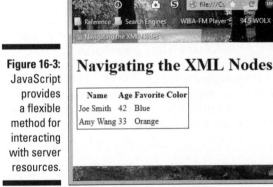

**Figure 16-3:** JavaScript provides a flexible method for interacting with server resources.

# Chapter 17

# Cleaning Up the Web with AJAX

C hapter 16 introduces you to XML, which is essentially a means of storing textual data in a structured way so that it retains its original context but is easily used by any platform. In that chapter, you see a basic example of what amounts to a database. This chapter looks at XML from a new perspective — as a means of exchanging data with a server and of updating parts of a Web page without reloading an entire page. This technology is called Asynchronous JavaScript and XML (AJAX). It isn't a new language but merely a new way to use existing standards to perform specialized tasks.

This chapter provides a simple overview of AJAX. You've probably seen AJAX at work in the past. This programming technique is used to create some of the effects used by Google Maps, Gmail, YouTube, and Facebook (amongst many others). When you complete this chapter, you'll know more about AJAX and how it can help you create applications that are more flexible and dynamic.

# Introducing AJAX

Many developers have heard of AJAX, assumed it was a special sort of language, and never went any further. AJAX isn't a new language; it's a reuse of existing technology to create a new way of dealing with updates to documents. You already know the technologies behind AJAX; all you need to do is apply them in a new way to gain some major advantages in presenting content online. The following sections describe AJAX and present some simple scenarios for using it to create dynamic pages on your site.

## Learning the benefits of AJAX

AJAX makes it possible to create dynamic applications that load and run faster and also use fewer network and server resources. The goal of AJAX is to allow changes to a page without having to reload the entire page. Using AJAX makes it possible to create applications that are quite fast without loading the server down with large requests. All the server has to do is send a small piece of data to the caller when requested. This small piece of data travels faster over the network, which means that request latency is also smaller.

One of the bigger reasons to use AJAX is that it's standards-based (created and administered by a standards group). There isn't some large company out there that controls AJAX. Because it's standards-based, AJAX runs on any newer browser and platform combination that supports the standards it uses. AJAX relies on these standards:

- ✔ **JavaScript:** You use JavaScript to write the code required to handle events at the browser, make requests to the server, and update areas on the page as needed.

- ✔ **Document Object Model (DOM):** JavaScript makes use of the DOM to gain access to specific locations on the page.

- ✔ **Cascading Style Sheets (CSS):** Using CSS makes it possible to create special effects during data updates. In addition, CSS makes the new data fit in with the existing page content.

- ✔ **eXtensible Markup Language (XML):** Any update is going to require some sort of data. XML is a perfect choice because it works anywhere.

- ✔ **XMLHttpRequest object:** Communication with the server requires a connection, and the XMLHttpRequest object creates this connection. Chapter 16 shows how to use a synchronous connection to insert XML data onto a page during the loading process. AJAX performs its tasks asynchronously.

## Understanding how AJAX works

AJAX doesn't perform magic. There's nothing behind the scenes that doesn't make sense once you understand it. In fact, AJAX performs its task by using a process that's similar to the one you've used for many of the examples in this book. The only difference is that AJAX performs the task over a network wire rather than locally in the same page or an external page in the same folder. Here's the sequence of events that occur when using AJAX.

1. An event occurs at the browser. (The nature of the event is irrelevant but generally involves a data request of some sort.)

2. JavaScript creates a new XMLHttpRequest object. In this case, the object will be configured to perform its work asynchronously using a callback function.

3. JavaScript sends the request to the server for processing. At this point, the page continues performing tasks as it normally does while waiting for a response.

4. The server receives the XMLHttpRequest object that JavaScript sent and processes it.

5. The server creates a response and sends it back to the browser.

6. The browser's callback function provided with the original request receives the response from the server.

7. The callback function performs any required post-processing of the response.

8. An update of the information onscreen occurs, and the user sees the result.

## Deciphering the XMLHttpRequest object

It may at first seem that XMLHttpRequest object is intensely complicated, but it really isn't if you take it apart and view it a bit at a time. In reality, most developers use only a few well-known methods and properties. However, it's entirely possible that developers would use more features of this object if they knew they existed. The following sections break the XMLHttpRequest object into two pieces: request and response. You use methods and properties to perform these two tasks, so it makes sense to review them from that perspective.

### Working with the request

To obtain resources from the server, you must make a request. After all, the server doesn't read minds. You build up a request by using methods and properties, and then you use the send() method to transmit the request you've built. The following list describes the properties normally associated with requests:

- ✔ timeout: Determines the time, in milliseconds, that the request will continue attempting to obtain a required resource from the server.

- ✔ withCredentials: Specifies that the request should include the user's credentials when set to true. The credentials allow access to secure resources on the server.

✔ `upload`: Provides the server with a `XMLHttpRequestUpload` object that contains data the server requires to fulfill a request.

Now that you have a better idea of which properties are available to make a request, it's time to look at the methods. The following methods are usually associated with making a request of some type:

✔ `open()`: Creates a new request. The request can include a number of arguments as defined in the following list in the order you provide them:

- `method`: Determines the method used to access the resource. The two valid choices are `GET` and `POST`.

- `URL`: Specifies the location of the resource on the server.

- `asynchronous`: Determines whether the request is made in a synchronous or asynchronous manner. The caller must provide a callback function when this flag is set to true (for an asynchronous request).

- `username`: Contains the user's logon name for secure resource access.

- `password`: Contains the user's password for secure resource access.

✔ `setRequestHeader()`: Creates a name/value pair to include with the request header. You supply the name and value as two separate arguments that the call uses to create the request header entry.

✔ `send()`: Transmits the request to the server. It sounds simple, but a number of features are in place to make the process more reliable than simply throwing a request out and hoping something happens. You can read about the entire process if you want at `http://www.w3.org/TR/XMLHttpRequest/#infrastructure-for-the-send()-method`. However, from a developer's perspective, how `send()` works isn't nearly as important as what `send()` returns. The `send()` method either returns data or an error. Here are the four most common errors you receive and why they happen:

- `network`: Something has happened to stop the request from reaching the server. In some cases, a Domain Name System (DNS) error causes the request to get lost before it reaches the server. In other cases, a Transport Layer Security (TLS) error occurs, which means that your application may not have the required credentials. In fact, network errors can come from a number of sources, but these are the two most common reasons.

- `abort`: The end user has cancelled the request. To cause this error, your application must call the `abort()` method.

- • timeout: A request has wandered about looking for the resource it needs and finally given up. Requests have a timeout value associated with them. Otherwise, the request could continue looking for a resource indefinitely if that resource doesn't exist.

- • request: There's a problem with the request. You normally have to dig deeper to find out precisely what the problem is. However, there are a number of common causes, including: requesting a non-existent resource, not providing a required argument, and providing information of the wrong type.

✔ abort(): Stops execution of the current request.

### *Working with the response*

The XMLHttpRequest object also provides a number of response properties and methods that you use to determine the success or failure of a request. Here are the properties that you commonly use when working with this object:

✔ status: Returns the HTTP status code. A status code of 200 means that the request completed successfully. Any other code normally reflects some sort of problem with the request process. You can find a list of status codes at http://www.w3.org/Protocols/HTTP/HTRESP.html.

✔ statusText: Returns the HTTP status as a textual value. For example, a status code of 200 returns a text value of OK. You can find a list of status text values and their associated codes at http://www.w3.org/Protocols/HTTP/HTRESP.html.

✔ readyState: Specifies the current state of asynchronous processing. The state can be any of these values:

- • 0: Request not initialized

- • 1: Server connection established

- • 2: Request received

- • 3: Processing request

- • 4: Request finished and response is ready

✔ responseType: Returns the value of the Content-Type response header. An application can use this value to determine how to react to the type of response the server has sent. The common return types are

- • "": An empty string indicates that the return type is unknown or that an error has occurred and there's no response to process.

- • arraybuffer: The data is in the form of an array.

- `blob`: The sender has used a Binary Large Object (BLOB) to store the data.

- `document`: The data appears as structured information in an XML document. Normally, the document is complete, rather than an XML fragment.

- `json`: The sender has used JavaScript Object Notation (JSON) to encapsulate the data.

- `text`: The information appears as plain text, which may mean that it lacks context and structure. However, some text formats are structured, such as Comma Separated Variable (CSV).

✔ `response`: Contains the entire response without any interpretation as an object.

✔ `responseText`: Contains only the text of a response when the `response Type` value is `" "` (the empty string) or `text`. This property returns nothing for other `responseType` values.

✔ `responseXML`: Contains only the XML document when the `response Type` value is `" "` (the empty string) or `document`. This property returns nothing for other `responseType` values.

The response methods help you interact with the response data in some way. Here are the response methods:

✔ `getResponseHeader()`: Obtains a specific response header value from the response object. You supply the value of the response header you want, such as `Content-Type`, as an argument to the method. There are no required response headers, and a server can create custom headers, but you can find a list of common response headers at `http://www. httpwatch.com/httpgallery/headers`.

✔ `getAllResponseHeaders()`: Creates an array of all of the response headers except those that are listed as `Set-Cookie` or `Set-Cookie2`.

✔ `overrideMimeType()`: Specifies the value of the `Content-Type` response header.

# Performing AJAX Tasks Using JavaScript

Using AJAX with pure JavaScript is a two-part process. First, you must send the request. Second, you must process the response. The following code shows the two parts of the process used to change just part of a page. You must execute this code on your server — it won't respond properly from the local drive. (You can find complete code for this example in the \Chapter 17 folder of the downloadable code as AJAX_JavaScript.HTML.)

```
// Create a connection to the server.
var Connect = new XMLHttpRequest();

function LoadDoc()
{
    // Specify which function to use on return.
    Connect.onreadystatechange = ProcessData;

    // Make the request.
    Connect.open("GET","Special.txt",true);
    Connect.send();
}

function ProcessData()
{
    // Verify the return status.
    if ((Connect.readyState == 4) &&
        (Connect.status == 200))
    {
        // Modify the <div> content.
        document.getElementById("ChangeText").innerHTML =
            Connect.responseText;
    }
}
```

The code begins by creating an XMLHttpRequest object, Connect, which is used to handle the connection with the server. This object is common to both requesting the data and processing it later.

When a user clicks Change the Text, the button calls LoadDoc(). The first step is to tell Connect where to find the function, ProcessData(), used to process the data later. The code then creates a request for Special. txt using the GET method. Notice that the open() function is set to use an asynchronous call rather than a synchronous call, which you might use when working with XML data.

The ProcessData() function receives input any time that the readyState changes for the connection. However, you don't need to process every change. The code begins by checking for a readyState of 4 and a status of 200, which means that the response has been successfully processed and is ready to use. When this combination occurs, the code changes just the text of the target <div> onscreen.

# Making AJAX Easier with jQuery

The example found in the "Checking browser and version" section of Chapter 2 introduces you to a valuable online library called jQuery. Using jQuery greatly reduces the amount of code you need to write to make AJAX work. In fact, creating an AJAX application becomes relatively simple. Of course, using jQuery always begins with defining the library source, as shown here. (You can find complete code for this example in the \Chapter 17 folder of the downloadable code as AJAX_jQuery.HTML.)

```
<script
    src="http://code.jquery.com/jquery-latest.js">
</script>
```

Using the latest jQuery version is always a good idea, but you can also download a local copy of jQuery to speed queries from http://code.jquery. com. This example relies on a simple button to execute the event handler shown here:

```
function ChangeText()
{
    $("#ChangeText").load("Special.txt");
}
```

The jQuery calls are preceded by a dollar sign ($). This call accesses a <div> with an id of ChangeText. It calls the load() function for that <div> with a resource of Special.txt. When you run the query, you see that the text in the <div> changes without loading the rest of the page.

# Chapter 18

# Making JavaScript Easier with jQuery

**In This Chapter**

▶ Understanding the jQuery library

▶ Working with the Google CDN

▶ Performing standard programming tasks with jQuery

▶ Creating event handlers using jQuery

**M**ost of the applications in previous chapters of the book use straight-forward JavaScript coding techniques. You write all the code required to perform a particular task. Writing your own code is a good way to figure out precisely how JavaScript works. Of course, it's also time consuming and error prone. The need to produce error-free applications quickly has created a demand for third-party libraries of common routines — code that a lot of developers need. jQuery is just one of many such libraries.

The reason that jQuery appears in this chapter is that it's one of the most used libraries for Web applications. In addition, you can use it without cost. That makes jQuery a good first choice for libraries. The first section of this chapter describes jQuery in further detail.

Previous examples in the book load jQuery directly from the jQuery site, which is a great idea if you plan to use just one library. However, as your skills grow and the complexity of the applications you create increases, you'll want to use other libraries. This chapter also examines one potential solution to the problem of working with multiple libraries, the Google APIs — essentially a means of accessing a number of these common libraries from a single site so that the user isn't constantly wondering whether allowing a particular library is safe.

The remainder of this chapter discusses ways in which you can use jQuery to make yourself more productive and to write better code in less time. A single chapter is barely enough to provide an overview of jQuery, so an overview is just what you get in the sections that follow.

It's important that you not get the idea that jQuery is the only product worth consideration out there. It would be impossible to explore all the possible libraries out there, even if you had an entire book to do it.

# Getting to Know the jQuery Library

There are many reasons to use jQuery within your applications. The most compelling are that

- ✔ Doing so will save you time.
- ✔ Using a library reduces the number of lines of code you must write.
- ✔ Relying on a standardized library provides a consistent manner of implementing application details.

In earlier chapters, you can see jQuery in action to an extent. For example, Chapters 2 and 17 rely on jQuery to perform some smaller tasks. In Chapter 2, the example in the section on checking browser and version shows a simple technique for detecting the browser making a request so you can service its request properly. Getting this information by using pure JavaScript would be cumbersome at best. In Chapter 17, the example in the section on making AJAX easier with jQuery is especially noteworthy because using jQuery reduces the number of lines of code used to create an AJAX application from six lines to a single line.

The jQuery library's also quite flexible. It won't fulfill every need, but it fulfills many of them. You can use jQuery to perform these sorts of tasks:

- ✔ Provide complex selectors for accessing elements on a page.
- ✔ Interact with Document Object Model (DOM) attributes with greater ease.
- ✔ Locate elements based on their relationship to other elements.
- ✔ Manipulate the DOM in some way.
- ✔ Perform Cascading Style Sheet (CSS)—related tasks with greater ease.
- ✔ Create and interact with events.
- ✔ Define special page effects.

✔ Perform Asynchronous JavaScript and XML (AJAX)—related tasks with greater ease.

✔ Interact with the browser.

✔ Ease creation and interaction with collections and other structures.

✔ Add and interact with special user interface widgets (plug-ins that make the user interface more interesting and useful).

Using jQuery also solves some issues that many developers face. For example, jQuery makes it possible to detect when a page is ready to manipulate using the `ready` event. This event ensures that your application won't try to execute code before the page has completed downloading and the document is configured for use. A failure to detect the ready state has caused problems for many developers because the JavaScript code will intermittently fail depending on whether the document was fully loaded at the time.

There are multiple sources for the jQuery library. However, you can always be certain of gaining access to the current version of the library using the following script tag. (You can find complete code for this example in the `\Chapter 18\Basics` folder of the downloadable code as `jQueryBasics.HTML`.)

```
<script
    src="http://code.jquery.com/jquery-latest.js">
</script>
```

The example relies on a button to perform a task. However, the page starts with the button disabled so that the user can't click it until the page is actually ready for use. You can set the control to the disabled state by using the `disabled` property as shown here:

```
<input id="btnMsg"
       type="button"
       value="Click Me"
       onclick="SayHello()"
       disabled=true />
```

To enable the control when the page is loaded and ready for use, the example relies on the jQuery `ready` event. The event automatically fires and enables the control so the user can interact with it. Here's the short jQuery script used to perform the task:

```
$(document).ready(
   function(){$("#btnMsg").attr("disabled", false);});
```

This code uses several new techniques, so review it carefully. You access jQuery using the dollar sign ($). The parenthesis after the $ indicates what part of the document to access.

When you want to access an object, you use the object's name without quotes. In this case, the code wants to access the document object. The code is assigning an anonymous function to the ready event.

An *anonymous function* is one that you create dynamically using JavaScript at runtime. The function has no name, and it's accessed in a specific way. You can't access the function from anywhere else because it has no name. The main advantage of using an anonymous function is that it makes your code concise. In addition, you can build functions on the fly by writing them to the page as needed. You can read about using anonymous functions at `http://helephant.com/2008/08/23/javascript-anonymous-functions`.

The anonymous function accesses the `<input type="button">` tag that has an id of btnMsg. When you want to access an element by id, you place the element's id value in quotes and precede the value with the pound sign (#). This function uses the jQuery `attr()` function to change the disabled attribute value to false so that the button is now enabled.

# Loading jQuery from Google CDN

Many developers use multiple libraries when creating an application because each library has something special to offer. Each reference to a source outside the current page can trigger a security message. This is a helpful feature of many browsers today that's often supported through a plug-in. Knowing where a page looks for resources can help keep a user's machine safe. However, when users begin seeing a lot of messages about sites they may not know about, many users throw up their hands and don't allow these external sites access to the page. Consequently, your application fails because it lacks access to the libraries it needs to work. The answer is to use a single source to access the libraries you need — a source that the user is likely to recognize and permit access to the browser page.

The Google Content Distribution Network (CDN) found at `https://developers.google.com/speed/libraries/devguide` is a series of libraries that you can use to create better applications. Google maintains all of these libraries on a common domain, `http://ajax.googleapis.com`, which means that users don't have to think so hard about each library you use in an application. All the user needs to do is approve use of a single domain. Many developers rely on the Google APIs site to gain access to libraries such as jQuery. You see it all the time when working with pages online. Figure 18-1 shows a listing of typical libraries found on the Google CDN.

**Figure 18-1:**
The Google
CDN makes
a number
of libraries
available for
use in appli-
cations.

When you want to use a particular library, you click its link on the page, and Google displays a script for accessing it. For example, when you want to use jQuery, you click its link to see a snippet similar to the one shown here. (You can find complete code for this example in the \Chapter 18\Basics folder of the downloadable code as GoogleCDN.HTML.)

```
<script
   src="http://ajax.googleapis.com/ajax/libs/jquery/1.8.3/jquery.min.js">
</script>
```

With a simple replacement of the src attribute in the example in the preceding section, you can use the Google CDN version of the library. Give it a try and you find that the example works just as it did before. For the purposes of this book, it doesn't matter which version of the library link you use, but the book does assume that you're using the 1.8.3 version of jQuery because that's the most current version available as of this writing.

Your application may depend on a specific version of the jQuery library. If this is the case, you can access the version you want from the Google CDN. Simply replace the 1.8.3 part of the URL with the version you want. The Google CDN hosts all versions of jQuery except versions 1.2.4 and 1.2.5 because these two versions weren't available for very long.

# Doing Things Easier with jQuery

Using jQuery to perform specific tasks makes life a lot easier for the developer. The following sections discuss and demonstrate a number of ways in which you can use jQuery to create applications faster and with fewer errors.

## Gathering elements with selectors

The act of selecting items on which to operate can prove time consuming. The examples in this book use only a few elements. A typical production page can contain a hundred elements or more quite easily. When you work with that many elements, trying to find a specific element becomes time consuming, especially when some of those elements are dynamically generated.

You can use jQuery to create the following types of selectors:

✔ **Basic:** Lets you access major document features. You use these selectors to perform a majority of tasks with jQuery. You can read more about them at `http://api.jquery.com/category/selectors/basic-css-selectors`. Here's a list of basic selectors that you commonly use:

- *All selector* (`"*"`): Selects all the elements in the document.

- *Object selector* (`object`): Selects the specific object types. The most commonly used object is `document`.

- *Class selector* (`".class"`): Selects a specific class as specified by the `class` attribute for an element. This selector always appears within quotes and is preceded by a period.

- *Element selector* (`"element"`): Accesses all the elements with a particular tag name, such as *p* for the <p> tag. This selector always appears within quotes.

- *ID selector* (`"#id"`): Chooses a specific element with the `id` attribute value specified. This selector always appears within quotes and is preceded by a pound sign (#).

- *Multiple selector* (`"selector1, selector2, selectorN"`): Selects each of the elements specified in the comma delimited list.

✔ **Attribute:** Provides access to attributes that have specific name/value pair combinations. For example, you could access every element that has a `value="SomeText"` name/value pair across different elements. Each of these selectors takes the form `$('a[name="value"]')`. You can use different operators to define the relationship between the name and its value. For example, the not-equal (`!=`) operator selects all attributes that aren't equal to the value specified by the attribute name you provide. You can see more of the operators and their descriptions at `http://api.jquery.com/category/selectors/attribute-selectors`.

✔ **Form:** Selects all of the elements on a form that reflect a specific element name/characteristic pairing. For example, you could choose to select all of the `<input>` elements that are checked using `$("input:checked")`. Many of these selectors are deprecated. You can read more about this selector type at `http://api.jquery.com/category/selectors/form-selectors`.

✔ **Hierarchy:** Allows selection of an element based on its relation to a currently selected element. For example, you can choose to select the parent of a child element. You can read more about this selector type at `http://api.jquery.com/category/selectors/hierarchy-selectors`. These selectors take several forms as described here:

- *Child selector* (`"parent > child"`): Specifies that the code should select all the children of a particular type given a specific type of parent. For example, if you want to select all the list item (`<li>`) elements that are children of an unordered list (`<ul>`), you use `$("ul > li")`.

- *Descendant selector* (`"ancestor descendant"`): Specifies that the code should select all the decedents of a particular ancestor element. For example, if you want to select all the `<input>` elements contained within a `<form>` element, you use `$("form input")`.

- *Next adjacent selector* (`"prev + next"`): Specifies that the code should select elements that follow a given element at the same level in the hierarchy. For example, if you want to select all `<input>` elements that follow a `<label>` element, you use `$("label + input")`.

- *Next siblings selector* (`"prev ~ siblings"`): Specifies that the code should select elements that follow a given element in the hierarchy. This selector differs from the next adjacent selector in that it also selects siblings. Consequently, if you want to select all `<div>` elements in a form, no matter where they appear in the hierarchy, you use `$("form ~ div")`.

✔ **Basic filter:** Provides you with essential aids for selecting one or a group of elements out of a list of elements based on a specific criterion. For example, you can use the animated filter to choose all the elements that are animated from a list of like elements. Most basic filters work on index values. For example, the first filter selects the first element in a list of elements. To use a filter, you add a colon (`:`) to another selector and then add the filter. For example, `$("tr:even")` selects the even-numbered `<tr>` tags from a list. You can read more about this type of filter at `http://api.jquery.com/category/selectors/basic-filter-selectors`.

*Filtering* is the process of reducing the size of a list of elements to reflect just the selections you need. In many cases, the selection process provides you with a crude list of element candidates. The filtering process refines this list so that you see only the elements you actually need.

✔ **Child filter:** Selects child elements that are the first, last, nth, or only child of their parent. You can read more about this type of filter at `http://api.jquery.com/category/selectors/child-filter-selectors`.

✔ **Content filter:** Chooses elements based on content criterion: specific content, no content at all (empty), partial content, or element parent. You can read more about this type of filter at `http://api.jquery.com/category/selectors/content-filter-selector`.

✔ **Visibility filter:** Filters elements based on their visibility. You can read more about this type of filter at `http://api.jquery.com/category/selectors/visibility-filter-selectors`.

✔ **jQuery extensions:** Provides assorted extensions to the CSS standard. Many of these extensions deal with functionality that jQuery adds to the JavaScript programming environment. However, some have curious flexibility. For example, you can use the button selector to select all the `<button>` and `<input type="button">` elements on a page by using a single selection. You can read more about this type of selector at `http://api.jquery.com/category/selectors/jquery-selector-extensions`.

## Working with programmatically generated elements

The section on nesting loops in Chapter 9 presents the `NestedLoop.HTML` example, which outputs a multiplication table as an HTML `<table>`. The output is correct but hardly interesting. The example in this section builds on that earlier example by adding a bit of special formatting to it, along with a `mouseover` effect — the section about Events in Chapter 12 describes the pure JavaScript approach to this technique. (You can find complete code for this example in the `\Chapter 18\Standard Tasks` folder of the downloadable code as `NestedLoop.HTML`.)

```
// Perform some basic formatting.
$("th:even").css("background-color", "lightblue");
$("th:odd").css("background-color", "lightgreen");
$("td:even").css("background-color", "lightgreen");
$("td:odd").css("background-color", "lightblue");
$("th, td").css("width", "50px");
```

```
// Add a special effect.
$("td").mouseover(
    function()
    {
        $(this).toggleClass("Selected");
    });
$("td").mouseout(
    function()
    {
        $(this).toggleClass("Selected");
    });
```

The formatting consists of selecting the `<th>` and `<td>` elements and then using a basic filter to choose between odd and even elements. The odd elements receive one background color, and the even elements receive another. The code then uses a multiple selector to apply the same width formatting to each of the cells. By combining selectors and selector filters, you can create some interesting effects with little programming. It's important to remember that this table is programmatically generated, so applying formatting to it could be difficult.

The special effect starts with the `<td>` elements. When a user hovers the mouse over a particular element, the code applies the Selected CSS formatting to it. Likewise, when the user places the mouse somewhere else, the effect is toggled back to the original formatting used by the `<td>` element. Toggling the formatting is a quick way to create a `mouseover` effect. Figure 18-2 shows typical output from this example.

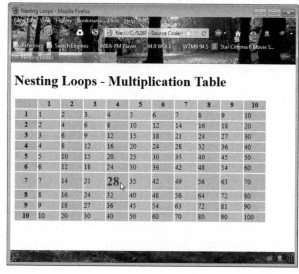

**Figure 18-2:** The table is a little nicer and includes a special effect now.

# Revisiting arrays with jQuery

Using jQuery can make it easier to work with arrays. The management tasks become easier, and you can use jQuery to interact with arrays in ways that would be hard using standard JavaScript code. The following list describes some of the most commonly used array-oriented features of jQuery:

- ✔ `jQuery.each()`: Makes it possible to iterate through an array or object without having to create the conditions used with a `for` statement. You can use this feature for arrays and collections of all sorts. For example, it's possible to use this feature to iterate over a list of `<div>` tags on a page. The idea is that this feature makes it possible to use a common strategy to interact with collections of all sorts. You can read more about this feature at `http://docs.jquery.com/Utilities/jQuery.each`.

- ✔ `jQuery.extend()`: Provides a technique for joining two objects and then returning the combination of the two as a modified object. For example, you can add the contents of one array to another array. However, this feature works with objects of all sorts. You can even use it to provide new functionality to the jQuery library. You can read more about this feature at `http://docs.jquery.com/Utilities/jQuery.extend`.

- ✔ `jQuery.grep()`: Filters an array using the specified expression and returns a new array containing just the elements that satisfy the conditions. This feature requires that you provide a function to perform the actual filtering, so it's incredibly flexible. You can read more about this feature at `http://docs.jquery.com/Utilities/jQuery.grep`.

- ✔ `jQuery.makeArray()`: Creates an array out of any object you provide as input. You can use any sort of list as input. For example, you could even obtain a list of a particular element type and turn that list into an array. You can read more about this feature at `http://docs.jquery.com/Utilities/jQuery.makeArray`.

- ✔ `jQuery.map()`: Translates an array of items into another array of items. You provide a function to perform the translation. The function receives the item to translate and its index in the array. A translation function can return a modified form of the item, the original item, null when the item is to be removed from the output, or a list of items that will be flattened into a single element in the resulting array. You can read more about this feature at `http://docs.jquery.com/Utilities/jQuery.map`.

- ✔ `jQuery.inArray()`: Locates the specified item in the array and returns an index to that item when found. If the function can't find the item, it returns a value of $-1$. You can read more about this feature at `http://docs.jquery.com/Utilities/jQuery.inArray`.

✔ jQuery.merge(): Creates a single array from two arrays. If the two items aren't true arrays but merely lists of items, use makeArray() to create a true array first. When the two arrays could contain duplication items, you can use the unique() function to remove the duplicates. You can read more about this feature at http://docs.jquery.com/Utilities/jQuery.merge.

✔ jQuery.unique(): Removes duplicate elements from an array of elements. This feature works only with elements and won't remove duplicate items from an array of strings or numbers. You can read more about this feature at http://docs.jquery.com/Utilities/jQuery.unique.

## Interrogating an array

The section on accessing array members in Chapter 4 shows how to access array members by using a simple for loop. A for loop works fine when the array is simple and you really are using an array. However, you might be dealing with a list of elements or a complex object of some type. In these cases, using a for loop may prove inadequate. The following example shows how you'd implement that Chapter 4 example using jQuery for comparison purposes. (You can find complete code for this example in the \Chapter 18\ Standard Tasks folder of the downloadable code as AccessArray.HTML.)

```
// Create the array and fill it with data.
var Colors = ["Blue", "Green", "Purple"];

// Define a loop to access each array element
// and display it on screen.
jQuery.each(Colors, function()
    {
        $("#Output").append(
            "Colors " +
            jQuery.inArray(this.toString(), Colors) +
            " = " + this + "<br />");
    });
```

In this case, the example relies on jQuery.each() to move between array members. This method works with any sort of object, not just arrays. You provide the array or object list you want to work with and a function to process the array as input. This example uses an anonymous function, but you can use a named function just as easily.

The example outputs the individual array members to a <div> with an id of Output. Because the output is collected through several passes, the code uses the append() method to append the output from each pass. The output is the word *Colors,* the number of the array element, an equals sign (=), and the value passed to the function.

Notice that the code uses `jQuery.inArray()` to obtain the index of the item passed through `this`. Because `this` is an object, you must convert it to a string by using the `toString()` method. Figure 18-3 shows typical output from this example.

**Figure 18-3:** The array and output are the same; the technique is different.

# Handling Events with jQuery

jQuery provides extension event-related functionality. Chapter 12 discusses events from the pure JavaScript perspective. In fact, the section on creating custom events in that chapter explains the technique required to create a custom event in JavaScript. Event-related tasks are quite doable with pure JavaScript, but using jQuery can make things simpler. The following sections describe the jQuery view of events and provide a simple example of how to use jQuery to address event-related needs.

## Understanding the event functionality

Events cover a number of areas: the event itself, the listener used to determine when an event has occurred, and the event handler used to react to the event. The following list describes how jQuery handles all these areas of event manipulation and more:

- ✔ `.bind()`: Assigns a particular event handler to an event. You can use any of the jQuery selectors for this method. For example, you could use a multiple selector to assign the same event handler to multiple events. You can read more about this feature at `http://api.jquery.com/bind`.

- ✔ `.blur()`: Binds an event handler to the `blur` event or triggers that event on the specific element. A `blur` event occurs when the element loses focus. You can read more about this feature at `http://api.jquery.com/blur`.

All specific event methods, such as .blur(), provide the means to send data to the event handler. Even if you don't send data to the event handler, it will still have access to the event and this objects.

- ✔ .change(): Binds an event handler to the change event or triggers that event on the specific element. A change event occurs whenever the content of an element changes. You can read more about this feature at http://api.jquery.com/change.

- ✔ .click(): Binds an event handler to the click event or triggers that event on the specific element. A click event occurs when the user clicks the specified element. You can read more about this feature at http://api.jquery.com/click.

- ✔ .dblclick(): Binds an event handler to the dblclick (double-click) event or triggers that event on the specific element. A dblclick event occurs when the user double-clicks the specified element. You can read more about this feature at http://api.jquery.com/dblclick.

- ✔ .delegate(): Assigns an event handler to all events that match the specified selector, now or in the future, based on the root elements you specify. For example, you can select all the <td> elements on a page and assign an event handler to the click event of all those elements. When a page dynamically adds more <td> elements, each of the added elements is also assigned to the event handler automatically. You can read more about this feature at http://api.jquery.com/delegate.

The jQuery documentation sometimes points out that a method is still usable, but has been superseded by another method. For example, you can still use the .delegate() method, but it has been superseded by the .on() method. By carefully checking for these library changes, you can often improve your ability to create useful applications with even less code.

- ✔ event.currentTarget: Provides access to the DOM element that's the target for an event. In most cases, this property is the same as the this object. You can read more about this property at http://api.jquery.com/event.currentTarget.

It pays to read the contributions made by other developers at the end of each documentation section. For example, the contribution for the event.currentTarget entry demonstrates at least one case in which this property isn't equal to the this object. These notes will help you avoid potential problems with the library.

- ✔ event.data: Provides access to additional event data that's provided to the handler during the binding process. You can read more about this property at http://api.jquery.com/event.data.

- ✔ event.delegateTarget: Specifies the element at which the event handler was assigned. This property is most useful when working with event handlers that are assigned using the .delegate() or .on() method, which allows the code to detect where an assignment is made and unassign the handler if necessary. You can read more about this property at http://api.jquery.com/event.delegateTarget.

- ✔ `event.isDefaultPrevented()`: Returns `true` when an event handler or other code has prevented the default processing associated with this event. You can read more about this method at `http://api.jquery.com/event.isDefaultPrevented`.

- ✔ `event.isImmediatePropagationStopped()`: Returns `true` when an event handler or other code has called `event.stopImmediatePropagation()` on this event. You can read more about this method at `http://api.jquery.com/event.isImmediatePropagationStopped`.

Many of the events described in this chapter are part of the DOM specification. You can find additional details about methods, such as `event.stopImmediatePropagation()`, in the DOM specification at `http://www.w3.org/TR/2003/WD-DOM-Level-3-Events-20030331/events.html`.

- ✔ `event.isPropagationStopped()`: Returns `true` when an event handler or other code has called `event.stopPropagation()` on this event. You can read more about this method at `http://api.jquery.com/event.isPropagationStopped`.

- ✔ `event.namespace`: Specifies the namespace that was in effect at the time the event was triggered. You can read more about this property at `http://api.jquery.com/event.namespace`.

- ✔ `event.pageX`: Returns the mouse position relative to the left edge of the document. You can read more about this property at `http://api.jquery.com/event.pageX`.

- ✔ `event.pageY`: Returns the mouse position relative to the top edge of the document. You can read more about this property at `http://api.jquery.com/event.pageY`.

- ✔ `event.preventDefault()`: Prevents the default processing from occurring. You can read more about this method at `http://api.jquery.com/event.preventDefault`.

- ✔ `event.relatedTarget`: Returns the element associated with a particular event. For example, when working with a `mouseover` event, this property returns the element that's being exited. You can read more about this property at `http://api.jquery.com/event.relatedTarget`.

- ✔ `event.result`: Returns the last value that was returned by this event handler, assuming there's a value to return. You can read more about this property at `http://api.jquery.com/event.result`.

- ✔ `event.stopImmediatePropagation()`: Prevents any other event handlers from being called. Essentially, this method tells the application that the event has been handled fully and no more processing is required. You can read more about this property at `http://api.jquery.com/event.stopImmediatePropagation`.

✔ `event.stopPropagation()`: Prevents parent event handlers from being called and being notified of the event. You can read more about this property at `http://api.jquery.com/event.stopPropagation`.

✔ `event.target`: Specifies the target of the event, including the decedent of an element. This property's useful for detecting event bubbling when compared with the `this` object. You can read more about this property at `http://api.jquery.com/event.target`.

✔ `event.timeStamp`: Specifies the time that the event was called in milliseconds since January 1, 1970. You can read more about this property at `http://api.jquery.com/event.timeStamp`.

✔ `event.type`: Defines the kind of event that has taken place. You can read more about this property at `http://api.jquery.com/event.type`.

✔ `event.which`: Specifies which key or button was pressed when processing a keyboard or mouse event. This property also normalizes event output for left- and right-handed mice so that a left button press is always 1, the middle always 2, and the right always 3. You can read more about this property at `http://api.jquery.com/event.which`.

✔ `.focus()`: Binds an event handler to the `focus` event or triggers that event on the specific element. A `focus` event occurs when the element receives focus for input or other data manipulation purposes. You can read more about this method at `http://api.jquery.com/focus`.

✔ `.focusin()`: Binds an event handler to the `focus` event or triggers that event on the specific element. A `focus` event occurs when the element or any element inside it receives focus for input or other data manipulation purposes. Unlike the `focus()` method, this method supports event bubbling so that a parent can handle child focus events. You can read more about this method at `http://api.jquery.com/focusin`.

✔ `.focusout()`: Binds an event handler to the `blur` event or triggers that event on the specific element. A `focus` event occurs when the element or any element inside it receives or loses focus for input or other data manipulation purposes. Unlike the `focus()` method, this method supports event bubbling so that a parent can handle child focus events. You can read more about this method at `http://api.jquery.com/focusout`.

✔ `.hover()`: Binds an event handler to both the `mouseenter` and `mouseleave` events or triggers those events on the specific element. A `mouseenter` event occurs when the mouse enters the control's boundary. A `mouseleave` event occurs when the mouse exits the control's boundary. You can read more about this method at `http://api.jquery.com/hover`.

✔ `.keydown()`: Binds an event handler to the `keydown` event or triggers that event on the specific element. A `keydown` event occurs when the user presses a particular key on the keyboard. You can read more about this method at `http://api.jquery.com/keydown`.

✔ `.keypress()`: Binds an event handler to the `keypress` event or triggers that event on the specific element. A `keypress` event occurs when the user presses a particular key on the keyboard. This event also registers repeated keystrokes that are generated when the user presses and then holds down the key. You can read more about this method at `http://api.jquery.com/keypress`.

✔ `.keyup()`: Binds an event handler to the `keyup` event or triggers that event on the specific element. A `keyup` event occurs when the user releases a particular key on the keyboard. You can read more about this method at `http://api.jquery.com/keyup`.

✔ `.mousedown()`: Binds an event handler to the `mousedown` event or triggers that event on the specific element. A `mousedown` event occurs when the user presses a particular mouse button. You can read more about this method at `http://api.jquery.com/mousedown`.

✔ `.mouseenter()`: Binds an event handler to the `mouseenter` event or triggers that event on the specific element. A `mouseenter` event occurs when the mouse pointer enters a particular element. You can read more about this method at `http://api.jquery.com/mouseenter`.

It may appear that some events that jQuery supports are precisely the same as JavaScript events. However, jQuery normalizes access to these events in many cases. For example, in the case of `mouseenter`, jQuery simulates the event so that it works the same with all browsers, regardless of the level of browser support provided. The `mouseenter` event (and other associated events) is normally supported only by Internet Explorer.

✔ `.mouseleave()`: Binds an event handler to the `mouseleave` event or triggers that event on the specific element. A `mouseleave` event occurs when the mouse pointer exits a particular element. You can read more about this method at `http://api.jquery.com/mouseleave`.

✔ `.mousemove()`: Binds an event handler to the `mousemove` event or triggers that event on the specific element. A `mousemove` event occurs when the mouse pointer moves within a particular element. You can read more about this method at `http://api.jquery.com/mousemove`.

✔ `.mouseout()`: Binds an event handler to the `mouseout` event or triggers that event on the specific element. A `mouseout` event occurs when the mouse pointer exits a particular element. You can read more about this method at `http://api.jquery.com/mouseout`.

✔ `.mouseover()`: Binds an event handler to the `mouseover` event or triggers that event on the specific element. A `mouseover` event occurs when the mouse pointer enters a particular element. You can read more about this method at `http://api.jquery.com/mouseover`.

✔ `.mouseup()`: Binds an event handler to the `mouseup` event or triggers that event on the specific element. A `mouseup` event occurs when the user releases a particular mouse button. You can read more about this method at `http://api.jquery.com/mouseup`.

✔ `.off()`: Removes an event handler that was added using the `.on()` method. It's possible to remove single event handlers or entire groups of event handlers. You can read more about this feature at `http://api.jquery.com/off`.

✔ `.on()`: Attaches an event handler for one or more events for the specified elements. This method is the replacement for the `.bind()`, `.delegate()`, and `.live()` methods. You can read more about this feature at `http://api.jquery.com/on`.

✔ `.one()`: Attaches an event handler for one or more events for the specified elements. The event handler executes once at most and then automatically removes itself. You can read more about this feature at `http://api.jquery.com/one`.

✔ `jQuery.proxy()`: Accepts a general function as input and returns a function that will always have a particular context. You can read about this feature at `http://api.jquery.com/jQuery.proxy`.

✔ `.ready()`: Fires when the document is ready for use after loading. This event assures that your code won't execute before the document is fully loaded and configured. You can read more about this event at `http://api.jquery.com/ready`.

✔ `.resize()`: Binds an event handler to the `resize` event or triggers that event on the specific element. A `resize` event occurs when the window is resized. You can read more about this method at `http://api.jquery.com/resize`.

✔ `.scroll()`: Binds an event handler to the `scroll` event or triggers that event on the specific element. A `scroll` event occurs when the document content's scrolled within the window. You can read more about this method at `http://api.jquery.com/scroll`.

✔ `.select()`: Binds an event handler to the `select` event or triggers that event on the specific element. A `select` event occurs when the user highlights content within an element. You can read more about this method at `http://api.jquery.com/select`.

✔ `.submit()`: Binds an event handler to the `submit` event or triggers that event on the specific element. A `submit` event occurs when the user sends the content of a form to the server. You can read more about this method at `http://api.jquery.com/submit`.

✔ `.trigger()`: Fires all the specified events for the target elements in the order in which they would normally occur if the user was performing the same task. You can read more about this method at `http://api.jquery.com/trigger`.

✔ `.triggerHandler()`: Fires all the specified events for the target elements in the order in which they would normally occur if the user were performing the same task. You can read more about this method at `http://api.jquery.com/triggerHandler`. This method varies from the `.trigger()` method in several important ways:

- This method doesn't cause the default behavior of an element to occur, such as a form submission.

- When using this method, only the first matched element is affected rather than all the elements that match the selection criteria.

- The events don't bubble up the DOM hierarchy. If the targeted element doesn't handle the event, nothing happens.

- You can't use this method to perform *chaining* (handling multiple events using a single handler). Instead, the method provides the return value of the last event handler that it executed. If no event handlers were executed or the event handlers didn't return a value, then the return value is undefined.

✔ `.unbind()`: Removes event handlers that were previously bound to an element by using one of the binding methods rather than the `.on()` method. When working with an event handler that was attached by using the `.on()` method, you must use the `.off()` method instead. You can read about this feature at `http://api.jquery.com/unbind`.

✔ `.undelegate()`: Removes all the event handlers attached to elements by using the specified selectors. You use this method with event handlers that were attached by using the `.delegate()` method. When working with an event handler that was attached using the `.on()` method, you must use the `.off()` method instead. You can read about this feature at `http://api.jquery.com/undelegate`.

The jQuery documentation lists myriad methods that are no longer in use. For example, you find documentation for the `.die()` method in the documentation. This method is deprecated. Likewise, the `.load()` method has been replaced by the `ready()` event. Avoid using deprecated methods because you can't be sure that jQuery will continue supporting them. You can find a list of deprecated methods and features at `http://api.jquery.com/category/deprecated`.

## *Working with events*

There are many ways to work with events by using jQuery. The following example shows how you can assign event handlers to two buttons using anonymous functions. In the first case, the event handler displays a simple message. In the second case, the event handler fires the `click` event of the first button. (You can find complete code for this example in the `\Chapter 18\Events` folder of the downloadable code as `Events.HTML`.)

```
$("#btnShowMessage").click(
   function()
   {
      alert("The event handler for " +
         this.id + " was called.");
   });

$("#btnFireEvent").click(
   function()
   {
      $("#btnShowMessage").click();
   });
```

In both cases, the buttons are accessed through their id values. Notice that the .click() method is used in two ways in the example. The first way is to assign an event handler to the click event. The second way is to fire the click event of btnShowMessage. Clicking either button displays the same message — the difference is how the event is fired.

# Chapter 19

# Using jQuery to Handle AJAX

C hapter 17 provides your first view of Asynchronous JavaScript and XML (AJAX). In that chapter, you obtain access to a simple file using straight JavaScript in the section on performing AJAX tasks using JavaScript. The section on making AJAX easier with jQuery in the same chapter shows how much easier it is to perform the task using jQuery. These simple examples demonstrate the usefulness of AJAX to the developer. This chapter takes the next step and introduces you to the full power of AJAX when coupled with the jQuery library.

Most AJAX scenarios don't deal with files on the server. In most cases, the server is asked to perform some type of data search or data manipulation and then return the results for display on the page. Keeping requests small and data transfers short helps improve overall efficiency so that everyone gets better results. AJAX helps make the entire process faster and easier. However, AJAX represents only part of the process. The server must also provide support for the requests. This chapter couples AJAX with server-side PHP Hypertext Processor (PHP) language strategies so that you can see the entire scenario that typically occurs.

This chapter explores only one typical scenario. There are many other server-side languages you can use to handle client requests. In addition, even though this chapter uses jQuery to make working with AJAX simpler, you could easily use straight JavaScript to perform the tasks or even rely on some other third-party library. As you read this chapter, think about the flow that's taking place between client and server. When you set up a solution of your own, consider how the technologies used in this chapter will work for your particular situation. You may find that you need to use some other strategy to accomplish the task, but the essential flow between client and server will be the same.

# Understanding the AJAX Object in jQuery

You can perform a broad range of tasks with AJAX. The essential goal is to reduce network traffic by reducing or eliminating the need to reload pages. Downloading a page requires quite a bit of time, especially when a site uses a lot of graphics to make a visual impact on the viewer. The more you can reduce the size of the data downloads, the more efficient your application becomes.

Using jQuery reduces the code the developer writes and makes the developer more efficient. The basic AJAX strategy remains the same. Consequently, this section isn't about making the application more efficient, it's about making the developer more efficient so there's more time to troubleshoot and optimize applications, rather than create new code.

The jQuery library provides access to a lot of AJAX functionality. It divides this functionality into four areas to make working with the library a little less cumbersome:

- Global AJAX event handlers
- Helper functions
- Low-level interface
- Shorthand methods

The following sections provide details about each of these areas of AJAX support in jQuery. Later in the chapter, you see some of these features at work as you review the process used to make a client-server configuration of an example application a reality.

## Considering the global AJAX event handlers

AJAX is an asynchronous environment, which means that your application makes a request and then, at some point later, receives a response. Your application continues to perform tasks while it waits for the response. To make such a scenario work, AJAX must rely on events to signal when data is ready for use or other actions have happened.

By default, these events are always fired at the times specified. You can turn global events off by changing the `global` property that's accessed using the `jQuery.ajaxSetup()` method described in the "Understanding the low-level interface" section, later in this chapter. Normally you want to keep global events turned on. However, if your application provides custom event handling or you use another third-party library that also provides these events, you may want to turn off global event handling. The following list

describes the global events that the jQuery library supports for use
with AJAX:

- ✔ `.ajaxComplete()`: Binds an event handler to the `ajaxComplete`
  event. An `ajaxComplete` event occurs when the application receives a
  response to a query (success or failure). You can read more about this
  feature at `http://api.jquery.com/ajaxComplete`.

- ✔ `.ajaxError()`: Binds an event handler to the `ajaxError` event.
  An `ajaxError` event occurs when the application receives an error
  response to a query. You can read more about this feature at `http://
  api.jquery.com/ajaxError`.

- ✔ `.ajaxSend()`: Binds an event handler to the `ajaxSend` event. An
  `ajaxSend` event occurs when the application is about to send a request
  to the server. The application could perform validation checks on the
  request before sending it to ensure that the request is complete and has
  a high probability of succeeding. Performing checks such as this one can
  greatly increase application efficiency by reducing errant requests.
  You can read more about this feature at `http://api.jquery.com/
  ajaxSend`.

- ✔ `.ajaxStart()`: Binds an event handler to the `ajaxStart` event. Every
  time the application sends a new request to the server, jQuery checks
  to determine whether there's an existing request. An `ajaxStart` event
  occurs when jQuery detects there's no current request. You can read
  more about this feature at `http://api.jquery.com/ajaxStart`.

- ✔ `.ajaxStop()`: Binds an event handler to the `ajaxStop` event. Every
  time the application receives a response from the server, jQuery checks
  to determine whether there's an existing request. An `ajaxStart` event
  occurs when jQuery detects there's no current request. This event also
  occurs when the last request in the queue is cancelled (meaning there
  are no more active requests). You can read more about this feature at
  `http://api.jquery.com/ajaxStop`.

- ✔ `.ajaxSuccess()`: Binds an event handler to the `ajaxSuccess` event.
  An `ajaxSuccess` event occurs when the application receives a successful response to a query. You can read more about this feature at
  `http://api.jquery.com/ajaxSuccess`.

## Working with the helper functions

The helper functions assist you in preparing data for submission in a request.
The requests you've seen in previous chapters deal with resources, such as a
text file. A request can also consist of a series of data fields used to describe
an entity that the client requires (as in a database application). These functions help you prepare such data for submission in the request:

✔ `jQuery.param()`: Accepts an object or array as input and returns a string containing the information in serialized form. The resulting string is suitable for use in either a request URL (as in a REpresentational State Transfer, or REST, request) or an AJAX request. You can read more about this method at `http://api.jquery.com/jQuery.param`.

✔ `.serialize()`: Accepts a series of form elements as input and returns an encoded string in serialized form. The resulting string is suitable for use in either a request URL or an AJAX request. To be included in the array, the element must have the `name` attribute defined. You can read more about this method at `http://api.jquery.com/serialize`.

✔ `.serializeArray()`: Accepts a series of form elements as input and returns a JavaScript array. The resulting array is ready for encoding as a JavaScript Object Notation (JSON) string. To be included in the array, the element must have the `name` attribute defined. You can read more about this method at `http://api.jquery.com/serializeArray`.

## Understanding the low-level interface

The low-level interface makes it possible to create arbitrary AJAX requests or to configure jQuery to make future requests. The following list describes the methods provided as part of the low-level interface:

✔ `jQuery.ajax()`: Allows the client to make a simple AJAX request by providing a resource URL. The client can optionally provide settings to override the default request settings. This method also allows configuration of the settings by calling the method without a resource URL. You can find out more about this method, along with a complete list of the settings it supports, at `http://api.jquery.com/jQuery.ajax`.

✔ `jQuery.ajaxPrefilter()`: Provides the means for attaching a function to the AJAX pre-filter. The pre-filter makes it possible to scan standard options for potential conflicts and to also add custom options to a request. This method can also be used to attach methods to create special effects, such as redirecting the request to a different URL as needed. You can read more about this method at `http://api.jquery.com/jQuery.ajaxPrefilter`.

✔ `jQuery.ajaxSetup()`: Configures the default settings for AJAX requests. These are the settings that jQuery uses when making a standard AJAX request without any overrides. You can read more about this method at `http://api.jquery.com/jQuery.ajaxSetup`. The options that this method can control appear at `http://api.jquery.com/jQuery.ajax`.

# Using shorthand methods

Most AJAX requests don't require any special manipulation of settings or encoding of request data. When you want to make a simple AJAX request, you can use these shorthand methods to make the call quickly. In many cases, you can make the request by using a single method call rather than writing a number of lines of code as you would when using straight JavaScript. The following list describes the shorthand methods:

- ✔ jQuery.get(): Makes a server request using the HTTP GET method. You provide the URL of the resource to obtain from the server. The method can optionally accept data to transfer with the request, a function to call when the request returns, and the type of data to return. You can find out more about this method at http://api.jquery.com/jQuery.get.

- ✔ jQuery.getJSON(): Makes a server request using the HTTP GET method. You provide the URL of the resource to obtain from the server. This method specifically returns the data in JSON format. The method can optionally accept data to transfer with the request and a function to call when the request returns. You can find out more about this method at http://api.jquery.com/jQuery.getJSON.

- ✔ jQuery.getScript(): Obtains a JavaScript script from the server and executes it. You provide the URL of the script to obtain from the server using the HTTP GET method. You can optionally provide a function to call when the request returns. You can find out more about this method at http://api.jquery.com/jQuery.getScript.

- ✔ .load(): Loads data found on the server. You provide the URL of the resource to obtain from the server. Unlike the global methods, such as jQuery.get(), this method provides a default handler, so it represents the fastest and easiest way to obtain data from the server. The method can optionally accept data to transfer with the request and a function to call when the request returns. You can find out more about this method at http://api.jquery.com/load.

- ✔ jQuery.post(): Makes a server request by using the HTTP POST method. You provide the URL of the resource to obtain from the server. The method can optionally accept data to transfer with the request, a function to call when the request returns, and the type of data to return. You can find out more about this method at http://api.jquery.com/jQuery.post.

# Discovering Server-Side Programming

It's entirely possible that your real world production application won't require any sort of server-side processing — that all your application will ever need is to grab resources in the form of scripts and files from the server. However, most real-world applications today have some need to perform server-side processing. You may need to access a database, perform a calculation, or return status information. The server can perform myriad tasks for the client, provided it has the required software. Because many organizations now rely on cloud-based solutions to just about every programming problem, it's important to have some idea of the activity that occurs during such processing. That's the sole intent of this section.

The following sections show how to use PHP as one possible means of providing extended processing functionality to clients that rely on AJAX to perform tasks. PHP is a good option because many servers support it, the language is platform independent, and you don't generally need many resources to use it. In fact, many hosted sites provide PHP access as part of their default setup, so your organization may already have the required support installed if you rely on a hosted site.

## Adding PHP support to your Apache server

If you installed the Apache server on your system using one of the techniques described in Chapter 2, you likely don't have PHP support installed on your server and will need to install it before you can proceed. The following procedure works for any of the platforms described in this book:

1. **Download the version of PHP you need from** `http://php.net`.

   You may be redirected to a different site from this main page. For example, the Windows binaries are found at `http://windows.php.net/download`. The examples in this book use the thread safe 5.4.9 version of PHP.

2. **Extract the file you've downloaded to the PHP directory (folder) on your machine.**

   The precise name will vary, but the examples in this book use `C:\php` as the source directory for PHP support. When changing the Apache configuration, you must supply the directory that you used to store your copy of PHP.

3. **Locate the `php.INI` development file in the `C:\php` folder and copy it to `php.INI`.**

You should now have a file named php.INI in the directory. This file contains the settings that configure PHP for use. The file you copied creates a development environment, but you should make a quick change to ensure that the environment runs with as few problems as possible.

4. **Open php.INI in a text editor and locate the line that reads short_open_tag = Off. Change this line to read**

   ```
   short_open_tag = On
   ```

   The reason for this change is that some commercial scripts don't provide the full PHP starting tag of <? PHP. They use <? instead, which is the short open tag. If you don't set this setting to On, your PHP configuration won't be able to read these commercial files.

5. **Save php.INI and close your text editor.**

6. **Open the Apache httpd.CONF file in a text editor.**

   This file is normally found in the Apache2.2\conf directory on your system. You must make sure you open the text editor in administrator mode, especially when working with a Windows system, or you won't be able to save the file when you're finished making changes. For example, when working with a Windows system, right-click the Notepad icon in the Start menu and choose Run As Administrator from the context menu.

7. **Locate the section that contains the LoadModule entries. Add a new line and type**

   ```
   LoadModule php5_module "c:/php/php5apache2_2.dll"
   ```

   This line adds support for your PHP installation.

8. **Locate the section that contains the AddType entries. Add a new line and type**

   ```
   AddType application/x-httpd-php .php
   ```

   This line tells the server what to do with PHP files you include on the server.

9. **Go to the end of the httpd.CONF file and add a new line. Type**

   ```
   PHPIniDir "c:/php"
   ```

   This line tells the server where to find the php.INI file you created earlier in this procedure.

10. **Save the changes to disk and close your text editor.**

11. **Restart the Apache server.**

    This step forces the server to install PHP support.

## Testing your PHP configuration

Even if you think you have PHP support installed, it's a good idea to test PHP support on your server. Otherwise, you won't know whether your PHP configuration is working before you move on to the next section. The following procedure helps you test your configuration:

1. **Create a new file with your text editor.**

2. **Type** <?php phpinfo(); ?> **in the file and save it as** `Test.php` **to the** `Apache2.2\htdocs` **directory on your system.**

3. **Open your browser and type** http://localhost/Test.php **in the address bar. Press Enter.**

   You should see the configuration information for your PHP setup as shown in Figure 19-1.

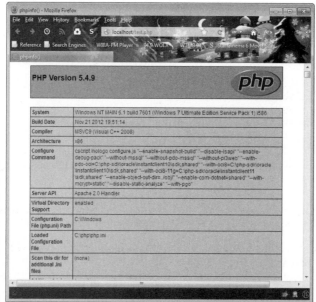

**Figure 19-1:**
A working
PHP
configuration
will show its
configuration
data when
queried.

## Creating the PHP script

The goal of this book isn't to make you a PHP developer — that's the goal of another book. However, to provide something to use for the AJAX portion of this chapter, you do need a simple PHP application. The example in this section performs simple addition. You send it two numbers, it adds them together, and then it returns the result. (You can find complete code for this example in the \Chapter 19\Math folder of the downloadable code as DoMath.PHP.) Here's the code needed to perform the task:

```php
<?php
   // Get the values from the query.
   $val1 = $_GET["val1"];
   $val2 = $_GET["val2"];

   // Perform the math operation.
   $result = $val1 + $val2;

   // Output the result.
   echo $result;
?>
```

The <?php line is standard in every PHP application. It tells the PHP interpreter to expect some code. If you really want to know more about PHP, try the tutorial at http://www.w3schools.com/php/default.asp. However, for this book, all you really need to know is that the <?php line starts code.

The first step is to retrieve data from the URL that the client sends to the server. The data is in the form of a query, and it contains two variables, val1 and val2. The example assumes that val1 and val2 are numbers, but if the client sends something else, the result will be a value of 0 because you need two numbers to perform addition.

The next step is to perform the math. The code creates $result, which contains the sum of $val1 and $val2.

The final step is to output $result. The call to echo works pretty simply. When a client calls using AJAX, it receives $result as a response. However, you can also test this script by using your browser:

1. **Save the file as DoMath.php in the Apache2.2\htdocs directory on your system.**

2. **In your browser, type** http://localhost/DoMath.php?val1=1&val2=2 **in the address bar. Press Enter.**

   You see 3 as the output.

3. **Try other values out and you find that the program always returns the value you expect.**

4. **Try values that won't work, such as the strings Hello and There for the values, and you find that the program outputs a 0 rather than crashing.**

# Retrieving Results from AJAX Calls

The PHP script described in the preceding section provides the perfect means for testing a more typical server solution with AJAX. Now it's time to build a few applications to see what jQuery can do for you when you're working with a situation that's more complicated than simply retrieving a file. Although your real-world situations will be more complex than the one described in the following sections, the process is going to be the same.

## Working with standard output

This example uses the `DoMath.php` script described in the "Creating the PHP script" section, earlier in this chapter, to perform math and change just the result field of a form on a page. You must use your server setup to make this example work because the server executes the PHP script and then returns the result. Using jQuery makes the process of working with AJAX significantly easier. This example differs considerably from the examples provided with the jQuery API. It provides a different view of how you can perform the task. The following code shows the form used for this task. (You can find complete code for this example in the `\Chapter 19\Math` folder of the downloadable code as `StandardTest.HTML`.)

```html
<form id="DataEntry">
   <h1>Scripting an Addition Routine with AJAX</h1>
   <div>
      <label>Value 1:</label>
      <input id="val1"
             name="val1"
             value="1"
             type="text" />
   </div>
   <div>
      <label>Value 2:</label>
      <input id="val2"
             name="val2"
             value="2"
             type="text" />
   </div>
   <div>
      <label>Result:</label>
      <span id="result"></span>
   </div>
   <input id="btnChange"
          type="button"
          value="Add the Numbers"
          onclick="PerformAdd()" />
</form>
```

The example uses standard `<input type="text">` controls for data input. Notice that you must define the `name` attributes for these controls, or the jQuery `.serialize()` method won't work. It's a good idea to assign the controls default values. The output is a simple `<span>`.

The application performs its task when the user clicks Add the Numbers, which is an `<input type="button">` control. This approach provides an alternative to using a submit style button. However, either approach works equally well. The advantage of this approach is that you can use a named function, `PerformAdd()`, to handle the `click` event. The following code shows how `PerformAdd()` does its work:

```
function PerformAdd()
{
    $("#result").load(
        "http://localhost/DoMath.php",
        $("#DataEntry").serialize());
}
```

As previously mentioned, the example places the output in a `<span>` with an `id` of `result`. You access this `<span>` by its identifier and call `load()` to fill it with information from the desired source. You provide the location of the source, which is `DoMath.php`.

The PHP script requires input data, which you add as a second argument. To obtain the data, you access the `<form>` tag, which has an identifier of `DataEntry`, and you call `serialize()`, which serializes every control that has a `name` attribute assigned to it. When using the default values, the serialized data is `val1=1&val2=2`. Taken together, the complete URL is `http://localhost/DoMath.php?val1=1&val2=2`, which is precisely the same as the test URL you use earlier in the "Creating the PHP script" section of the chapter. Figure 19-2 shows typical output from this example.

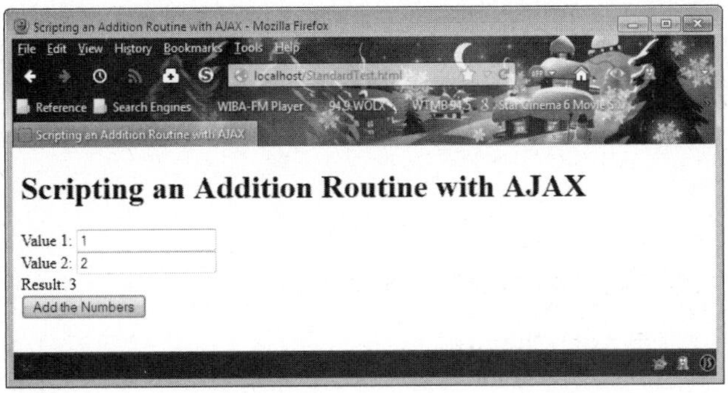

**Figure 19-2:**
The example adds two values together and shows the result without reloading.

Scripting an Addition Routine with AJAX - Mozilla Firefox

File Edit View History Bookmarks Tools Help

localhost/StandardText.html

Reference  Search Engines  WIBA-FM Player  94.9 WQLX  WTMB-FM  Star Cinema 6 Movie

Scripting an Addition Routine with AJAX

## Scripting an Addition Routine with AJAX

Value 1: 1
Value 2: 2
Result: 3
Add the Numbers

# Investigating the benefits of JSON

Chapter 16 explains how to use XML with JavaScript. Working with XML provides a cross-platform, cross-browser solution for storing data that also works with just about every programming language on the planet. It really isn't possible to get any more generic than XML. However, XML can be difficult to parse into a form that the computer can understand. Consequently, developers looked for an easier way to store complex data. JavaScript Object Notation (JSON) is one of the new solutions that developers have created.

Like XML, JSON works with any platform and with any browser. Using jQuery makes working with JSON easy. Interestingly enough, PHP provides the functions required to translate complex PHP data into JSON format. Creating a complex example that includes databases, PHP scripts, and complex server data is outside the scope of this book, but you can read about the PHP end of JSON at `http://php.net/manual/book.json.php`. The example in the sections that follow is a little more modest, but you get the flavor of how JSON and jQuery can work together to make it easier to interact with complex data.

## Creating the JSON data

As its name implies, JSON relies on JavaScript objects to store information. You actually use object literals as described in the section on working with object literals in Chapter 5 to store data.

This example stores the JSON data on disk in a file. (You can find complete code for this example in the `\Chapter 19\JSON` folder of the downloadable code as `Test.JSON`.)

```
{
  "Users" :
  [
    {
      "Name" : "George Smith",
      "Number" : 28,
      "Birthday": "\/Date(377244000000)\/"
    },
    {
      "Name" : "Amy Jones",
      "Number" : 41,
      "Birthday": "\/Date(414914400000)\/"
    },
    {
      "Name" : "Sammy Wang",
      "Number" : 33,
      "Birthday": "\/Date(-147380400000)\/"
    }
  ]
}
```

The data consists of a group of users. There are three users in the file. Each user entry has the same fields associated with it: Name, Number, and Birthday. Notice that strings appear in quotes. Numbers appear without quotes. JSON doesn't actually provide support for standard object types, so this example uses one of the types you commonly see. If this file contained a Boolean value, it would appear as true or false without quotes. In sum, JSON supports these data types:

- ✔ String
- ✔ Number
- ✔ Boolean
- ✔ null

In addition, JSON files support two structure types: object literal and array. This example demonstrates both structure types for you so that you know how to handle them in JavaScript using jQuery.

### Viewing the JSON data onscreen

The preceding section explains the data file used for this example. The form for this example includes the heading and an <input type="button"> control. When the user clicks the button, it calls ViewData, which is shown in the following example code. (You can find complete code for this example in the \Chapter 19\JSON folder of the downloadable code as ViewJSON.HTML.)

```
function ViewData()
{
    // Obtain the data from disk.
    $.getJSON("Test.json",
        function(data)
        {
            // Create an array to hold the data.
            var items = [];
            // Parse the data by looking at
            // each entry in the Users object.
            $.each(data.Users,
                function(key, value)
                {
                    items.push("<li>" +
                        value.Name + "<br />" +
                        value.Number + "<br />" +
                        (new Date(
                            parseInt(value.Birthday.substr(6)))
                        ).toDateString()
                        + "</li>");
                });
            // Place the result in an unordered list.
            $('<ul/>', {html: items.join("")}).
                appendTo('body');
        });
}
```

The example begins by calling .getJSON(), which loads Test.json from the drive and places the content in data. The anonymous function accepts data as input. To create the output for this example, the code creates an empty array, items. Using items simplifies the code.

The next step is to process each of the user entries in the Users array found in Test.json. The code calls .each() and passes it data.Users, so that the loop will process each of the object literals it contains. The anonymous function receives a key and value pair for each of the user entries.

To access each of the key/value pairs for the object literal entries, you interact with the appropriate properties: Name, Number, and Birthday. Processing Name and Number is straightforward — simply pass them to the output as is.

To process the odd-looking .NET date, you must separate the text part from the numeric part of the string and then turn that value into an integer that contains the number of milliseconds since January 1, 1970. If you want to provide a date earlier than January 1, 1970, you use a negative number of milliseconds. The number of milliseconds is used to create a new Date() object. The code calls toDateString() to provide nicer-looking output.

At this point, items contains three array elements, each of which is a list item <li> tag containing facts about the users. The code creates a new unordered list <ul> tag and places items within it by calling join(). The resulting list is added to the current document by using the appendTo() method. Figure 19-3 shows the output from this example.

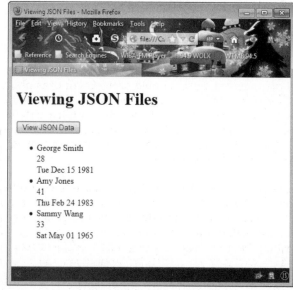

**Figure 19-3:** JSON provides a friendly way to store data that requires less parsing than XML.

# Chapter 20

# Animating the Web

· · · · · · · · · · · · · · · · · · · · · · · · · · · · · · · · · · · · · · · · · · · · · · ·

· · · · · · · · · · · · · · · · · · · · · · · · · · · · · · · · · · · · · · · · · · · · · · ·

*E*veryone likes special effects. You see special effects everywhere today. Of course, they appear in movies, but even common billboards often have special effects. From the glittery lights that festoon children's shoes to the blinking of Christmas lights, life has become a festival of special effects. It isn't too surprising that special effects also appear on Websites, and those sites that lack special effects are often called boring or sometimes aren't noticed at all. Some developers equate special effects to eye candy — to the glitz that attracts the attention of the consumer, sometimes at the expense of useful content.

Special effects do have useful purposes. One of the most important reasons to use special effects is to focus user attention. A mouseover effect can help people interact with a page with greater ease, especially when lighting conditions or other environmental factors make it hard to see the cursor. Helping the user to focus means that you get better input from the user and the user has a better experience from the application.

In many cases, special effects appear as widgets that you can use to better convey the sort of input that a user should provide. For example, a text box works perfectly well for inputting a range of values, but it doesn't tell the viewer anything (such as the fact that the input is within a certain range). If you replace that text box with a slider control, suddenly the user understands that any value within a specified range is acceptable. In addition, it's easier for the user to set the specified range.

You can also use special effects to turn abstractions into concrete concepts for the user. The use of a *slide effect* (where an element slides into and out of view) can help the user to understand that the user interface contains hidden features that are accessible when the user needs them, but which will stay out of the way when the user doesn't. Using other special effects can help a user understand the urgency of a particular input or see the data controlled by the input in a real-world perspective. In short, special effects need not be limited to pure glitz. The purpose of this chapter is to introduce you to some of the special effects that you can add to applications by using products such as the jQuery UI.

# Getting to Know jQuery UI

Previous chapters, especially Chapters 18 and 19, demonstrate the usefulness of jQuery in working with data and performing other low-level tasks in your application. The jQuery UI library (`http://jqueryui.com`) works with the user interface. You use it to add new kinds of interactions, expand the number of controls at your disposal, create special effects, and perform utilitarian tasks, such as positioning user interface elements precisely.

All these examples require that you provide a link to the jQuery UI as well as jQuery. They also use the jQuery Cascading Style Sheet (CSS) that helps create a pleasant presentation. These external elements make the coding task easier. Make sure you include the following entries in the heading of the file for each of the examples:

```
<script
    src="http://code.jquery.com/jquery-latest.js">
</script>
<script
    src="http://code.jquery.com/ui/1.9.2/jquery-ui.js">
</script>
<link
    rel="stylesheet"
    href="http://code.jquery.com/ui/1.9.2/themes/base/jquery-ui.css" />
```

You can always download the required files if desired. However, this approach makes it easier for your application to receive required updates. The following sections introduce you to jQuery UI and help you understand how you can use these features to create more interesting applications.

## Considering interactions

The way in which a user interacts with an application is important. When a set of interactions seems contrived or proves inconvenient, users have to concentrate too hard on what the application should be able to do and how to obtain that result, which makes them lose focus on their work goal. Many business users are currently in the process of moving from desktop applications to browser-based applications for at least part of their work. Consequently, these users often anticipate having desktop-like features in their browser-based application solutions. The following sections describe some jQuery UI features that help you provide that desktop experience to your users.

### Dragging content from one location to another

Sometimes a user needs to reposition screen elements to make them easier to see or work with. Creating an environment in which the user can move items around need not involve writing reams of code. In fact, all you really need is a single method call, draggable(). The following code shows the method used to create a draggable paragraph in this example. (You can find complete code for this example in the \Chapter 20\jQueryUI folder of the downloadable code as DragContent.HTML.)

```
$(function()
  {
      $("#MoveMe").draggable();
  });
```

This code is interesting because it actually creates a jQuery anonymous function that extends the jQuery environment rather than working with any particular page feature. The focus of this call is a paragraph with an id of MoveMe. All you need to do is access that member and call draggable() to make it move around. Try the downloadable example and you find that you can move the paragraph anywhere you want on the page.

To create a movable box, this example relies on a custom style. The style creates a border, allows plenty of room for the text, and then centers the text both horizontally and vertically. Here's the style used for this example:

```
#MoveMe
{
    border: solid;
    width: 200px;
    height: 5em;
    text-align: center;
    line-height: 5em;
}
```

Many developers experience problems vertically centering text within a <p> tag. You can find a number of ways to perform this task. However, one of the easiest ways to get the job done in a platform- and browser-consistent manner is to use the line-height style as shown in the example. The trick though is to set the height and line-height styles to the same value — the text will always appear in the middle.

### Dropping items into containers

Sometimes a user needs to drag an item to a container and drop it in the container. There are many instances of this process in current applications. For example, the concept of dragging an item to a trash can and dropping it to delete it is consistent across all platforms. If you want to send an item to the printer, you drag its icon to the printer icon and drop it there.

Of course, to create this effect, you must have one item that's draggable and another item that's droppable. The preceding section describes how dragging works. The following code shows how dragging and dropping can work together to create this desirable user interaction. (You can find complete code for this example in the \Chapter 20\jQueryUI folder of the downloadable code as DropContent.HTML.)

```
$(function()
  {
      $("#MoveMe").draggable();
      $("#FillMe").droppable(
        {
            drop: function(event, ui)
            {
                $(this)
                    .addClass("Filled")
                    .html("Filled!");
            }
        });
  });
```

This example uses the same code for the MoveMe <p> tag. A second <p> tag, with the id of FillMe, acts as a container. When a user drags MoveMe to FillMe, the code calls the anonymous function associated with the drop event. Notice how the example begins with the event name, followed by a colon (:), followed by the anonymous function to handle that event. The droppable() method supports these events:

✔ create: Indicates that the droppable item has been created.

✔ activate: Indicates that a draggable item is active. You can use this event to change the droppable item style so that the user can see where to drop an item.

✔ deactivate: Indicates that the user has stopped dragging an item. You can use this event to change the droppable style back to its original state.

✔ over: Fires when the draggable item is over the top of the droppable item. You can use this event to indicate when the user should release the mouse to drop the item into the container.

✔ out: Fires when the draggable item has moved out of the droppable item container. You can use this event to tell the user that it's no longer possible to drop an item into the container.

✔ drop: Tells the droppable item (the container) that it has received a draggable item.

You can create an event handler for any of the events you want to handle in your code. In fact, there are several opportunities for special effects that would focus the user's attention.

### Resizing display elements

The wide variety and types of screens used to display information make it
necessary to allow the user to resize elements as needed. In most cases, you
can simply allow the user to make the element any size. However, there may
be situations where you need to monitor the amount of resizing so that you
can tailor content to meet the needs of the container. The following example
shows how to resize an object and monitor its size. (You can find complete
code for this example in the \Chapter 20\jQueryUI folder of the downloadable code as ResizeContent.HTML.)

```
$(function()
   {
      $("#ResizeMe").resizable(
         {
            minWidth: 200,
            minHeight: 60,
            resize: function(event, ui)
            {
               $("#Content")
                  .html("Width: " +ui.size.width +
                     "<br/>Height: " + ui.size.height);
            }
         });
   });
```

This example is interesting because it shows how to set properties as well
as respond to events. In this case, the minWidth and minHeight properties
keep the element a specific minimum size — the user can't make the element
smaller.

The code also responds to the resize event. There's a special requirement
for resizing you need to know about. The resizing container is separate from
the content element. Here's the HTML for this example:

```
<div id="ResizeMe">
   <p id="Content">
      Resizable Paragraph
   </p>
</div>
```

When you want to write content to the screen, you must use the content
element, not the container element. Otherwise, the sizing handles will disappear, and the user won't be able to resize the element after the first time. In
this case, the current size of the container appears as part of the ui object
passed to the resize event handler. You access the information though the
size.width and size.height properties, as shown in the code. Figure 20-1
shows a typical example of how the output appears.

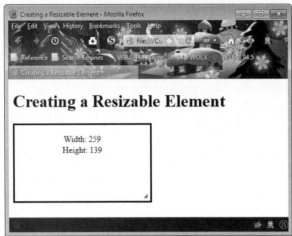

Figure 20-1:
The container must be separate from the content when resizing.

### Selecting items onscreen

Making it possible to select from a list of items reduces the chance that the user will enter incorrect information. It will also increase application reliability and reduce the potential for security issues, such as injection attacks (see the article at `http://www.zdnet.com/sql-injection-attack-what-is-it-and-how-to-prevent-it-7000000881/` for details). The user becomes more efficient as well. Fortunately, HTML5 already comes with a number of selection controls, but you may find that these controls don't quite fulfill your needs at times. In this case, a custom selection technique implemented with jQuery might answer the need. A selection sequence can consist of a `<div>` and a series of `<p>` tags, as shown here. (You can find complete code for this example in the `\Chapter 20\jQueryUI` folder of the downloadable code as `SelectContent.HTML`.)

```
<div id="Selections">
    <p id="Red">Red</p>
    <p id="Green">Green</p>
    <p id="Blue">Blue</p>
    <p id="Purple">Purple</p>
</div>
```

Notice that the `<div>` acts as a container and the `<p>` tags act as items within the container. No matter how you implement your custom list (and it need not be the arrangement shown), it must have a container/item arrangement like the one shown here. When you have the arrangement in place, you can create a selection and tracking mechanism like the one shown in the following code:

```
// Create an array to track the selections.
var Selections = new Array();

// Handle the selects and unselects.
$(function()
    {
        $("#Selections").selectable(
            {
                selected: function(event, ui)
                {
                    // Verify the item hasn't already
                    // been added.
                    if (Selections.indexOf(ui.selected.id ) ==
                        -1)

                        // Add the id of the selected item
                        // to the array.
                        Selections.push(ui.selected.id);
                },

                unselected: function(event, ui)
                {
                    // Find the location of the unselected
                    // item in the array.
                    var Index =
                        Selections.indexOf(ui.unselected.id);

                    // Remove that item.
                    Selections.splice(Index, 1);
                }
            });
    })

// Display the results.
function ShowResults()
{
    alert("You have selected: " + Selections);
}
```

The Array, Selections, keeps track of the current selection list. To make
the <div>, Selections, selectable, you use the selectable() method.
This example uses two events, selected and unselected, to keep track
of the current selections. When the user selects a new item, the selected
event handler verifies that the item doesn't already appear in Selections,
and then it pushes the new item onto Selections.

The unselected event handler must perform two tasks. First, it must locate
the unselected item using the indexOf() method. Second, it must use
splice() to remove that item from Selections.

This example doesn't provide any fancy output, but you can see for yourself
how well the selection methodology works. Click Show Selections to display

the list of selected items. The `ShowResults()` event handler displays a list of the selections for you. In a production application, you could just as easily process each of the selected items.

A final piece to this particular application is the need to define one special style. You must provide a means for the display to register the selected state of a particular item, which means providing values for the `.ui-selected` style, as shown here:

```
#Selections .ui-selected
{
    background: black;
    color: white;
}
```

When a user selects an item, the background turns black with white text so the user can see a visual change. You could also modify the text as a second means of helping the user see the selection.

### Making items sortable

Certain kinds of sorting are easy for computers to do. For example, a computer can put items in alphabetical order much faster than a human can, especially when the list is long. However, sorts aren't always logical. You may want the user to sort a list of items by personal preference or other criteria that the computer can't even understand. In these cases, you need a means of allowing manual sorts, and this example gives you just what you need. The following example lets a user sort items by unspecified criteria. (You can find complete code for this example in the `\Chapter 20\jQueryUI` folder of the downloadable code as `SortContent.HTML`.)

```
$(function()
    {
        $("#SortMe").sortable();
    })

function ShowResults()
{
    // Create the output string.
    var Output = "The sort order is:\n        ";

    // Locate each of the required items and
    // add them to the string.
    $("#SortMe p").each(
        function(index, element)
        {
            Output += element.innerHTML.substr(74);
        });

    // Display the result.
    alert(Output);
}
```

The `sortable()` call is all that you need to do to make the list visibly sortable. The user can place the elements, whatever those elements might be, in any order desired. To make this call work, however, you do need to create a container, a `<div>` in this case, and a list of items, `<p>` tags in this case. The `SortMe id` goes with the `<div>`.

Accessing the items in order is also a requirement. Otherwise, there's no point in letting the user sort the items. In this case, it's actually easier to use other jQuery functionality to obtain the list of elements in the order in which they appear and process them that way. `ShowResults()` demonstrates one technique for performing this task. You begin by creating the appropriate selector, which begins with the `<div>`, `SortMe`, and ends with each `<p>` tag it contains. The anonymous function receives both an `index` and an `element` argument. By checking the `innerHTML` property of the element, you can obtain the moniker for that `<p>` tag. The result is displayed in a dialog box.

This example also makes use of a special jQuery UI CSS style. This style creates a double-ended arrow that helps the user understand that each item can move up or down in the list. You create it using a `<span>` like this:

```
<span class="ui-icon ui-icon-arrowthick-2-n-s"></span>
```

You can find a list of these icons at `http://jquery-ui.googlecode.com/svn/tags/1.6rc5/tests/static/icons.html`. It's important to create icons that match the way your list appears onscreen. Figure 20-2 shows a typical output of this application, including the list in the order that I personally decided to sort them.

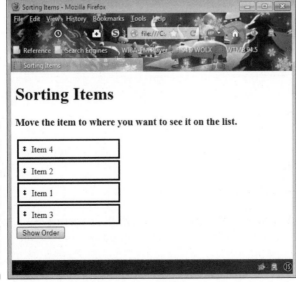

**Figure 20-2:** Sortable lists make it possible for users to place items in order of personal preference.

# Understanding the widgets

Widgets are specialty controls you can use to create special effects on a page. The advantage of these controls is that they can make your application easier to use and more appealing as well. The disadvantage of widgets as a whole is that they can be overused or used incorrectly.

A widget is only a good idea when it materially adds to the usefulness and accessibility of your application. When you find yourself admiring the pizzazz that a widget adds to the application rather than how it makes the user work faster or with greater ease, reconsider using the widget — your application may work a lot better without it.

HTML5 already comes with a number of useful generic controls of all sorts. For example, if you need a standard check box for your application, rely on HTML5 to provide it. The controls described in the following sections are special in some way. For example, the Accordion widget makes it easy to focus user attention by hiding unused elements from sight. The jQuery UI library does provide access to additional widgets that aren't discussed in the sections that follow. Most widgets, such as Button, have HTML5 counterparts and aren't quite as useful for that reason.

## Using the Accordion widget

You use the accordion to hide any page element from view. When a user selects a category, the elements in that category become visible, and the elements from all other categories are hidden. The effect is to focus user attention and make the user more efficient in performing specific tasks. The following code is all you need to make this feature usable. (You can find complete code for this example in the \Chapter 20\Widgets folder of the downloadable code as Accordion.HTML.)

```
$(function()
    {
        $("#Configuration").accordion();
    });
```

However, the secret in this case is the way you create the tags for your page. Figure 20-3 shows how the form appears to the user. Notice that the Accordion widget hides settings that the user isn't focusing on. When the user clicks Background Color, the Foreground Color options are hidden from view. Likewise, clicking Options presents those controls.

The controls in each area don't matter to the Accordion widget, but the HTML5 formatting does. This form also includes a submit button. If you don't configure the controls properly, the submit button becomes part of the accordion effect, and clicking it no longer submits the form. Here's a condensed view of the HTML5 for this example:

```html
<form id="ConfigForm"
      method="get"
      action="Accordion.html">
   <div id="Configuration">
      <h2>Foreground Color</h2>
      <div>
         <input id="FGRed"
                type="radio"
                name="Foreground"
                value="Red"
                checked="checked" />
         <label for="FGRed">Red</label><br />
... More inputs and labels ...
      </div>
      <h2>Background Color</h2>
      <div>
         <input id="BGRed"
                type="radio"
                name="Background"
                value="Red"
                checked="checked" />
         <label for="BGRed">Red</label><br />
... More inputs and labels ...
      </div>
      <h2>Options</h2>
      <div>
         <input id="Sounds"
                type="checkbox"
                name="Sounds"
                value="SpecialSounds" />
         <label for="Sounds">Use Special Sounds</label>
         <br />
         <input id="Effects"
                type="checkbox"
                name="Effects"
                value="SpecialEffects" />
         <label for="Effects">Use Special Effects</label>
      </div>
   </div>
   <input id="ChangeConfig"
          type="submit"
          value="Change Configuration" />
</form>
```

Figure 20-3:
The
Accordion
widget
focuses
user
attention.

Notice that you must place the headings control groups within a separate `<div>` and then label that `<div>` as the one you want to use for the accordion effect. A separate `<div>` houses the individual controls for a specific group. The submit button is part of the form, but it's outside the `Configuration` `<div>`. When you click the Change Configuration button, you see that the form works as it should by examining the address field content. Using the defaults, you see an address field that contains `http://localhost/Accordion.html?Foreground=Red&Background=Red` when you click Change Configuration (assuming you're using the server setup to test the example).

### Using the Autocomplete widget

Whenever possible, provide the user with specific inputs for forms you create to help the user work more quickly and reduce security risks. For example, instead of providing a text box and asking the user to type the name of a state, provide a combo box that the user can use to choose a state. Even with the best planning, though, you sometimes encounter situations where you must allow the user to provide a freeform answer in a text box — an error-prone method of input at best. The Autocomplete widget makes it possible to reduce the risk of input errors by suggesting the most common responses to such questions. Using this widget isn't quite as good as providing a specific answer, but it's the next-best thing.

The following code shows how you implement an Autocomplete widget for a text box. (You can find complete code for this example in the `\Chapter 20\Widgets` folder of the downloadable code as `Autocomplete.HTML`.)

```
// Create a list of common colors.
var Colors =
[
    "Red",
    "Orange",
    "Yellow",
    "Green",
    "Blue",
    "Purple",
    "White",
    "Black",
    "Gray"
]

$(function()
    {
        // Set up the autocomplete function, complete
        // with a list of common colors.
        $("#ColorEntry").autocomplete({source: Colors});
    })
```

To make this widget work, you create an array that contains a list of common entries. This list should be as complete as possible to ensure that the user can find a desired choice in most cases. The list also serves to help the user understand what input is desired.

When configuring the `autocomplete()` method, you include the `source` option. This is one of the few instances where you must include an option to ensure the widget works properly. Notice that the option and its associated value aren't quoted. Figure 20-4 shows typical output from this example. In this case, typing the letter *R* displays every option that contains that letter. Typing additional letters refines the list of available choices.

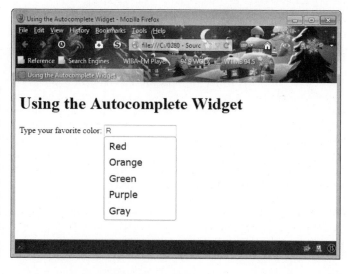

**Figure 20-4:**
Use the Auto-complete widget to provide the user with a list of common choices.

### Using the Datepicker widget

There are situations where HTML5 currently provides a solution for a particular need, but few vendors have implemented it yet. This is the case with the date and time support for HTML. Only Opera and Chrome provide support for the date and time features. For example, if you want to add a date to a form, you can use the date input type as shown here:

```
<label for="Date">Enter a Date: </label>
<input id="Date"
       type="date" />
```

The default date is today. When the user clicks on the field, the application displays a date picker control, but only when you use Opera or Chrome. Until the other vendors provide date and time support, it's still necessary to use the jQuery UI Datepicker widget to ensure that all of your users can enter a date with ease. The following code shows how to use the Datepicker widget. (You can find complete code for this example in the \Chapter 20\Widgets folder of the downloadable code as Datepicker.HTML.)

```
$(function()
  {
      $("#DateEntry").datepicker();
  })
```

DateEntry is a standard <input type="text"> control. When the user clicks the control, jQuery UI automatically displays a calendar like the one shown in Figure 20-5.

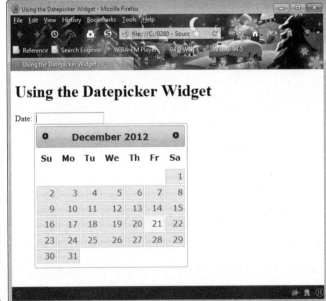

**Figure 20-5:**
The
Datepicker
widget
makes
entering
dates much
easier.

## Using the Progressbar widget

Users are impatient, and sometimes a process takes a while to complete. A file downloads only so fast, and some transactions become bogged down on the server. A progress bar makes it possible for the developer to keep the user informed about the progress of a task. Modern programming strategies try to keep the user from waiting at all by performing longer tasks in the background, but sometimes a user can't proceed until the task is done. This is the time you need to rely on a progress bar to keep the user from attempting to stop the process before it completes.

The following example shows how to use a progress bar. In this case, the progress bar is updated through a timing loop. Each time the timer expires, the progress bar is updated, and the timer is reinstituted. The result is that the progress part indicator moves from left to right and that the timer eventually stops when the indicator moves all the way to right. (You can find complete code for this example in the \Chapter 20\Widgets folder of the downloadable code as Progressbar.HTML.)

```
// Configure the progress bar.
$(function()
  {
     $("#Progress").progressbar({value: 0});
  })

// Create a variable to hold the timer object.
var Timer;

// Create a variable to hold the total timeout.
var Timeout;

function StartTimer()
{
   // Initialize the timeout.
   Timeout = 0;

   // Set the progress bar maximum value.
   $("#Progress").progressbar(
      "option", "max", parseInt($("#StartValue").val()));

   // Create the timer variable.
   Timer = window.setTimeout(UpdateTimer, 100);
}

function UpdateTimer()
{
   // Get the maximum value.
   var MaxTime =
      $("#Progress").progressbar("option", "max");

   // Check for the end of the timing cycle.
   if (Timeout >= MaxTime)
      return;
```

```
    // Update the Timeout value.
    Timeout += 100;

    // Update the percentage completed.
    $("#PercentDone").text(
        Math.round((Timeout/MaxTime)*100));

    // Set the progress bar value.
    $("#Progress").progressbar("value", Timeout);

    // Create the timer variable.
    Timer = window.setTimeout(UpdateTimer, 100);
}
```

The first task is to create the progress bar itself by calling `progressbar()`. Notice that you must provide an initial value as input. However, the progress bar configuration isn't complete — the call to `StartTimer()` later will perform some additional configuration tasks.

The `StartTimer()` function is called when the user clicks Start Timer on the form. This function initializes two global variables. `Timer` is a timer object used to animate the progress bar. `Timeout` is the current elapsed time in milliseconds. This function also configures the `max` option for the progress bar. The indicator is a percentage of the current `value` and the `max` value properties. The maximum value is provided by the user through an `<input type="text">` control, `StartValue`.

Whenever `Timer` expires, it calls `UpdateTimer()`. `UpdateTimer()` obtains the maximum time value from the progress bar and places it in `MaxTime`. It then verifies that `Timeout` is less than `MaxTime`. When `Timeout` finally reaches `MaxTime`, the progress bar has reached 100 percent, and it's time to stop the timer.

The next step is to update `Timeout` to the next value. Every iteration advances `Timeout` by 100 milliseconds.

After updating `Timeout`, the example updates the onscreen percentage, which is stored in a `<span>` with an `id` of `PercentDone`. It also updates the progress bar's value attribute so that the bar moves to the next position.

A timer fires only once. To create the next loop of the iteration, the example must reset `Timer`. When the next 100 millisecond wait is over, `UpdateTimer()` is called again and the process begins anew.

### Using the Slider widget

Sliders give the user the ability to input a value visually — as part of a whole. A slider ensures that the user inputs a correct value within a range of values, so you don't need to worry about security issues or incorrect values. As a result, sliders provide a valuable means of allowing variable input. The following example shows how to use a slider in your application. (You can find complete code for this example in the \Chapter 20\Widgets folder of the downloadable code as Slider.HTML.)

```
$(function()
  {
    $("#Slider").slider(
      {
        // Set the maximum slider value.
        max: 50,

        // Perform tasks when the value changes.
        change: function(event, ui)
        {
          // Display the current slider value.
          $("#Value").text(
            $("#Slider").slider("value"));
        }
      });
  })
```

In this case, the code sets the maximum slider value to 50. The minimum value defaults to 0. However, you can set both the maximum and minimum values to any starting or stopping position. Even though the example doesn't show it, the Slider can have more than one handle, so it can represent a range. This flexibility means that you can ask the user to input both a starting and a stopping point.

One of the most commonly used events is change. The example displays the new value each time the user finishes moving the handle. However, the way in which you use the output depends on your application. Generally, you use the output to provide data input or application control. However, it's a good idea to display the actual slider value so the user knows the actual input value.

### Using the Spinner widget

Some, but not all, browsers support the <input type="number"> tag. This tag provides a spinner input for working with numeric input, so the user can simply click up or down arrows to change the numeric value of an input. Because it's important to provide users with easy methods for entering data correctly, the Spinner widget is an important addition to your toolkit. Not only does it work with all major browsers, but you can also add features such as input validation, as shown in the following example. (You can find complete code for this example in the \Chapter 20\Widgets folder of the downloadable code as Spinner.HTML.)

```
$(function()
  {
     // Create the spinner and place a reference
     // to it in ThisSpinner.
     var ThisSpinner = $("#Spinner").spinner(
        {
           // Set the minimum and maximum values.
           min: 1,
           max: 5,

           // Add validation.
           change: function(event, ui)
           {
              // Check for minimum and maximum value
              // compliance.
              if (ThisSpinner.spinner("value") < 1)
                 ThisSpinner.spinner("value", 1);

              if (ThisSpinner.spinner("value") > 5)
                 ThisSpinner.spinner("value", 5);
           }
        });

     // Set the initial value.
     ThisSpinner.spinner("value", 1);

     // Provide a means for returning the current value.
     $("#GetSpinValue").click(
        function()
        {
           alert(ThisSpinner.spinner("value"));
        }
     );

     // Create buttons for all buttons on the form.
     $("button").button();
  });
```

In this case, the example begins by creating a variable to hold the Spinner widget. You can use this technique with any of the widgets to make them easier to work with. This example needs to access the Spinner widget in several ways, so using a variable makes sense.

To ensure the user enters only values in the correct range, you must set the min and max options. However, these options control input only when the user works with the spinner. To verify that manual input is also correct, you must create a handler for the change event. All that this function does is check whether the value() method returns a number between 1 and 5. If not, the code uses the value() method to set the numeric value appropriately.

Validation events, such as `change`, occur when the control loses focus. When you type an incorrect value into the control, the example doesn't fix it immediately. The fix occurs when the control loses focus. To see this event-handling for yourself, type an incorrect value into the control and then click outside the control so it loses focus. You see the control provide a correct value in place of the one you typed.

Eventually, you need to access the widget's value to send it to the server or use it in other ways. This example also creates an event handler for a `<button>` control, `GetSpinValue`. When a user clicks this button, it displays the current value.

### Using the Tabs widget

Many developers use tabbed interfaces to reduce application complexity. If you can focus the user's attention on one item at a time, you reduce the potential for errant input. This example provides an alternative to the example shown in the "Using the Accordion widget" section earlier in this chapter. As with that example, you begin with a simple function call. (You can find complete code for this example in the `\Chapter 20\Widgets` folder of the downloadable code as `Tabs.HTML`.)

```
$(function()
  {
     $("#Configuration").tabs();
  });
```

The trick for this example is in the HTML tags, just as it was for the Accordion widget example. There are some important differences in how you create the two pages to obtain the desired appearance, as shown in the following code:

```
<form id="ConfigForm" method="get" action="Tabs.html">
   <div id="Configuration">
      <ul>
         <li><a href="#Tab1">Foreground Color</a></li>
         <li><a href="#Tab2">Background Color</a></li>
         <li><a href="#Tab3">Options</a></li>
      </ul>
      <div id="Tab1">
         <input id="FGRed"
               type="radio"
               name="Foreground"
               value="Red"
               checked="checked" />
         <label for="FGRed">Red</label><br />
... More inputs and labels ...
      </div>
      <div id="Tab2">
         <input id="BGRed"
               type="radio"
```

```
                      name="Background"
                      value="Red"
                      checked="checked" />
            <label for="BGRed">Red</label><br />
... More inputs and labels ...
        </div>
        <div id="Tab3">
            <input id="Sounds"
                   type="checkbox"
                   name="Sounds"
                   value="SpecialSounds" />
            <label for="Sounds">Use Special Sounds</label>
            <br />
            <input id="Effects"
                   type="checkbox"
                   name="Effects"
                   value="SpecialEffects" />
            <label for="Effects">Use Special Effects</label>
        </div>
    </div>
    <input id="ChangeConfig"
           type="submit"
           value="Change Configuration" />
</form>
```

Notice that the `<h2>` elements are gone in this case. Instead of using headings to define the separation between elements, you provide an unordered list (`<ul>`) instead. The list must contain a `href` to each of the `<div>` elements in the page. There isn't any difference in the page content. Figure 20-6 shows typical output from this example.

**Figure 20-6:** Tabs focus the user's attention, just as the accordion interface does.

## Effects run amok

There has been a tendency as of late to overdo all sorts of special interface features. A designer will choose an artsy font that looks cute but is nearly impossible for anyone without perfect vision to read. Certain color combinations that look fine to someone with full color vision are impossible for someone who has colorblindness to see. Some graphics actually interfere with everyone's ability to use the application — despite adding an interesting feel. However, the worst of all of the offenses in modern applications are effects run amok. The lack of self-control on the part of designer and developer alike make users wonder what is happening. A window that appears out of nowhere and serves no useful purpose except to annoy the user truly is a form of insanity that no one needs.

When creating an application, avoid using effects if possible. When you do use effects, make sure they serve a useful purpose and that the user can easily understand the reason for the effect. For example, a message dialog box that appears in the upper-right corner of the display to tell the user that a process, such as printing, has completed, and then fades from view after a couple of seconds, is an example of a useful effect that the user will understand and appreciate. On the other hand, option boxes that slide out for no apparent reason and block the user's view of the screen are an example of an annoying effect. Worse still are unhelpful help dialog boxes that pop up in the middle of the display to remind the user about the presence of an application feature that the user is already using. Often, these dialog boxes don't actually tell the user how to use the feature, so the dialog box doesn't provide anything the user doesn't already know.

To make a change, you click the tab that contains the information you want to see. You make changes as normal. Clicking the Change Configuration button sends the changes to the server. If you test this example by using the same process you did for the accordion example, you get precisely the same results — only the interface appearance has changed.

# Defining the effects

Special effects can add pizzazz to your site. They can turn mundane information into something with that special sparkle that people will remember long after they've read the material you provide. Using special effects correctly can draw the user's attention to a particular area of the page or help the user understand a process when using an animated sequence. The point is that effects are normally an addition to the page, not the main focus of it. Effects normally don't present any sort of information, but they can enhance the impact of information you do present. The following sections describe some of the more interesting effects that you can create using jQuery UI.

### Creating an animation by manipulating classes

Using CSS classes can have an interesting effect on the presentation of information onscreen. jQuery UI makes it possible to use CSS classes to perform animations in four different ways:

✔ Adding a class

✔ Removing a class

✔ Switching between classes

✔ Toggling a class

In all four cases, the effect doesn't occur immediately — you provide a time delay to make the transition between presentations slow enough for the user to see. (You can find complete code for this example in the \Chapter 20\ Animations folder of the downloadable code as ManageClasses.HTML.)

```
$(function()
   {
      $("#ChangeClass").click(function()
         {
            $("#SampleText").addClass(
               "Effect", 1500, RemoveClass);
            return false;
         });

      function RemoveClass()
      {
         $("#SampleText").removeClass(
            "Effect", 1500, "easeOutBounce");
      };

      $("#SwitchClass").click(function()
         {
            $(".Normal").switchClass(
               "Normal", "Effect", 1500, "easeInElastic");
            $(".Effect").switchClass(
               "Effect", "Effect2", 1500,
               "easeOutElastic");
            $(".Effect2").switchClass(
               "Effect2", "Normal", 1500,
               "easeInOutElastic");
            return false;
         });

      $("#ToggleClass").click(function()
         {
            $(".Normal").toggleClass("Effect", 1500);
            return false;
         })
   })
```

There are three buttons on the front of the page: Add/Remove Class, Switch Between Classes, and Toggle Between Classes. Each of these buttons is assigned an event handler as shown. The `RemoveClass()` function is a callback for the Add/Remove Class button. After the transition for the event handler has ended, the code automatically calls this function.

All of these animations work in precisely the same way — they add or remove classes to or from the specified element. In this case, a `<div>` named `SampleText` is the target of the animations. The difference between the method calls is how they perform their task. The `addClass()` method performs a straightforward addition of a class. You supply the name of the class to add as the first argument. If the class already exists for the element, nothing happens. Likewise, the `removeClass()` method removes the specified class from the element. Again, you supply the name of the class to remove as the first argument.

The `switchClass()` method switches between one class and another. You can use it to create multiple transitions. For example, this example shows how to switch between three transitions. The `Normal` class is replaced with `Effect`, `Effect` is replaced with `Effect2`, and `Effect2` is replaced with `Normal`. Consequently, you see the animations rotate between three classes. You supply the name of the class to remove as the first argument and the name of the class to add as the second argument.

The `toggleClass()` method adds or removes a class depending on whether the class is assigned to the element. In this case, the code adds `Effect` when `SampleText` lacks it and removes `Effect` when `SampleText` has it applied. You supply the name of the class to toggle as the first argument.

jQuery UI can't animate all styles. For example, there's a transition between having the text left justified and having it centered in this example. This transition can't be animated. What you see is that the effect occurs at the end of the animation. In addition, some effects are animated, but they aren't animated in the way you might expect. For example, if an element changes color, the new color is used throughout the animation, but you see it gradually fade in.

Each of these method calls includes a time delay of 1500 milliseconds. This value indicates the amount of time in which the animation occurs. The default setting is 400 milliseconds, which is a little hard for most people to see. However, this argument is optional, and you don't have to supply it to make the method work.

The `addClass()` method includes another optional argument, a callback function. The callback function is called when the animation is over. The example uses the callback function to toggle the effect. However, a callback could be used for any number of purposes. For example, you could use it to create a validation sequence to ensure that users enter the correct data for form fields that have incorrect information.

An animation can also use an *easing function*. This function determines how the animation appears onscreen. The default setting is to use the swing easing function, which provides a gentle transition that most users will appreciate. However, you might want a little more pizzazz or at least a different effect. You can see a list of easing functions at `http://api.jqueryui.com/easings`. This example uses a number of different easing functions so that you get an idea of how they work.

### Defining a color animation

If you want to perform an actual color animation in your application, you need to use the `animate()` method. This method seems to be a work in progress because the documentation for it isn't nearly as nice as the other documentation for jQuery UI. The method does seem to work for all the target platforms and browsers for this book, but you'll want to experiment to ensure that it will work for every browser you need to target. The color will actually transition in this case. It's also possible to control the text colors to a large degree. The following example shows the most commonly used transitions. (You can find complete code for this example in the `\Chapter 20\ Animations` folder of the downloadable code as `Animate.HTML`.)

```javascript
$(function()
  {
      // Track the normal state.
      var State = true;

      $("#ChangeColors").click(
          function()
          {
              if (State)
              {
                  // Set to the changed state.
                  $("#SampleText").animate(
                      {
                          backgroundColor: "#0000ff",
                          color: "white",
                          borderColor: "#ff0000",
                          height: 100,
                          width: 600
                      }, 1500);
              }
              else
              {
                  // Set to the normal state.
                  $("#SampleText").animate(
                      {
                          backgroundColor: "#7fffff",
                          color: "black",
                          borderColor: "#00ff00",
                          height: 50,
                          width: 400
                      }, 1500);
```

```
            }

            // Change the state.
            State = !State;
        }
    )
})
```

If you're thinking that this code looks like it works similar to CSS, it does, but the `animate()` method provides a significantly reduced list of features it can change. You can change many features of the text and the container that holds it, including both the width and height. However, you can't change things like the kind of border used to hold everything — even though you can change the color of the border. The jQuery UI documentation states that `animate()` supports these properties:

✔ `backgroundColor`

✔ `borderBottomColor`

✔ `borderLeftColor`

✔ `borderRightColor`

✔ `borderTopColor`

✔ `color`

✔ `columnRuleColor`

✔ `outlineColor`

✔ `textDecorationColor`

✔ `textEmphasisColor`

The library-supplied examples (those provided by the vendor on the vendor's site) show that a few other properties are supported, including `width`, `height`, and `borderColor`. Use these non-published properties with care. Even though they work now, they may not be supported in future releases of the library.

### Managing element visibility using effects

Many applications require that you show or hide elements at different points of application execution. It may be something as simple as not needing the element at that particular time (such as a progress bar). In most cases, you simply want the element to go away. Whether the user notices the disappearance is immaterial to the application's functionality. However, you may want the user to notice the change in some situations. For example, a user might select an option that makes other options inaccessible. Using a special effect to make this more noticeable could be helpful.

The jQuery UI library provides several means of controlling element visibility in an animated manner. The fact that the element is shown or hidden doesn't change, but the way in which the application shows or hides it does. For example, you could use a slide effect to show that a new element has been added due to a choice the user has made. There are four main methods of animating elements by using this technique:

- Use an effect where the element visually changes.
- Show a hidden element by using an effect.
- Hide an element by using an effect.
- Toggle an element's visibility by using an effect.

The effect that you choose for working with an element controls how jQuery UI visually manages it. For example, an explode effect causes the element to break into pieces, with each piece moving in a different direction off screen. The following keywords define the sorts of effects that you can use (you can find additional details at `http://api.jqueryui.com/category/effects`):

| | | |
|---|---|---|
| blind | fade | scale |
| bounce | fold | shake |
| clip | highlight | size |
| drop | puff | slide |
| explode | pulsate | transfer |

In addition to the actual effect, you can use an easing function to make the effect more pronounced or special in other ways. You can see a list of easing functions at `http://api.jqueryui.com/easings`. The following example shows how to use all four approaches for working with element visibility. There are actually four buttons used for the example, but element visibility limits you to seeing just three at a time because you can't show an element that's already visible or hide an element that's already hidden. (You can find complete code for this example in the `\Chapter 20\Animations` folder of the downloadable code as `Visibility.HTML`.)

```
$(function()
    {
        // Keep track of the element hidden state.
        var Hidden = false;

        $("#Effect").click(
            function()
            {
                $("#SampleText").effect(
                    "bounce", "easeOutBounce", 1500);
            });

        $("#Show").click(
```

```
              function()
              {
                  Hidden = false;

                  $("#SampleText").show(
                      "slide", 1500, ChangeButtonState);
              });

          $("#Hide").click(
              function()
              {
                  Hidden = true;

                  $("#SampleText").hide(
                      "explode", 1500, ChangeButtonState);
              });

          $("#Toggle").click(
              function()
              {
                  Hidden = !Hidden;

                  $("#SampleText").toggle(
                      "scale", {percent: 0}, 1500,
                      ChangeButtonState);
              });

          // Set the button state as needed.
          function ChangeButtonState()
          {
              if (Hidden)
              {
                  $("#Show").attr("hidden", false);
                  $("#Hide").attr("hidden", true);
              }
              else
              {
                  $("#Show").attr("hidden", true);
                  $("#Hide").attr("hidden", false);
              }
          }
      }
  })
```

The example begins by creating a variable, Hidden, to track the state of the
element. When the element is hidden, the Show button is displayed. Likewise,
when the element is displayed, the Hide button is displayed as well. This
functionality is controlled by a callback function, ChangeButtonState().

The code for the Effect button simply performs an effect on the element,
SampleText. In this case, you see the bounce effect. The performance
of this effect is modified by the easeOutBounce easing function, and the
entire animation lasts 1500 milliseconds. The actual visibility is unchanged,
but the user sees an animation of the element onscreen. You could use this

technique to point out fields that have incorrect information or require additional information. Of course, you can also use it to perform any other sort of simple animation desired — including a looped animation, where the animation is constantly replayed.

The `Show` and `Hide` button codes work hand-in-hand to hide or display `SampleText`. The `Show` button uses the `slide` effect, and the `Hide` button uses the `explode` effect. Both perform the task over 1500 milliseconds. Notice that both event handlers set the state of `Hidden` directly because the state is an absolute based on the task that the button performs. The event handlers also provide `ChangeButtonState()` as a callback function. The animation calls this function after the animation has completed to set the button state correctly.

The `Toggle` button works like a combination of the `Show` and `Hide` buttons — the event handler simply toggles the `SampleText` visual state. Because the state isn't known, the value of `Hidden` is also toggled. In this case, the event handler calls the `scale` effect, which requires an additional argument in the form of `percent`. Make sure you check the effects to determine whether they require additional arguments — most don't. When the animation completes, the application calls `ChangeButtonState()` to reconfigure the user interface as needed.

# Canvasing Your Web Page

HTML5 includes the concept of a canvas. As with the artist's version of the physical canvas, you use the HTML5 canvas to draw images onscreen. Using the canvas makes it easier to manage various sorts of drawings that you need to convey information to the user. The following sections provide additional details about the canvas from a JavaScript perspective and then demonstrate how to use the canvas with the Google Maps API to draw a map onscreen.

## Understanding what the canvas does

A canvas is simply a drawing area onscreen. To create a canvas, the browser you interact with must support HTML5. This means that you need to use newer browser versions, such as Internet Explorer 9.

You also need to have an understanding of the source of the canvas and how the canvas works with the client's browser. The canvas relies on an actual `<canvas>` tag. To draw something onscreen, you provide an `id`, a `height`, and a `width` property for the `<canvas>` tag like this:

```
<canvas id="MyCanvas"
        height=500
        width=600 />
```

The size of the canvas is always in pixels. When you have a canvas to use, you can create a context to it by obtaining a reference to the canvas element and calling `getContext()` with the type of context you want, such as 2D. The context lets you use various drawing commands to create graphics onscreen. A discussion of precisely how the canvas works is outside the scope of this book. You could quite easily create several books on the topic and not cover the topic thoroughly. A great tutorial on the topic appears at `http://www.html5canvastutorials.com`. You could also read *HTML5 Canvas For Dummies* by Don Cowan (Wiley) for additional information.

The important issue for this chapter is precisely where the canvas comes from. Most tutorials assume that the client relies on local JavaScript functionality to perform the task. A simple application could use this approach, but most of the applications you'll create will rely on server-based canvases. In this case, you supply a `<div>` as a container to hold the `<canvas>` that the server sends to the client. The advantage of this approach is that the server can create a wealth of graphics for the client and send the cached `<canvas>` tags to every client that needs them — creating an efficient method for sharing graphics. Many developers find this approach confusing, which is why this chapter approaches the canvas from the server-based perspective using the Google Maps API.

## Creating a simple Google API application

This chapter doesn't provide a detailed look at the Google Maps API, which is relatively complex. What it does provide is a simple look at something you could easily expand into a full-fledged application later. Many organizations use maps for all sorts of interesting purposes. The article at `http://blog.smartbear.com/software-quality/bid/242126/using-the-google-maps-api-to-add-cool-stuff-to-your-applications` provides some additional ideas on how you can use the Google Maps API with your browser-based application.

### Obtaining a developer key

To use this example, you must obtain a developer key. Google provides two kinds of keys: paid and free. You need only the free key for this example. The paid key does provide considerably more flexibility, and you'll likely need it for any full-fledged application you create. However, for experimentation purposes, the free key works just fine. You can obtain this key at `https://developers.google.com/maps/licensing`. Make sure you understand the terms of service fully before you begin working with the Google Maps API. You can also find some additional assistance in using the Google Maps API with JavaScript at `https://developers.google.com/maps/documentation/javascript/tutorial`.

### Creating the application

It's best to create the code for this example in several steps. The first is to add the usual jQuery references used in the remainder of the chapter. In addition, you also need to add a reference to the Google Maps API, as shown here. (You can find complete code for this example in the \Chapter 20\ GoogleAPI folder of the downloadable code as GoogleAPI.HTML.)

```
<script type="text/javascript"
    src="https://maps.googleapis.com/maps/api/js?key=Your Key Here&sensor=false">
</script>
```

This example won't work at all unless you replace the words, *Your Key Here*, with the key that you receive from Google. Consequently, this particular step is important because it's the one step you must perform even if you're using the code downloaded from the book's site.

Now that you have all the required references in place, it's time to create a canvas to draw the map. The canvas is simply a <div> with an id: <div id="MapCanvas"></div>. You must provide style information that gives the <div> size or else the map won't appear onscreen, even when Google sends it to you. The example uses the following style information:

```
#MapCanvas
{
    height: 90%;
    width:100%;
}
```

In addition to the canvas, the example provides two text boxes for input and a button that you can use to request a new map. There isn't anything too complex about the interface, but it gets the job done. The code for this example uses many of the jQuery and jQuery UI tricks you've already seen in other places in the book, as shown here:

```
$(function()
    {
        // Track the current latitude using a
        // spinner control.
        var Latitude = $("#latitude").spinner(
            {
                min: -90,
                max: 90,
                step: .1,

                change: function(event, ui)
                {
                    if (Latitude.spinner("value") < -90)
                        Latitude.spinner("value", -90);
                    if (Latitude.spinner("value") > 90)
                        Latitude.spinner("value", 90);
                }
```

```
    });

    // Track the current longitude using a
    // spinner control.
    var Longitude = $("#longitude").spinner(
        {
            min: -180,
            max: 180,
            step: .1,

            change: function(event, ui)
            {
                if (Longitude.spinner("value") < -180)
                    Longitude.spinner("value", -180);
                if (Longitude.spinner("value") > 180)
                    Longitude.spinner("value", 180);
            }
        });

    // This function actually displays the map on
    // screen.
    function GetMap()
    {
        // Create a list of arguments to send to Google.
        var MapOptions =
        {
            center: new google.maps.LatLng(
                        Latitude.spinner("value"),
                        Longitude.spinner("value")),
            zoom: 8,
            mapTypeId: google.maps.MapTypeId.ROADMAP
        }

        // Provide the location to place the map and the
        // map options to Google.
        var map = new google.maps.Map(
            document.getElementById("MapCanvas"),
            MapOptions);
    };

    // The example provides two methods of getting a
    // map: during page loading or by clicking Get Map.
    $(window).load(
        function()
        {
            GetMap();
        });

    $("#submit").click(
        function()
        {
            GetMap();
        });
})
```

To make it easier to browse an area, the example provides spinner controls for the latitude and longitude inputs. These spinners work much like the spinner example described in the earlier "Using the Spinner widget" section of this chapter. However, moving an entire degree at a time wouldn't make the application very useful, so the two spinners change the inputs by a tenth of a degree at a time. (Even this setting may be too large, so you might want to change it.) Notice the use of the `step` option to perform this task. Latitudes range from 90 degrees north to –90 degrees south, so the example reflects this requirement. Likewise, longitudes range from 180 degrees west to –180 degrees east of Greenwich, England. You can read more about latitude and longitude at `http://geography.about.com/cs/ latitudelongitude/a/latlong.htm`.

The `GetMap()` function performs the actual task of obtaining the map. To do this, your application must create a list of map options. The example shows a simple, but typical, list. The most important of these options is where to center the map. In this case, the map automatically centers itself on Milwaukee, Wisconsin, but you can change the settings to any location you want. The example uses a zoom factor of 8, and you'll see a road map. The Google Maps API actually provides a number of map types that you can try.

There are two times when `GetMap()` is called. When the application loads, you see Milwaukee, Wisconsin (unless you change the default settings). After you change the inputs, you can also click Get Map to display a new location. Figure 20-7 shows typical output from this application.

**Figure 20-7:**
The example can show any location for which you have a longitude and latitude.

# Part VI
# The Part of Tens

Enjoy an additional Part of Tens article about ten cool sites you can emulate at `http://www.dummies.com/extras/html5programmingwith javascript`.

# In this part . . .

- ✔ Discover techniques for combining elements to create better user interfaces.

- ✔ Create a slideshow application you can extend to work in a number of environments.

- ✔ Work with both date and time pickers to make it easier to enter these values correctly.

- ✔ Consider how applications could possibly change in the future and what your role in that future development environment will be.

# Chapter 21

# Ten Incredible HTML5 and JavaScript Examples

*T*his chapter brings many of the elements in the rest of the book together into useful pieces that you could combine to create a site of your own. The examples are short, practical ways to use HTML5 and JavaScript together to add interest, functionality, and flexibility to any site. The examples do rely on jQuery (described in Chapter 18) and jQuery UI (explored in Chapter 20) to perform tasks, as will most production sites you visit today. No one wants to reinvent the wheel, so using third-party libraries such as jQuery and jQuery UI just makes sense.

If you find that one of the examples doesn't work directly from the down-loaded code folder, try placing it on your test server. Many browsers won't display information unless it is received from a server. For example, most of these examples fail in Chrome unless you place them on your test server (see Chapter 2 for instructions on installing the Apache server). The platform can make a difference as well. Linux appears to be the pickiest when it comes to using a test server rather than simply opening the example from the down-loaded code folder.

## Using online resources

This book provides you with a wealth of interesting and useful ideas for working with HTML5 and JavaScript, but it only scratches the surface of what's possible. Make sure you use online resources to your benefit. For example, there are entire sites devoted to helping you find third-party add-ons for the jQuery UI library, such as 20 Awesome jQuery UI Resources (`http://www.technoread.net/webdesign/javascript-a-jquery/item/358-20-awesome-jquery-ui-resources`). You should also check out 65 Excellent jQuery Resources (`http://speckyboy.com/2008/04/02/65-excellent-jquery-resources-tutorials cheat-sheetsebooksdemosplugins`) for some outstanding ideas of how to extend jQuery to meet specific needs. If you want even more jQuery tutorial type examples, check out the W3Schools site at `http://www.w3schools.com/jquery`.

In addition to using online resources to work with libraries and other tools, there aren't any developers who have everything about HTML5, CSS, or JavaScript memorized — it's simply impossible to do so. The best developers memorize the features they use most often, and then rely on online references to fill in the gaps. You can find an HTML5 reference at `https://developer.mozilla.org/docs/HTML/HTML5`, CSS reference at `https://developer.mozilla.org/docs/CSS`, and JavaScript reference at `https://developer.mozilla.org/docs/JavaScript/Reference`. The point is, don't try to reinvent the wheel — rely on online sources to help you find the information and resources you need to create amazing sites in the shortest time possible.

# Creating an XML-Based Menu

Many browser-based applications employ menus to make it easier for users to make selections. Hard-coding these menus may seem like a good idea, but doing so makes updates more difficult. Using a database or XML file to hold the menu options makes it possible to update the menus by using a tool without actually changing the application code. The following example shows one technique for creating a menu that stores its data in an external XML file. (You can find complete code for this example in the \Chapter 21\XMLMenu folder of the downloadable code as XMLMenu.HTML.)

```
$(function()
  {
     $(window).load(
        function()
        {
           // Create a connection to the file.
           var Connect = new XMLHttpRequest();

           // Define which file to open and
           // send the request.
```

```
            Connect.open("GET", "XMLMenuData.xml", false);
            Connect.setRequestHeader(
                "Content-Type", "text/xml");
            Connect.send(null);

            // Place the response in an XML document.
            var Response = Connect.responseXML;

            // Place the root node in an element.
            var MenuEntries = Response.childNodes[0];

            // Start at the upper levels and move down.
            if (MenuEntries.children.length > 0)
                ProcessEntries(MenuEntries.children);

            // Make the menu entries public.
            $("#Menu").append(MenuData);

            // Create the menu onscreen.
$("#Menu").menu();
        }
    );

    var MenuData = "";

    function ProcessEntries(Nodes)
    {
        for (var i = 0; i < Nodes.length; i++)
        {
            // Store the current node and add it
            // to the menu.
            var ThisNode = Nodes[i];
            MenuData +=
                "<li id='" + $(ThisNode).attr("id")
                    + "'>" +
                "<a href='" + $(ThisNode).attr("target")
                    + "'>" +
                $(ThisNode).attr("caption") + "</a>";

            // Check for submenus and process them.
            if (ThisNode.children.length > 0)
            {
                MenuData += "<ul>";
                ProcessEntries(ThisNode.children);
                MenuData += "</ul>";
            }

            // End the current node.
            MenuData += "</li>";
        }
```

```
        // Return to the caller.
        return;
    }
});
```

The `(window).load()` event handler looks like it contains a lot of code, but you've already worked through quite a bit of it in the section on loading XML with JavaScript in Chapter 16. Instead of loading a customer data file, the example loads menu entries. After the code loads the menu entries, it processes them into the HTML unordered list format required to create a menu. You can see typical source code for such a menu at `http://jqueryui.com/menu`. In fact, the HTML isn't much different from the menu demonstrated in the section on creating JavaScript-based menus in Chapter 13. After creating the unordered list dynamically, the code appends it to a `<ul>` element, `Menu`, and turns `Menu` into a jQuery UI menu by calling `menu()`. Typical output from this example looks like the menu in Figure 21-1.

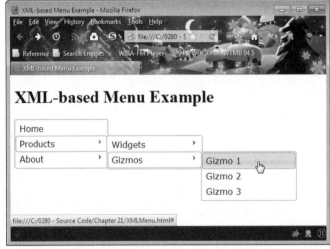

**Figure 21-1:** This dynamic menu can change without changing the underlying code.

The secret to this menuing system is the recursive function, `Process Entries()`. This function creates the unordered list content dynamically by parsing the XML entries that you provide. It doesn't matter what the XML contains, as long as the entries are formatted correctly. Each list entry appears within an `<li>` tag that includes an `id` attribute. You use the `id` to enable or disable menu entries as needed later. The tag content consists of an `<a>` tag with an `href` attribute that points to the location where the menu will take the user when clicked. The only part the user sees is the `caption` attribute of the XML entry.

Recursion occurs when the XML entry contains children, or submenus. When the current node contains children, the `ThisNode.children.length` property is greater than 0, and the code calls `ProcessEntries()` recursively with the children of the current node. Because of the way that this feature is constructed, you can create menus of any depth without special programming as long as the host system has the required resources.

The XML file must be constructed in a specific way to work with the example. The elements must appear in the order you want them presented onscreen, and submenus must appear nested appropriately within their parent menus, as shown here:

```xml
<?xml version="1.0" encoding="UTF-8"?>
<Menu>
    <Entry id="Home"
           caption="Home"
           target="#" />
    <Entry id="Products"
           caption="Products"
           target="#">
        <Entry id="ProductsWidgets"
               caption="Widgets"
               target="#">
            <Entry id="ProductsWidgets1"
                   caption="Widget 1"
                   target="#" />
            <Entry id="ProductsWidgets2"
                   caption="Widget 2"
                   target="#" />
        </Entry>
        <Entry id="ProductsGizmos"
               caption="Gizmos"
               target="#">
            <Entry id="ProductsGizmos1"
                   caption="Gizmo 1"
                   target="#" />
            <Entry id="ProductsGizmos2"
                   caption="Gizmo 2"
                   target="#" />
            <Entry id="ProductsGizmos3"
                   caption="Gizmo 3"
                   target="#" />
        </Entry>
    </Entry>
    <Entry id="About"
           caption="About"
           target="#">
        <Entry id="AboutLocation"
               caption="Location"
```

```
                target="#" />
       <Entry id="AboutContact"
              caption="Contact Us"
              target="#" />
       <Entry id="AboutSupport"
              caption="Customer Support"
              target="#" />
    </Entry>
</Menu>
```

This XML contains all the menu entries for the example. As you can see, there is nothing to differentiate the menu entries except their position in the hierarchy. This generic method of laying out the menu makes it possible to move menu elements around as needed without having to change anything except the entry's position. Every entry must include the id, caption, and target attributes shown. The target always points to the location where the user goes when the menu entry is clicked.

# Creating an XML-Based Tabbed Interface

It's possible to use XML files (or databases) to hold just about anything related to a browser-based application. In this example, you see how to create a jQuery UI tabbed interface by using data stored in an XML file. However, this example incorporates a major difference from the previous XML example — it relies on jQuery to get the XML file rather than relying on handwritten code to perform the task (as is shown in the example in the preceding section). The code is shorter; somewhat easier to understand; and, most important of all, more likely to work with browsers that you didn't originally test as part of the initial application design. The following code shows the jQuery method of creating a tabbed interface. (You can find complete code for this example in the \Chapter 21\XMLTab folder of the downloadable code as XMLTab.HTML.)

```
$(function()
   {
      // Create variables to hold temporary data.
      var TabHeads = "";
      var TabContent = "";

      // Obtain the XML data file and process it.
      $.get("XMLTabData.xml", function(data)
         {
            // Locate each Heading entry and use it to
            // create a tab heading.
```

```
        $(data).find("Heading").each(function()
            {
                TabHeads +=
                    "<li><a href='" +
                    $(this).attr("href") +
                    "'>" + $(this).attr("caption") +
                    "</a></li>";
            });

        // Append the data to the heading area.
        $("#Headings").append(TabHeads);

        // Locate each Content entry and use it to
        // create the tab content.
        $(data).find("Content").each(function()
            {
                TabContent +=
                    "<div id='" + $(this).attr("id") +
                    "'>" + $(this).text() + "</div>";
            });

        // Append the data to the tab content area.
        $("#Tabs").append(TabContent);

        // Complete the process by displaying the
        // tabs.
        $("#Tabs").tabs();
    });
});
```

This example isn't doing anything radically new. It's still retrieving and parsing an XML file — it just makes jQuery perform all the heavy lifting. The get() method obtains the XML file, XMLTabData.XML, and places the content in data. The function is executed when the data retrieval is complete, so it acts as a callback for an asynchronous data read.

Parsing the file is as easy as asking jQuery to use find() to locate something in the XML file. Here is the XML file used for this example:

```
<?xml version="1.0" encoding="UTF-8"?>
<Tabs>
    <TabData>
        <Heading id="Tab1"
                 href="#Tabs1"
                 caption="Tab 1" />
        <Heading id="Tab2"
                 href="#Tabs2"
                 caption="Tab 2" />
```

```
        <Heading id="Tab3"
                 href="#Tabs3"
                 caption="Tab 3" />
    </TabData>
    <TabContent>
       <Content id="Tabs1">
          This is some content for Tab 1.
       </Content>
       <Content id="Tabs2">
          This is some content for Tab 2.
       </Content>
       <Content id="Tabs3">
          This is some content for Tab 3.
       </Content>
    </TabContent>
</Tabs>
```

All of the heading information appears within the `<Heading>` elements. So, the code asks jQuery to `find()` each of the `<Heading>` elements and process them one at a time using the `each()` method. The `each()` method creates a loop that automatically provides access to individual `<Heading>` elements through the `this` variable. Tab headings are stored in an unordered list (`<ul>`), `Headings`, that is already part of the HTML for the example page.

The content for each tab appears in `<div>` elements that are appended after the `<ul>` element, `Headings`. The content could be anything — including controls as used for the previous tabbed interface example demonstrated in the section on using the Tabs widget in Chapter 20. The most important issue to consider is how to store information in the XML file. You escape any tags so that they're not misinterpreted as XML elements. (See Chapter 16 for a table of typical replacement characters.)

As with the headings, the code uses `find()` to locate each of the `<Content>` elements in the XML file and convert them to the HTML required to create the tab content. The `each()` method creates the loop used to process each element one at a time. Figure 21-2 show typical output from this example.

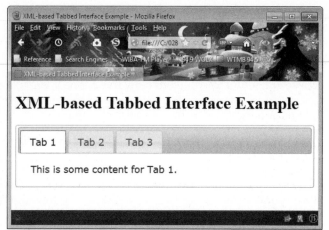

**Figure 21-2:**
Dynamic tab configuration is just as easy as creating dynamic menus.

# Displaying a Slideshow

Slideshows have become a method for doing everything from displaying pictures to describing processes to advertising. You find slideshows all over the place for good reason — graphics can communicate in ways that words can't. No one is quite sure who said, "A picture is worth a thousand words" (although you can get some ideas at http://www.phrases.org.uk/meanings/a-picture-is-worth-a-thousand-words.html), but the phrase certainly holds true. The right graphic says quite a lot to the right person.

It shouldn't be too surprising to find that jQuery aficionados have created a host of slideshow add-ins to make working with slideshows significantly easier. The example in this section relies on an easy-to-use plug-in from SlidesJS (http://www.slidesjs.com). To use the plug-in with your own code, you need to download a copy of the current product from the developer's site. However, this plug-in is just the tip of the iceberg. You can find 20 interesting slideshow plug-ins on the Vandelay Design site at http://vandelaydesign.com/blog/web-development/jquery-slideshow. There are 25 plug-ins described on the Webdesigner Depot site at http://www.webdesignerdepot.com/2011/08/25-jquery-image-galleries-and-slideshow-plug-ins. These are just some of the slideshow plug-ins available for jQuery, which is just one of many JavaScript libraries. In short, slideshows are important enough to warrant all sorts of attention.

This example helps you create a slideshow using five images and the SlideJS plug-in for jQuery. Make sure you download SlideJS by clicking Download on the host site described in the first paragraph, unarchive the downloaded .ZIP file, and place the slides.jquery.JS file found in the \slides\ Slides\source folder in the \Chapter 21\Slideshow folder of the downloadable source code. You also need to copy the global.CSS file found in the \slides\Slides\examples\Standard\css to the example directory. These references incorporate the files into the example:

```
<link rel="stylesheet" href="global.css">
<script src="slides.min.jquery.js"></script>
```

The following code shows the HTML for this example. (You can find complete code for this example in the \Chapter 21\Slideshow folder of the downloadable code as Slideshow.HTML.)

```
<div id="container">
   <div id="example">
      <div id="slides">
         <div class="slides_container">
            <a href="#">
               <img src="CactusBlossom.jpg"
                    width="600"
                    height="450" /></a>
            <a href="#">
               <img src="FirstSnow.jpg"
                    width="600"
                    height="450" /></a>
            <a href="#">
               <img src="MountainView.jpg"
                    width="600"
                    height="450" /></a>
            <a href="#">
               <img src="NankingCherry.jpg"
                    width="600"
                    height="450" /></a>
            <a href="#">
               <img src="SquashHarvest.jpg"
                    width="600"
                    height="450" /></a>
         </div>
      </div>
   </div>
</div>
```

The organization of the HTML is important because the plug-in expects to see certain elements in certain places and with specific names. You can overcome many of these issues by modifying the global.CSS file, but the best option is to simply use the author's naming scheme in your own code. The HTML shown here is extremely simplified from the samples that come with the product. Consider this a "Hello World" sort of example — it shows the simplest implementation you can create. The SlidesJS plug-in provides considerable flexibility in displaying the slideshow, which is one reason you want to try this plug-in for your application.

The default CSS for the plug-in does create a few problems, and the author documents several places in global.CSS where you need to make changes. For example, you need to modify the styles to accommodate the size of your pictures. Rather than actually change the global.CSS file, this example places the changes directly in the Slideshow.HTML file like this:

```
<style>
    .slides_container
    {
        width: 600px;
    }

    .slides_container a
    {
        width: 600px;
        height: 450px;
    }

    #slides .prev
    {
        font-size: medium;
    }

    #slides .next
    {
        left: 615px;
        font-size: medium;
    }

    h1
    {
        font-size: 20px;
        font-family: serif;
        text-align: center;
    }
</style>
```

The main purpose for these changes is to make the output a little more read-able and accommodate the size of the pictures. The actual code used to make the example work is short. Here is all you need to display the pictures in a slideshow format:

```
$(function()
    {
        $("#slides").slides(
        {
            generateNextPrev: true,
        });
    });
```

The generateNextPrev option tells the plug-in to add Next and Prev buttons to the output. You can also use graphic buttons if desired. There are all sorts of options you can use, but they're all optional. However, you must provide some method for moving between pictures, and adding the Next and Prev buttons is the simplest way to accomplish this task. Figure 21-3 shows the output from this example.

**Figure 21-3:** Slideshows can help you convey all sorts of information by using graphics.

# Employing Custom Spinners

All the jQuery UI widgets lend themselves to customization. Most of the changes you make deal with using built-in features correctly. You can also work with the CSS that jQuery UI employs to format the widgets to produce special effects. Of course, if nothing else, you can always use JavaScript to modify the actual widget behavior as needed. The point is that you can change widgets, such as Spinner, to meet specific needs without having to reinvent the wheel. The modifications are usually short and easy to do, which means you don't have to start from scratch with an idea you have to code by hand.

Spinners are popular because you can use them to control user input in a number of ways. The idea is to provide control for data that is normally variable, so you can't use something like a drop-down list. One of the most interesting uses of spinners is shown on the Ben Knows Code site at `http://benknowscode.wordpress.com/2012/10/18/exploring-the-new-jquery-ui-spinner-beyond-the-basics`. In this case, the author shows how to perform tasks such as moving the location of the arrows and creating an alphabetical spinner.

Spinners normally deal with numeric input. However, you might have a need for alphabetic input instead. To create an alphabetic input, you need to give the appearance of letters without actually using letters, because the Spinner widget works only with numbers. (You can find complete code for this example in the `\Chapter 21\Spinner` folder of the downloadable code as `Spinner.HTML`.)

```
$(function()
   {
       var CurrentValue = 65;

       var ThisSpinner = $("#Spinner").spinner(
          {
              // Set the minimum to the code for A
              // and the maximum to the code for Z.
              min: 65,
              max: 90,

              // When the user starts to spin the spinner,
              // convert the value to a number and hide the
              // text from view.
              start: function(ui, event)
              {
                  ThisSpinner.spinner("value", CurrentValue);
                  $("#Spinner").css("color", "white");
              },

              // When the user stops spinning the spinner,
              // save the numeric value, convert it to a
              // letter and display the text onscreen.
              stop: function(ui, event)
              {
```

```
        CurrentValue =
            ThisSpinner.spinner("value");
        ThisSpinner.spinner("value",
            String.fromCharCode(CurrentValue));
        $("#Spinner").css("color", "green");
    }
});
});
```

The code begins by creating a variable, CurrentValue, that tracks the numeric value of the spinner. The value, 65, is the numeric equivalent of the letter *A*. So, the spinner starts with a value of A, but it stores this value as the number 65.

Creating the spinner, ThisSpinner, comes next. You must set minimum and maximum values that reflect the numeric values of *A* and *Z*. This same technique can work for any series of letters. You could just as easily use lowercase letters, if desired. For that matter, any series will work, including special characters. It's even possible to use this approach for enumerated values.

The simplest approach provides handlers for the start and stop events. When the user clicks one of the two arrows, it starts a spin event. The change occurs, and then the spin stops. For the spinner to work correctly, the value attribute must contain a numeric value. The code sets value to CurrentValue, which is the code that equates to the currently selected letter. However, at this point, you can see the numeric value as text in the spinner, which is distracting. To keep this from happening, the event handler also sets the text color to white, so the user can't actually see the text onscreen.

The stop event handler stores the new spinner value in CurrentValue. It then converts the numeric value from a number, such as 65, to a letter, such as *A*. The code then changes the text color to green so the user can see the letter onscreen.

This example also changes a few of the widget styles. These styles are listed as part of the jQuery UI CSS file at http://code.jquery.com/ui/1.9.2/themes/base/jquery-ui.css. In this case, you don't want the user to be able to type more than one character, so the width of the widget is changed to accept just one letter. In addition, the text color is changed to green, as shown here:

```
.ui-spinner
{
    width: 45px;
}

.ui-spinner-input
{
    color: green;
}
```

Using a combination of events and CSS lets you create all sorts of custom effects with any of the jQuery UI widgets. All you need to do is experiment a little to create some really interesting output.

# Working with Timepickers

Users need to enter time values as well as date values. The jQuery UI library comes with a Datepicker widget (see http://jqueryui.com/datepicker), which is fine but not quite enough for modern applications. Fortunately, there is a solution in the form of a third-party plug-in on the Trent Richardson site at http://trentrichardson.com/examples/timepicker. To use this plug-in, you add the following reference to your code. (You can find complete code for this example in the \Chapter 21\Timepicker folder of the downloadable code as Timepicker.HTML.)

```
<script
    src="http://trentrichardson.com/examples/timepicker/jquery-ui-timepicker-
            addon.js">
</script>
```

All you need to do is add a simple <input> tag to your code and provide an id value for it. This widget has a number of forms. For example, you can request both a date and time if desired. The simplest form is to request the time by using the following code:

```
$(function()
  {
      $("#TimeSet").timepicker();
  })
```

As with most widgets, you can configure the Timepicker using various options, which are considerable. There aren't any events to handle except those that are provided by jQuery UI natively. The default settings present a 24-hour clock, but you can override the presentation and use a 12-hour clock if desired. Figure 21-4 shows typical output from this example.

**Figure 21-4:**
Users now have an easy method for adding time values to forms.

# Creating a Standardized Look with CSS

Hand-coding the design for your site is a perfect way to create inconsistencies that will drive your users crazy. Unfortunately, not everyone is an artist or has the aesthetic sense of a designer. You may find that you require help with creating a good look for your site. Using any of the publicly available CSS samples can help you create a standardized look. It's easy to customize these samples to meet your specific needs. Add a few graphics of your own (or mix and match those you find in the public domain online), and the site looks completely customized.

The following list of sites can provide you with a great start toward creating a standardized look (you can also perform a search online for "free CSS3 templates" to find more ideas). (Some of these suggestions are free — others require a payment of some type.)

- **Blueprint:** `http://www.blueprintcss.org`
- **Dynamic Drive CSS Library:** `http://www.dynamicdrive.com/style`
- **Free CSS:** `http://www.free-css.com`
- **Free CSS Templates:** `http://www.freecsstemplates.org`
- **Malo:** `http://code.google.com/p/malo`
- **templatemo.com:** `http://www.templatemo.com`
- **templateworld:** `http://www.templateworld.com/ free_templates.html`
- **YUI:** `http://yuilibrary.com/yui/docs/cssgrids`

In addition to actual CSS style sites, it pays to visit sites that provide access to tools for generating CSS and associated HTML5 code. For example, you find a list of such tools on the Smashing Magazine site at `http://coding. smashingmagazine.com/2011/06/10/useful-html-css-and-java script-tools-and-libraries`. It's also possible to create a custom form of the jQuery UI interface for your particular needs using the ThemeRoller tool at `http://jqueryui.com/themeroller`. Simply configure the interface as you want it to appear and download the custom version of jQuery UI for your site. Adobe also provides a number of interesting tools and services on the Edge Tools and Services site at `http://html.adobe.com/edge/`.

# Displaying a Category and Detail Data View

There are many situations where you need to provide a master/detail view. Of course, the most common use for such a view is in database applications where you present data such as the orders associated with a particular client. The view is used in many other places though. The Windows Explorer application uses a master/detail view in presenting the folder hierarchy in one pane and the content of the select folder in the other. The example application shows categorized data and the details of that data. Like every other master/detail view you've ever seen, the categories and their associated content appear in the left pane and the selected item in the right, as shown in Figure 21-5.

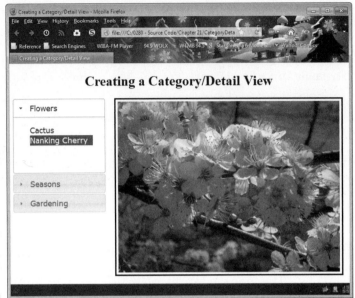

**Figure 21-5:**
A category/
detail view
provides
a useful
method of
presenting
information
to the user.

What you're actually seeing here is a combination of the jQuery UI Accordion widget and the Selectable interaction — both of which are discussed in Chapter 20. The following code shows how to create the HTML for the left pane shown in Figure 21-5. (You can find complete code for this example in the \Chapter 21\CategoryDetail folder of the downloadable code as CategoryDetail.HTML.)

```
<div id="Categories">
   <h2>Flowers</h2>
   <div>
      <ol id="FlowerSelect" class="Selections">
         <li id="Cactus">Cactus</li>
         <li id="Nanking">Nanking Cherry</li>
      </ol>
   </div>
   <h2>Seasons</h2>
   <div>
      <ol id="SeasonSelect" class="Selections">
         <li id="Nanking">Nanking Cherry</li>
         <li id="Mountain">Mountain View</li>
         <li id="Harvest">Squash Harvest</li>
         <li id="Snow">First Snow</li>
      </ol>
   </div>
   <h2>Gardening</h2>
```

```
<div>
   <ol id="SeasonSelect" class="Selections">
      <li id="Nanking">Nanking Cherry</li>
      <li id="Harvest">Squash Harvest</li>
   </ol>
</div>
</div>
```

The right pane consists of a <div> and <img> combination. The <div> has an id of DrawingContainer, whereas the <img> has an id of Drawing. Normally, these components would appear one over the other. You need to create some CSS in order to obtain the required appearance. Here is the CSS for this example:

```
<style>
   h1
   {
      text-align: center;
   }

   #Categories
   {
      width: 220px;
   }

   .Selections .ui-selected
   {
      background: blue;
      color: white;
   }

   .Selections
   {
      margin: 0;
      padding: 0;
      width: 150px;
      list-style-type: none;
   }

   #DrawingContainer
   {
      width: 533px;
      height: 400px;
      border: solid;
      position: absolute;
      left: 250px;
      top: 80px;
   }
```

```
    #Drawing
    {
        width: 523px;
        height: 390px;
        margin: 5px;
    }
</style>
```

Notice that the width of Categories is such that the DrawingContainer can appear to the right of it. The Selections are set up to fit fully in Categories. When setting the width of Selections, you must account for the indent that jQuery UI automatically provides as part of the Accordion widget. The most important part of the DrawingContainer setup is the left setting, which must be configured to accommodate the Accordion widget to the left of it. The size of Drawing is such that the application can maintain the aspect ratio of the images it will display. With some additional work, you could allow for images of multiple sizes to fit easily within the space — the example images are all the same size.

The example requires surprisingly little code to perform its work. That's because jQuery UI does most of the heavy lifting for you. The act of displaying the image is surprisingly easy because of the way the <img> tag work. Here is all the code you need to make this example work:

```
$(function()
    {
        // Create an Accordion as a means to
        // organize the data.
        $("#Categories").accordion();

        // Choose a particular image based on the
        // user's selection. Display it using the
        // src attribute of the <img> tag.
        $(".Selections").selectable(
            {
                selected: function(event, ui)
                {
                    switch(ui.selected.id)
                    {
                        case "Cactus":
                            $("#Drawing").attr(
                                "src", "CactusBlossom.jpg");
                            break;
                        case "Nanking":
                            $("#Drawing").attr(
                                "src", "NankingCherry.jpg");
                            break;
```

```
                case "Mountain":
                    $("#Drawing").attr(
                        "src", "MountainView.jpg");
                    break;
                case "Harvest":
                    $("#Drawing").attr(
                        "src", "SquashHarvest.jpg");
                    break;
                case "Snow":
                    $("#Drawing").attr(
                        "src", "FirstSnow.jpg");
                    break;
            }
        }
    });
});
```

A production application might perform some additional work with the input handling, but testing will show you that the application is fully functional now, and there is little the user can do to cause the application to crash. The trick is in the `ui.selected.id`. Each of the selections has a unique `id` value that the `switch` statement can capture. All that you need to do then is modify the `src` attribute of the `<img>` tag to match the desired drawing.

# Selecting Data Using a Calendar

Calendars are an essential part of daily living. Everyone uses them for various purposes. It's not just a matter of keeping track of appointments — calendars are used for all sorts of other date-related uses. For example, most blogs include a calendar where you can choose from posts made during a specific timeframe.

It's entirely possible that someone could write a short book on calendar usage in applications. When it comes to JavaScript-compatible calendars, most developers would probably start with an event-based calendar such as Full Calendar (`http://arshaw.com/fullcalendar`). However, you should keep your options open. The list of 35 different calendar plug-ins found on the Tripwire Magazine site at `http://www.tripwiremagazine.com/2012/11/jquery-calendar-date-pickers.html` is only the tip of the iceberg. There are literally hundreds of different calendar plug-ins you could use for your application. The example in this section relies on the Date Picker jQuery plug-in found at `http://www.eyecon.ro/datepicker`. It's a simple plug-in that you can use for something like a blog to choose content based on the date it was produced.

To start this example, download the Date Picker plug-in and place the
datepicker.CSS and datepicker.JS files in the downloaded source
code folder. Before you can use the Date Picker jQuery plug-in, you need
to add some references for it to your page. The following code adds the
correct references. (You can find complete code for this example in the
\Chapter 21\CalendarSelect folder of the downloadable code as
CalendarSelect.HTML.)

```
<link rel="stylesheet"
      media="screen"
      type="text/css"
      href="datepicker.css" />
<script type="text/javascript"
        src="datepicker.js"></script>
```

The Date Picker plug-in is quite flexible. For example, you can set it to
allow single or multiple date selections. The default is to use multiple
dates. You can also choose features such as the starting day of the week.
The full set of options and events appears at http://www.eyecon.ro/
datepicker/#implement. The calendar appears as part of a container tag,
such as <div>, <span>, or <p>. Here is the code used to create the calendar
for this example:

```
$(function()
  {
    $("#DateSelect").DatePicker(
      {
        // Set the initial configuration.
        flat: true,
        date: "2013-03-01",
        current: "2013-03-01",
        calendars: 1,
        starts: 0,

        // Process date changes.
        onChange: function(formatted, dates)
        {
          // Display the selected date.
          $("#SelectedDate").text(
            dates.toDateString());

          // Display a thought for the day.
          switch (dates.toDateString())
          {
            case "Fri Mar 01 2013":
              $("#Thought").text("Thought One");
              break;
            case "Mon Mar 04 2013":
              $("#Thought").text("Thought Two");
```

```
                                break;
                    case "Tue Mar 05 2013":
                        $("#Thought").text("Thought Three");
                        break;
                    default:
                        $("#Thought").text("No Thought");
                        break;
                }
            }
        });
    });
```

In this case, the calendar is set up to present the days in the current month, with Sunday as the starting day of the week. It displays only one calendar at a time, and the selected date is 1 March 2013.

The important event to handle is onChange(). This event is fired whenever the user chooses another date. The event handler receives a Boolean value, formatted, that defines whether the dates are formatted in some way. The dates argument contains a single date, when the calendar is in single-selection mode, or a date array, when the calendar is in multiple-selection mode. The example displays the selected date, along with a string selected by certain dates. You can change this code to match any selection requirement you might have. Figure 21-6 shows typical output from this example.

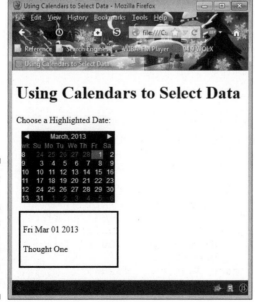

**Figure 21-6:** Use a calendar to help users visualize date-oriented information choices.

# *Developing a User-Configurable Interface*

jQuery UI provides a number of methods for creating a user-configurable interface. The draggable interaction, demonstrated in the example of dragging content in Chapter 20, is the best place to begin. After a user drags an interface component from one location to another, you can store the user's choices in a cookie (as demonstrated in the section on using cookies in Chapter 15). Using just these two techniques together would allow you to create a basic user-configurable interface.

Most developers don't have time or resources to write a user-configurable interface completely from scratch. The best approach is to locate a third-party library, preferably one that's free, that meets your specific needs. Of course, you need to perform some configuration to get the look you want, but the basic library should provide most of what you need. Fortunately, there are many libraries and templates available to make your job easier. The following list tells you about a few of the more common and usable libraries and templates available (although, there are many others):

✔ **Alloy UI:** `http://www.liferay.com/community/liferay-projects/alloy-ui/overview`

✔ **Dijit (based on dojo):** `http://dojotoolkit.org/reference-guide/1.8/dijit/index.html`

✔ **JxLib:** `http://jxlib.org`

✔ **LivePipe UI:** `http://livepipe.net`

✔ **script.aculo.us:** `http://script.aculo.us`

✔ **Sigma AJAX UI Builder:** `http://sourceforge.net/projects/ajaxuibuilder`

✔ **UKI:** `http://blog.ukijs.org/`

✔ **xui:** `http://xuijs.com`

It's important to remember that hand-writing JavaScript code is necessary only when you need particular effects. Many developers rough out their designs by using a Content Management System (CMS). A CMS provides a word processor-like interface for creating content online. They were initially used to create blog posts, but many developers have turned to them for site content as well. The three most popular CMSs are

✔ **Drupal:** `http://drupal.org`

✔ **Joomla!:** `http://www.joomla.org`

✔ **WordPress:** `http://wordpress.org`

# Devising a Simple Survey Form

Most sites include a number of forms. You find forms used for contact information, surveys, sales, and a host of other tasks. A form provides a means for two-way communication between the user and the site owner.

As with many other JavaScript programming requirements, you can find third-party products to help you create surveys. For example, The Wufoo Form Gallery (`http://www.wufoo.com/gallery/templates/surveys/market-research-survey`) contains a number of templates focused on market research.

Developers make more work for themselves than necessary when creating forms by using text boxes instead of other controls. Whenever possible, reduce the risk of incorrect entries by users by limiting the user's choices to specific answers. Using controls with predetermined values (check boxes, option [radio] buttons, drop-down lists, and many others described in this book) is always a better choice than using a text box. When you must use a text box, make sure you use features such as `maxlength` to reduce the potential for security issues.

The simple survey for this example asks four questions: name, age, gender, and reason for visit. The point of this example is the technique rather than creating something fancy. Except for the name, the other three inputs use controls that strictly control user input so there isn't any chance of getting incorrect information from a type perspective. Of course, the user can still choose to use options that don't reflect real-world values. The following code shows how to submit the form by using jQuery syntax. (You can find complete code for this example in the `\Chapter 21\Survey` folder of the downloadable code as `Survey.HTML`.)

```
$(function()
   {
      // Submit the form.
      $("#Submit").click(function()
         {
            $("#Test").submit(
               function()
                  {
                     // Verify that the name field
                     // contains information.
                     if ($("#Name").val().length == 0)
                        {
                           alert("You must provide a name!");
                           return false;
                        }
```

```
                    // If the name field contains data,
                    // allow the submission.
                    return true;
                });
            });
        });
```

Notice that the example still validates the Name field to ensure that the user has typed a value. The Name field is also length limited. You could possibly verify that the user hasn't typed numbers or special characters. However, at some point, you simply can't add any more validation and must deal with incorrect entries should the user want to make them. Figure 21-7 shows how this form appears.

**Figure 21-7:**
A simple form used to provide feedback on a site.

The example shows a few other interesting techniques. In this case, the form uses the get method and sends the output to another page. Figure 21-8 shows typical output from this example when the user clicks Submit on the form.

The code retrieves the data directly from the `location` object. A complete URL consists of the location, followed by a question mark (?), followed by the data. Each name/value pair is separated by ampersands (&) from the other data elements. In addition, the name/value pairs consist of a variable name, the equals sign (=), and a value. The following code shows how the example separates this information to display it onscreen. (You can find complete code for this example in the `\Chapter 21\Survey` folder of the download-able code as `ReadData.HTML`.)

**Figure 21-8:**
The
example
shows an
output page
containing
the survey
data.

```
$(function()
    {
        // Obtain access to the data and place
        // each item in an array.
        var Variables =
            $(location).attr("href").split("?")[1];
        var VarArray = Variables.split("&");

        // Display the data items onscreen.
        $("#Name").text(VarArray[0].split("=")[1]);
        $("#Age").text(
            VarArray[1].split("=")[1].replace(/\+/g, " "));
        $("#Gender").text(VarArray[2].split("=")[1]);
        $("#Reason").text(VarArray[3].split("=")[1]);

        // Go back to the previous form.
        $("#GoBack").click(function()
            {
                window.location = "Survey.html";
            })
    });
```

The Age data is especially interesting because the spaces are replaced by
plus signs (+) during transmission. To put the spaces back in, you use a
global replace (using the /g switch). However, the + also has to be escaped.
So, to specify a global replacement of the +, you must use /\+/g.

The example also makes it possible to go back to the survey form. It does this
by providing a button. Clicking the button changes the window.location
value to the URL of the survey.

# Chapter 22

# Ten Thoughts About the Future of Web Development

*W*here do you go from here? It's a common question. People get to a particular point in a journey and wonder what comes next. By the time you reach this point in the book, you've experienced a good deal of what's possible with a combination of HTML5 and JavaScript, even if you haven't quite mastered it yet. It's natural to wonder what these new skills will garner — where they might take you in the future. This chapter discusses some of the things that could happen in the future. A word of warning about any prognostication — the future has a habit of making everyone look just a bit foolish — we expect one thing and get something different.

## Automating More Tasks

It doesn't take a crystal ball to see that developers are overwhelmed and that technology seeks to correct this problem by automating more development. This book uses more than a little automation in the form of libraries. Expect to see more libraries, templates, and tools in the future. You shouldn't expect that your code will ever write itself or that the role of the developer will simply go away. Human interaction will always be needed. However, Content Management Systems (CMSs) such as WordPress (`http://wordpress.org`) show the direction that technology is taking. Developers will become more specialized and take on more complex tasks in the future, which means you really need to polish your skills.

# Developing Applications That Run Anywhere

At one time, you needed to know the platform your application would run on extremely well. In fact, there was a time when an application might not run on a system with a slightly different processor because applications were written to use every feature that a processor provided. The trend today is to write applications that run anywhere, regardless of the platform the user employs. The whole Bring Your Own Device (BYOD) movement makes it necessary for developers to write applications that don't care about what platform they use. To discover more about BYOD, read the Gartner report at `http://www.gartner.com/it/page.jsp?id=2136615`.

The emergence of BYOD makes it necessary to create code that checks the platform and makes adjustments when necessary. This is one of the reasons that using libraries, rather than rolling your own custom solution, will become even more important. The person writing a library can add all the required checks and provide code needed to make an application work on a particular platform. Everyone who uses the library automatically gains the functionality that the library provides. As of this writing, jQuery (`http://jquery.com`) is probably the most popular solution for writing applications that work everywhere, but you need to keep your options open and constantly research new solutions (see Chapter 18 for a discussion of jQuery).

# Using Standards for Every Application

Browser developers are becoming more and more aware of the need to follow standards when writing their code. However, vendors are still extremely competitive, so you find that the browsers meet the standards and then add something extra in the way of features or programming functionality. It's a problem because you can't be sure that the vendor will continue to support the addition. The use of the addition also makes your application unusable with other browsers because these other browsers will lack the addition. In short, you need to adhere to the standards even when browser vendors don't quite make the grade. Using just the standardized features and avoiding the extras will save a lot time and heartache later.

Look for vendors to continue moving toward more standardized browsers, with extras. Currently, some browsers don't quite meet the standards or implement the standards in different ways. In the future, the standards will become more stable, and everyone will implement them the same way. Using libraries can help you overcome the glitches in browser implementations today.

# Creating a Desktop Environment with a Browser

As people begin using more and more devices that don't look like each other or rely on the same operating system, the desktop environment as you know it today will eventually disappear. Your future word processor will appear in a browser, not on the desktop. In fact, people are moving in that direction already. Desktop applications are large, cumbersome, and hard to learn. They don't work well on multiple platforms, and people can't use the device they prefer in a particular situation. Browser applications are flexible — they work anywhere. Even though you might rely heavily on desktop applications today, in the future you'll likely use a browser equivalent that works precisely the same on every device you own.

# Using a Centralized Data Store

Businesses have more money invested in data today than just about anything else. The data that a business relies upon to make sales, track inventory, and perform other tasks has become so critical that a business could become insolvent without it. The problem with data is that it's not a physical asset — it resides as electrical impulses. Creating backups and then storing the information where nothing can harm it has become a nightmare, especially for smaller businesses. You can expect businesses to rely more on central data stores as people move toward browser-based applications. The security and reliability of central data stores continue to improve, and when people start using browser-based applications for daily tasks, using a central data store will make strong business sense as well. You may not require much in the way of local storage in future systems.

# Creating Mobile-friendly Applications

More and more industry experts are pointing toward decreased PC sales as an indicator that the age of the PC is over — that new devices are taking its place. Of course, there's an immense installed base of PCs worldwide, so any thoughts that anyone is entertaining about the imminent demise of the PC are unfounded.

What is more likely going to happen is a relatively long period of chaos where no one vendor stands out and no one platform takes the lead in computing, which means your applications need to run on anything the user might choose to use, especially in the mobile device category. Although no one is likely to write a book like *War and Peace* using a smartphone, expect to find users working with applications on everything from smartphones to tablets. In fact, many industry pundits are beginning to ask whether 2013 will be the year of the tablet. (See `http://www.pcmag.com/article2/0,2817,2414200,00.asp` as an example of such a prediction.)

The use of browser-based applications will make the transition less painful than it might otherwise be. The browser translates the platform-independent application into something a specific platform can use, but only if the browser understands the application. Make sure your applications use common libraries and templates, rely on standards, and make no assumptions about the device the user is using for interaction.

# Developing Accessible Applications

An *accessible* application is one that accommodates people with special needs. A *special need* can encompass a broad range of requirements. For example, about 8 percent of the male population is colorblind, but only 0.5 percent of the female population experiences this problem. (See `http://www.vischeck.com/faq/#c0_f5`.) If your site uses color combinations that make it impossible for those with colorblindness to see the content, you leave out a huge percentage of the potential user base.

In fact, around 20 percent of the population of the United States is recognized as having some sort of special need requiring some sort of accommodation. (See `http://specialneedsplanning.net/statistics`.) The number of special needs requirements will increase as the population grows older. For example, many people now require larger text to accommodate failing eyesight, and others require closed captioning to address failing hearing. When your site ignores special needs, you leave out potential buyers for your products or users of the content you present.

The best place to discover the details about creating accessible sites is the W3C site at `http://www.w3.org/standards/webdesign/accessibility`. There are also free tools you can use to check your site for problems, such as Vischeck (`http://www.vischeck.com/vischeck/vischeckImage.php`) and the Web Accessibility Evaluation Tool (`http://wave.webaim.org`). I've also written a book on the topic, *Accessibility for Everybody: Understanding the Section 508 Accessibility Requirements* (Apress; `http://www.amazon.com/exec/obidos/ASIN/1590590864/datacservip0f-20`). You can read posts associated with this book on my blog at `http://blog.johnmuellerbooks.com/categories/263/accessibility-for-everybody.aspx`.

# Building New Application Types

Online development has spurred a new age of creativity for developers because the medium makes possible applications that can't work effectively on the desktop. For example, the Web service is impossible to create at the desktop. Sharing data on a scale of such huge proportions requires the Internet. The same holds true for centralized backup, Massively Multiplayer Online (MMO) gaming, and social media such as Facebook. None of these applications can exist at the desktop level. Look for the pace of creativity to maintain its current pace or even increase as developers see new potential in the range of tasks an application can perform on the Internet.

Agitation of the platforms used for computing, the use of new applications, and a decidedly different perspective for how computing devices are used sounds interesting and exciting. However, there's a curse that expresses the potential for disaster appropriately, "May you live in interesting times." It's purportedly of Chinese origins, but the source is considerably newer than that and not from China at all. (See `http://www.phrases.org.uk/meanings/may-you-live-in-interesting-times.html`.) Even so, the truth of the curse rings true. During these interesting times, you need to exercise caution in assuming a technology will survive or even become remotely useful.

# Thinking More About Users

In the early days of PCs, only a geek could love computers, and even the geeks became frustrated at times. The introduction of the Graphical User Interface (GUI) made it possible for power users to become involved with PCs. As computers gained processing power and developers came to better understand the needs of users, interfaces became easier and easier to use even while they become capable of performing more work. Given that this trend has been going on for 31 years, you can expect it to continue.

Today computers rely heavily on intuitive gestures and hardware that works with humans in a way that human users can anticipate. Your application reaches the pinnacle of success when it becomes completely invisible to the user, yet performs every task the user expects. Expect the addition of touch-based and gesture-based computing to become prevalent in browser-based applications.

Of course, the question is, what comes after touch and gesture? Look for flexible displays to become not only practical, but prevalent. (See `http://www.engadget.com/tag/flexible+display` for some articles on the topic — the article at `http://www.oled-info.com/flexible-oled` tells how they work.) Some people think that computers will eventually be printed on clothing or accessories such as purses. Some people may actually have technology embedded in their bodies in new ways — although this would be a somewhat radical change for people who have grown up without such technology. (See the latest version of *Total Recall* for ideas on how this might work.) As platforms change, your application will also need to change.

# Expecting Unexpected Connections

Many developers today ask the question, "How can I use that?" All sorts of data sources, technologies, code libraries, templates, and so on are available for experimentation today. During the writing of this book, I spent several days just playing with various technologies to see what I could do with them. Other developers are doing the same thing. With this in mind, you need to consider the fact that you can't envision how others will use your code. You can envision only what you originally intended for the code to do. As part of the development process, you need to expect unexpected uses for your code. Your application could become something quite different from what you initially expected. This is the reason that creating well-documented, well-organized applications is so important. When you have invented a new wheel, you must expect that others will use it.

# Index